Beyond
Survival and Philanthropy

American Jewry and Israel

Edited by
Allon Gal
Alfred Gottschalk

Hebrew Union College Press
Cincinnati

Published in association with the Ben-Gurion Research Center and the Center for North American Jewry, Ben-Gurion University of the Negev.

The editors express their appreciation to Richard J. Scheuer, patron of learning, whose generosity made this conference and publication possible.

Library of Congress Cataloging-in-Publication Data

Beyond survival and philanthropy: American Jewry and Israel / edited and introduced by Allon Gal and Alfred Gottschalk

    p. cm.
    Includes bibliographical references.
    ISBN 0-87820-218-8 (alk. paper)
    1. Jews–United States–Attitudes toward Israel–Congresses. 2. Israel and the diaspora–Congresses. I. Gal, Allon. II. Gottschalk, Alfred.

DS132. B39 2000
305.892'4073   dc21

                                                                              00-021248

Printed on acid-free paper in the United States of America
Typeset by Posner & Sons Ltd., Jerusalem, Israel
Distributed by Wayne State University Press
4809 Woodward Avenue, Detroit, MI 48201

Contents

Preface

This volume is based on the conference "North American Jewry and Israel: Beyond Survival and Philanthropy," which took place in Kiryat Sede Boker and Jerusalem in July 1996. The sponsors were the Center for North American Jewry and the Ben-Gurion Research Center of Ben-Gurion University of the Negev, and the Hebrew Union College–Jewish Institute of Religion. Both the conference and the book represent the pioneering efforts of these institutions as they endeavor to define the future quality of relationships between Israel and American Jewry and address important issues that confront them in the twenty-first century. Crucial and radical choices must be made with regard to these issues, which are by nature so complex that they require the total resources of the Jewish people, globally, to address them.

The early period of the State of Israel was a time of austerity and great difficulties with respect to security conditions and the economy. These difficulties masked the equally important internal political and religious conflicts that begged for early resolution but were never resolved. Consequently, issues of religion and state, the relationship of Diaspora Judaism to Israel, and the legitimization of the Diaspora's existence still confront us.

In addition, the problems of assimilation, acculturation, intermarriage, and feelings of alienation are, in our view, of significance and no less important today than they were in the 1940s. What was unique in that period, however, was a pervasive aura of Jewish solidarity, which is to be envied when one looks at the Jewish world today, where divisions are much more apparent and appear to be much more serious and irreconcilable. Yet we believe that beneath all the apparent dissonance there is even today a psychic and spiritual unity that holds the Jewish people together. When one considers all the difficulties that arose since Herzl pronounced that he had created the Jewish State at the conclusion of the First Zionist Congress in 1897, one marvels at what has been achieved. All of the prognostications of the demise of the Jewish people have come to naught. No one would have dreamt in 1948 that by the year 2000 Israel would be on the threshold of being the largest Jewish population center in the world, that the infra-structure of the country would reflect a healthy economy, or that the ingathering of the Jews of Ethiopia and the former Soviet Union would give rebirth to a whole generation of Jews whom history had written off as lost or forgotten.

Yet there is still much to be accomplished to unify us as a people. In the realm of the Hebrew language and culture, wider and more intensive learning can be an important instrument of self-identification for Jews in the Diaspora. Even in Israel, the quality of Jewish education, although improving, is still not at an enviable level. We need to facilitate travel to Israel–for whatever reason–for greater numbers of Jews in the Diaspora in the hope that this coming together will foster a sense of concern and feelings of empathy among all Jews. Most important, there is a continuing need for dialogue, for the shar-ing of diverse views and opinions–indeed, an on-going global forum–to formulate and address the crucial and radical choices that lie before us. All of this can herald the advent of a pluralism un-dreamed of before and crucial to the future of Israel and the Jewish people. It is our hope that the next century will bring to realization ever more profoundly the dreams and aspirations first held so pre-cious in the thought of those who created the idea of a Jewish State and those who actually shaped it.

* * *

The seeds of this conference were planted in the summer of 1994, at an informal meeting of Israelis and North American Jews during a "Moriah" international gathering in Zikhron Ya'akov. Those were the days when the peace process was consistently and most promisingly developing; and the issue that came up was: What will hold the Diaspora and Israel together once the traditional "crisis glue" eventually melts down and the familiar and practiced Israeli call for aid retreats to the remote background of our communities' lives?

Those present were of differing Jewish philosophies and differing political inclinations, but it is interesting that they shared the same basic concerns and feelings regarding that question. Even if the peace process would encounter difficulties and complications, they felt that the old "survivalist" pattern in Israel–Diaspora relations was going to exhaust itself. And they also felt that it was not historically inevitable that the end of this traditional pattern must mean the demise of the great Israel–Diaspora partnership.

Although they possessed no fully persuasive answers, all present believed that Jewish togetherness, elusive as it is, is something unique and to be cherished. And that belief led them to meet again and further discuss this complex subject. They wanted an analysis, and they also wanted positive concrete responses to the new historical situation.

The result of these concerns and yearnings was the decision—by the initiating group and, largely, colleagues and friends in the Reform movement—to convene an international conference that would candidly discuss the new situation. Before our conference materialized, however, the shocking assassination of Yitzhak Rabin occurred. In early November 1995, the Prime Minister had been expected to attend the General Assembly in Boston. The Jewish community there—and elsewhere in the U.S.—knew that Rabin intended to deliver a "shalom message" to American Jewry that would revise his previously harsh criticism of the reluctant attitude of the American Jewish political establishment regarding the peace process. All knew by then that he was thoughtfully going to express general appreciation of the community and also to recognize its immense potential for advancing prospects for peace.

Alas, this strategic alliance for good, under Rabin's leadership, did not take place. But his legacy—a very Jewish, noble, inspiring one—mobilizes us still. Sustaining the peace process, uplifting the Israel–Diaspora relationship, and confronting the challenge posed "beyond security and philanthropy" have all become interwoven into one ideological matrix. Thus, we of Ben-Gurion University of the Negev and of the American Reform movement decided even more purposefully to proceed with preparations for the conference.

We also thought it crucial to assign a special session to the issue of cultural pluralism as a tribute to the memory and legacy of Rabin. We expected humanistic and open-ended discussions at this session that would be our kind of Judaic response to the assassin's chauvinism and religious fanaticism. In a tragic way, though, the assassination colored the entire conference and spurred us to strive for a deeply positive answer regarding the two communities' relationship. Indeed, the sublime values of the sanctity of life, enlightened and creative Judaism, and the peaceful development of Israel—all these offered themselves as the most essential elements in our reshaped solidarity.

Our value-oriented search, however, has not undermined the scholarly analysis of past and present. We trust then that this volume will contribute both to a better understanding of our relations and to their enhancement.

* * *

We are grateful for the active cooperation of the President of Ben-Gurion University, Professor Avishai Braverman, who emphasized the call of the Negev's broad horizons as a limitless canvas for a productive Israeli–American Jewish partnership. We are thankful too to Dr. Tuvia Friling, Director of the Ben-Gurion Research Center at the Sede Boker campus, who heartily joined our enterprise, underscoring that the essential legacy of David Ben-Gurion stood for mission-committed Jewish partnership meaningfully interwoven into the free world's fabric.

We would like to thank our colleagues at the Center for North American Jewry—in addition to those who presented papers herein included—who graciously chaired sessions and otherwise contributed to the success of this three day conference: Professor Robert Liberles, the Chair of our Executive Committee; Professor Walter Ackerman, Professor Mark Gelber, and Dr. Hanna Yablonka.

We are warmly indebted to Mr. Milton Forman of New York City and Ms. Ruth Wolman of Cambridge, Massachusetts, who generously supported the conference. We are deeply grateful too to Mr. Richard J. Scheuer, Governor and Chairman of the Jerusalem School Committee, Hebrew Union College–Jewish Institute of Religion, who nurtured the conference from its inception, inspiringly contributed to its discussions, and supported the publication of this volume.

The late Dr. S. Zalman Abramov, Chair, Board of Overseers, Jerusalem School, HUC–JIR, Michael Rukin, Chair, Combined Jewish Philanthropies, Boston, and Rabbi Uri Regev, Director, Israel Religious Action Center, all enriched the enterpise in significant ways. Rabbi Baruch Gold of the Blechner Chair in Jewish Tradition and Values at Ben-Gurion University coordinated the event; and Rabbi Shaul R. Feinberg, Associate Dean of HUC–JIR, Jerusalem, most devotedly and always in good spirits helped to plan the conference and carried its organizational burden. Rabbi Sheldon Zimmerman, the new President of the HUC–JIR, spiritedly endorsed this joint project.

For their efforts in the publication of this volume, we must express our thanks and appreciation to Dr. Michael A. Meyer, chair of the Publications Committee of the Hebrew Union College Press, to Barbara

Selya, its managing editor, and to Cynthia Marmer, executive secretary to Dr. Gottschalk, who served as editorial assistant.

Our spouses, Snunit and Dee, sharing with us the trauma of Rabin's assassination as well as the challenge of the conference, have helped us in so many ways to get things done.

Allon Gal
Alfred Gottschalk

NEW DIMENSIONS

Steven M. Cohen and Charles S. Liebman

Israel and American Jewry in the Twenty-First Century
A Search for New Relationships

Our Values

Any analyses and recommendations concerning the relationships between Israel, Israeli Jews, and American Jews are informed by the values of the writer. Accordingly, in thinking about these issues, we wish
to make our own values clear at the outset. Our primary commitment
is to the Jewish people, a commitment that precedes our concern with
Israel, Israeli Jews, or American Jews. We firmly believe that the Jewish people is entitled to a state of its own and that Israel should remain
a Jewish state. We also believe that the good of Israel, Israeli Jews, and
the Jewish people is best served by the existence of a strong and vibrant
American Jewish community with close links to Israel. These links, not
aliyah per se, are our primary concern. They should be strengthened
by enriching the cultural relationships between Israeli and American
Jews. In such relationships, Israeli Jews may well feel like senior partners, giving more than they receive. But American Jews, for their part,
also have what to give; in particular, they constitute important allies in
the battle to preserve a Jewish state and in the definition of what the
Jewishness of Israel should mean.

On Asking the Right Question

Like others, we are increasingly anxious about the prospects for a
healthy and vital relationship between the two largest Jewish communities in the world. In the past, the concern that traditionally animated
Israelis in general and policy makers in particular was that American
Jews would refuse to support Israeli policies. Such concerns emerged
most prominently during the Sinai War, the Intifada, and whenever

3

Israeli policies were opposed to those of the American government. At these points, Israeli policy makers feared that when the positions of Israeli and American officials clashed, American Jews would favor the policies of their own government rather than those of Israel. In part drawing upon classic Zionist images of *galuti* Jews, Israeli policy-makers, at least until quite recently, portrayed American Jews as insufficiently committed to standing up for Israel against American public opinion. Many Israelis see American Jews as troubled by issues of "dual loyalty," that is, as being seen by others as more loyal to Israel than to the United States.

We are arguing that, whatever its merits in the past, the "dual-loyalty" paradigm no longer serves to illuminate our understanding of American Jews' relationship with Israel.

In focusing on such matters as support or loyalty, Israelis, their leaders in particular, therefore, have severely misjudged American Jews and concerned themselves with the wrong issue. The question was never whether American Jews would oppose Israel, much less support U.S. government policy in opposition to Israel. The issue was—and still is—the level of interest that American Jews express about Israeli affairs. In fact, opposition to Israeli policy, as reflected for example in the "Who Is a Jew?" issue, or opposition to Likud policies during the Intifada, or opposition to the peace process today, is a sign of a healthy interest in and commitment to Israel. In surveys of American Jews conducted by one of us in the 1980s, those most critical of Israeli policies were also most attached to Israel (Cohen 1985, 1987, 1989a, 1989b, 1990a). (Relative to American Jews, Israelis are more attached to Israel and more critical of their leaders' policies.) Israel would be fortunate if it could sustain the kind of interest that characterized American Jewry at its most critical moments.

Unfortunately, what we are observing today is growing indifference on both sides (Cohen 1989b and 1992). Jews in Israel and in the U.S. care about each other less than they have in the past. Israel is coming to occupy a smaller and narrower place in the consciousness of American Jews. (We make this claim despite evidence from social surveys of relative stability in Israel-attachment measures through the early 1990s; see Cohen 1996). Among Israelis the situation is similar—though, as we shall see, it takes on a somewhat different form.

Why is the Relationship Troubled?

The analysis of the problem has by now become commonplace. In broad strokes, since the inception of the Zionist movement, Diaspora Jews in affluent societies (of which American Jewry has been the largest and most powerful) have pursued a largely two-dimensional relationship with the Jewish community of Israel (first the Yishuv, and then the State). One dimension consisted of lobbying their national leaders to lend Israel economic, military, and diplomatic support. The other dimension comprised fund-raising. They sought to support social welfare needs that largely flowed from the rescue of Jewish refugees and their resettlement in Israel More generally, the funds were meant to lend material support to a society perceived as having to devote a disproportionate share of its resources to security needs. We refer to this relationship, which embraces political advocacy and philanthropic activism, as the "Mobilized model."

We now appear to be in the midst of a steady erosion in the Mobilized model, an erosion that is unlikely to be reversed in the near future. Objectively, Israel no longer requires the financial and political assistance it once did, and, subjectively, American Jews no longer feel compelled to offer it.

The Decline of the Mobilized Model—Or the Passing of the "Golden Age"

To gain perspective on the Mobilized model, and to understand why it now seems to be running out of steam, we need to turn back to what may be its Golden Age, the decade immediately following the Six Day War (1967–1977). For it was then that American Jewish political advocacy and philanthropic activity on behalf of Israel reached its zenith, and Israel became—and remains until this day—the number one item on the Jewish public agenda, surpassing liberal politics and the fight against antisemitic discrimination. At that time (1967), the rise to prominence of the Israel cause occasioned a dramatic turnabout in political mobilization and, more particularly, in the readiness of American Jews to confront American political leaders in an aggressive and forthright fashion.

The impact of Israel on fund-raising is also well known. Both the Six Day War and the Yom Kippur War propelled levels of giving to UJA/Federation campaigns to new heights. Especially in Israel's early years, the Jewish State was in dire need of financial aid. In the absence of large scale assistance from other governments, American Jewry was the logical target for rendering that support. Another factor enhanced the relationship between Israeli officials and American Jewish philanthropic leaders. During the early years of the State, the Israeli government feared political intervention from American Zionist leaders. Philanthropic leaders, unlike the Zionists, were less involved in domestic Israeli politics and were quite content to contribute money, which Israel desperately needed, in return for status rewards. Israeli leaders were prepared to lavish attention and honors on UJA and Jewish Federation leaders. When, beginning in the late 1960s, Israel assumed an increasingly important place on the public agenda of American Jewish life, those status rewards increased in value. To state matters crudely, the value of an invitation to dinner with the Israeli Ambassador, or a picture shaking hands with an Israeli general, or a signed photograph of an Israeli prime minister was worth considerably more after the June War.

During this period (1967–77), several factors enhanced Israel's prominence in the consciousness of American Jews and on the agendas of their political and philanthropic organizations (Cohen and Fein 1985). They illustrate the special character of that period, and the unlikelihood of its return. The key factors included:

1. The dramatic lead-up to the Six Day War, the War itself, and the Yom Kippur War. No one has explained with certainty why the two wars, the June War in particular, had the impact it did. But there can be no question that many American Jews, including many of their leaders, discovered in themselves deeper emotional links with Israel and its survival than they had heretofore realized.

2. The emergence of the Holocaust as a central symbol of Jewish life. This phenomenon was embodied in the slogan "never again," in the sense that the Holocaust threat was seen as a constant of Jewish history and that Israel was the obvious location for its recurrence. In addition, no doubt many American Jews harbored guilt feelings about what they or their parents had not done during the years of the Holocaust.

3. The blatant Jew-hatred that energized the Arab enemies, and the unambiguous character of the Arab–Israel conflict. After 1967, the Israelis, seeking peace, were threatened by seemingly villainous and violent Arab neighbors. Moreover, the apparent isolation of Israel among nations that ranged from hostile to indifferent also evoked strong emotional resonances.

4. The erosion of the liberal political coalition, which had provided

a context of meaning for many American Jews and their major organizations. We must recall that the central force that energized American Jewish organizations until the end of World War II was the defense against antisemitism. But after the war, doors that heretofore had been closed to Jews—in universities, in large corporations, in financial institutions, and even in social clubs—were now opened. Jewish organizations that had previously worked to fight antisemitism and shape a more tolerant America now sought new programs with new content to justify their existence. Centered around the notion of Jewish liberalism in general, and the struggle for Black equality in particular, the new programs served as a mandate of the Jewish tradition and the first line of defense against a potential re-emergence of antisemitism.

But in the late 1960s the Black struggle took on an anti-white and antisemitic turn. Black organizations focused their attention—and their protests—on the economic disparity between Blacks and whites, rather than on legal discrimination. They protested not so much the lack of equality in opportunity (an agenda congenial to the Jewish world view), but the lack of equality in results (an agenda at odds with the traditional civil rights orientation of most Jewish organizations).

In the space of a few years, the older and more moderate Black leadership, which had emphasized coalitions with Jews and other liberals, was displaced by younger militants. Jews who had held prominent positions in Black organizations were displaced. The new leaders tended to dismiss the Jewish contribution to legal desegregation and the assistance that Jews had accorded the Blacks in their struggle for civil rights. In addition, some new Black organizations and leaders were strongly anti-Israel.

5. The emerging legitimacy of ethnic assertiveness among American whites. The early 1970s witnessed a surge of interest in European (white) ethnicity, partly as a response to Black militancy, that undoubtedly overflowed into Jewish precincts. As one prominent federation leader said, "If Black can be beautiful, surely Jewish can be beautiful." This woman, heretofore identified with nearly assimilationist tendencies in Jewish life, was now found actively engaged in aggressively pro-Israel programs.

6. The awakening of the Soviet Jewry movement. which provided American Jews with yet another important Israel-related objective and focus of mobilization.

7. The coming of age of a highly educated, relatively affluent third generation of American Jews. This generation was so secure in its sense

of being American that it harbored little fear of the charges of "dual loyalty" that had dissuaded a prior generation from pursuing an aggressive pro-Israel stance.

These factors coincided at a particular moment in history. They operated synergistically to propel Israel to the fore of the American Jewish consciousness, to the extent that it came, for a time, to dominate, if not reshape, that consciousness. Obviously, short of another unusual confluence of similar circumstances, we cannot anticipate the re-emergence of the passionate political and philanthropic activism that characterized the Mobilized model in its Golden Age. In addition, one other important trend has served to erode commitment to political advocacy and philanthropic generosity. In the last five to ten years, Israel has become less in less need of the financial and political support that American Jews have provided.

Another Reason: A Stronger Israel

Politically and militarily, Israel is perceived as basically secure. The collapse of the USSR, the subsequent agreements with the PLO, the treaty with Jordan, and recognition by other Arab states have significantly diminished the level of international hostility and the likelihood of significant, sustained violent clashes. The long-term prospects for Israel's security may not be as sanguine as some on Israel's left may believe, but it is perception that is significant.

In addition, the Israeli economy has been growing quickly and steadily during the 1990s. With relatively moderate inflation, increased foreign investment, declining unemployment, and abundant signs of conspicuous consumption, it is difficult for Israel's advocates to argue on behalf of economic assistance to absorb the diminished flow of new immigrants. Hence, the case for Israel as a beneficiary of Jewish largesse and of Jewish political support has never been weaker.

Philanthropic Decline

From the American Jewish side, several factors have conspired to reduce in absolute and relative terms the share of philanthropic funds designated for Israel. Perhaps the most significant constraint has been the stagnant level of donations to Jewish federations (which may, in fact, reflect declining passions for Israel). In contrast with the "Golden Age" of mobilization when donations grew substantially, the past twenty years and more have witnessed declines in contributions in real, inflation-adjusted terms. Not only has the total Jewish charitable pie shrunk over the years, but the Israeli share of philanthropic contributions, and certainly the contributions to the Jewish Agency and related services, has declined as well.

Nothing on the horizon suggests an increase in dollars destined for Israel, any time soon. We may divide the American Jewish philanthropic pie into three slices: one destined for Israel and other overseas needs; one devoted to what has been termed, of late, "Jewish continuity" (formal and informal programs of Jewish education, camping, trips to Israel, etc.), and one designated for a variety of Jewish human services (hospitals, nursing homes, family and children's agencies, Jewish Community Centers, etc.).

The advocates of more money to Israel are currently at a relative disadvantage. The Jewish continuity advocates have at their disposal a powerful issue, recently identified, and one that strikes at the core of concerns for the very survival of the Jewish philanthropic system itself. The human services advocates point to huge cutbacks in U.S. and local government support of all social service agencies, of which the Jewish-sponsored agencies have been receiving in the neighborhood of $2.5 billion annually before the 1995–96 cutbacks came into effect. Advocates for these two sectors, in other words, can point to newly realized, legitimate, and pressing crises in their spheres, and they argue that Israel itself is better able to make up the shortfall in funds for what are essentially nation-building tasks that ultimately benefit the Israeli taxpayer.

The advocates for a larger Israeli share of the philanthropic pie suffer another disadvantage: the Jewish continuity and human service agencies are locally based, clearly visible, and a constituent part of the community. Israeli social agencies, and those who lead them, are several thousand miles away, lacking the ability to maintain visibility based on frequent informal contact with those who decide on how the American Jewish philanthropic dollar shall be divided.

Public and Private Spheres

Another factor that has diminished the significance of the Mobilization model relates to the distinction between public and private spheres of Judaism in America. The public sphere refers to Jewish organizations, politics, and fund-raising. Its rhetoric is sprinkled with such themes as community, solidarity, and peoplehood, or such slogans as "Keep the Promise," and "We are One." In contrast, the private sphere of Jewish identity relates to family, ritual, synagogue, religiosity, and education. Its rhetoric is characterized by such terms as spirituality, meaning, search, and journeys. Its language is softer, more comforting, non-judgmental, and, these days, more personally engaging.

Obviously, Judaism encompasses both the public and the private spheres. It is composed of an ethnic dimension that evokes the sense of a common history, communal obligations, even a national or quasi-national identity. The private dimension, more spiritual and narrowly religious, encompasses aspects of the individual Jew's relationship to God. Whereas the Jewish tradition insists upon and socializes Jews to both public and private commitments, the decline of the tradition has been accompanied by the bifurcation of these two spheres, as they have become increasingly distinctive aspects of Jewish life.

Of primary importance for our present concern is that over the last several years, the public sphere has declined, whereas the private sphere has been holding its own. Thus, with respect to indicators in the private realm, day school enrollments are up, Jewish studies courses have proliferated, and the publication of Jewish books has increased dramatically. Levels of ritual observance have risen among Orthodox and Conservative Jews. Softer evidence points to continued ferment and creativity in Jewish feminism, and in what has been called the Jewish spiritual renewal movement.

But Jewish life in the public sphere seems to be in decline, involving fewer and fewer Jews, whose commitments seem to be increasingly tenuous. We already noted the stagnation in contributions to Jewish federations; more broadly, there is diminished mobilization around political causes (of all sorts), rapidly aging memberships of mass Jewish organizations, and a decline in volunteerism, particularly when comparing women born after World War II (now middle-aged and younger) with their older counterparts.

Links between American Jews and Israel, one might argue, have been hitched to the wrong horse. Because involvement with Israel has been primarily political and philanthropic, the historic ties of American Jews with Israel have been weakened by the declining interest in Jewish politics and philanthropy. Because Israel has had little real meaning in American Jewish religious, spiritual, or cultural life, the relative vitality in recent years in these areas does little to renew interest in things Israeli.

Who Needs American Jews?

American Jewish policy makers need not rely on theoretical analyses by social scientists to learn that their political and philanthropic contributions are no longer prized by Israelis. They need only listen to the leaders of Israel who have been telling them in loud and clear voices: "We don't need you."

Notwithstanding the popularity of the Labor Party with most non-Orthodox American Jewish leaders, the voices expressing disdain for American Jewish assistance were heard most clearly after the 1992 Labor Party victory. In his first visit to the U.S. after his election as Prime Minister, Yitzhak Rabin told AIPAC officials that Israel no longer needed their help lobbying Congress and the Administration. He announced that, from then on, Israel would handle her own lobbying. Shortly thereafter, Finance Minister Avraham Shochat commented that Israel no longer needed over-priced Israel Bonds—that Israel could (and soon would) borrow more cheaply on the open markets. Yossi Beilin, serving as Deputy Foreign Minister, observed on several occasions that Israel no longer needed Diaspora contributions for social programs. And, in repeated statements, President Ezer Weizmann announced that Israel needed nothing at all from the Diaspora, with the single exception of young Jewish bodies coming on aliyah.

These statements reflect a genuine underlying mood of self-confidence, even triumphalism, bred by personal, economic, political, military, and diplomatic achievements. As Israeli leaders came to see their country as more secure and successful, they began to reject the old model of Israel-Diaspora relations, which, in retrospect, is somewhat humiliating to both partners. On the one hand, it denies that Israel is a secure and independent state. On the other hand, it attributes only a utilitarian or instrumental role to Diaspora Jews, whose partnership with Israeli Jews is based only on their contributions to Israel's well-being. The title of Matti Golan's recent book, *Money for Blood*, expresses this point of view.

It is not at all clear that the Mobilization model will be replaced by a healthier one. Those Israelis who are popularly identified as post-Zionists, while numerically few, occupy influential positions in the country's cultural life. They prefer a less obviously Jewish state for a combination of reasons. One may be their own alienation from Judaism; another might be their sense that dissociating the state from its

Jewish roots is necessary to provide its Arab citizens with full equality; or, that it might help integrate Israel into the region. They have little problem rejecting ties with American and other Diaspora Jewries. Their voices have become increasingly strident in the last few years, and may well gain further ascendancy if the peace process continues, security problems abate, and Israeli Arabs demand a greater voice in shaping the meaning of Israeli nationality.

If the most involved American Jews are to remain linked to Israel, if Israel is to play a significant role in the consciousness of a substantial number of American Jews, then additional models of connection—and new expressions of need—will have to emerge. These must be based on an understanding of the currents in American life that mold the culture of American Jews and the divisions among the Jews themselves.

Currents in American Life Molding American Jewish Culture

American Judaism, like American religion in general, is adaptationist rather than radical (Liebman 1977). That is, American Judaism takes its physical as well as its cultural environment as a given, rather than as something to be rejected. It is, as a rule, non-judgmental about broad social and cultural norms. The values American Jews have adopted, mostly unconsciously, are those of the professional, intellectual, upper middle classes, who also dominate the American media—that is, the values of what Christopher Lasch has called the *New Class* (Lasch 1995).

This adaptationist stance has two very important implications for Israel–Diaspora policies. First, American values and culture have helped forge a Judaism that is, in many respects, unlike its counterpart(s) in Israel. Second, it means that policies seeking to enhance the relationship of American Jews with Israel must take account of these values. We will argue that these values tend to undermine American Jewish ties to Israel and to Israeli Jews. Hence, if these links are to be strengthened, those who are responsible for projecting Israel to American Jews must seek a delicate balance: they need to acknowledge the power of these values, yet seek at the same time to either challenge them or even transform them.

American Judaism is characterized by four distinctive features: universalism, moralism, personalism/individualism, and voluntarism (Liebman and Cohen 1990). Each feature merits some elaboration.

1. **Universalism** is the idea that the Jewish tradition has a message for all people, not only for Jews, that Judaism is open to the messages of other traditions and cultures, and that Jews ought to be involved with improving the lot of all people, not just Jews alone. This impulse finds expression throughout the public rhetoric of American Jewry. One example is found in the most recently published Sabbath and Holiday prayer book for the Conservative movement, which states that: "From one group to one humanity has been our goal."

As part of a study of American Jewish identity (Cohen and Eisen forthcoming), when asked about her interest in oppressed Jews, a middle-aged mother in Queens (a part of New York not especially known for its liberal excesses) responded:

> I think you should do things for the community in which you live. I mean it's okay if you want it to be for Jewish causes, but I don't think the work you do should be based on religion. Maybe I can identify a little more [with oppressed Jews] because I'm Jewish, but I feel sad for all people that are oppressed. There may be a slight difference in the way I feel [about Jews] because I am Jewish, and believe it or not, I'm not very proud of it.

American Jews, as a whole, are only comfortable in supporting Israel when Israeli policies are perceived as consistent with universalist and moralist values (moralism is described below). That helps explain one reason why philanthropic and political support for Israel was historically projected as support for needy Jews, for refugees from oppression, or for a state under siege. When unconstrained by Jewish particularist values, universalism undermines the idea of a special relationship between American Jews and Israel, Israeli Jews, or, indeed, any other Jews. After all, if all people are to be treated equally without regard to race, religion, national origin, sex, and most recently, sexual preference, how can American Jews feel totally comfortable in maintaining a special relationship with, let alone granting preference to, Israelis?

2. **Moralism**. Moralism was defined by the sociologist Marshall Sklare as the idea that "religious man is distinguished not by his observance of rituals but rather by the scrupulousness of his ethical behavior" (Sklare and Greenblum 1979: 89). Moralism is the opposite of ritualism, a perspective that finds significance and transcendence in the performance of certain religiously or culturally ordained acts for their own sake.

A recent random sample survey of members of Conservative congregations asked for reactions to the statement, "A Jew can be religious even if he or she isn't particularly observant." Note that the statement didn't refer to what it means to be a good Jew but what it means to be a "religious" Jew. We may further observe that after the Orthodox, Conservative synagogue members are the most traditionally observant group among American Jews. Nevertheless, seventy-six percent of the respondents agreed that a Jew could be religious even if he or she wasn't particularly observant. Even *hiloni* Israelis, we believe, would respond differently. For them, "religious" Jews are identified by observance only, which is one reason non-observant Israelis are not "religious" in their own minds.

In an interview with the editors of *Yahadut hofshit*, a publication of the Secular Israeli Movement for a Humanist Judaism (*Tnu'ah hilonit yisraelit le-yahadut humanistit*), Dr. Yair Auron, lecturer on Contemporary Jewry in the Seminar of the Kibbutzim, stated:

> One of the great failures of Jewish-Zionist education is ... [that] we hardly ever affirm the legitimacy of different contemporary religious expressions. The young secularist has only a faint knowledge of non-Orthodox expressions [of Judaism]. He generally adopts the perspective of Israeli Orthodoxy with regard to these movements (1994: 21)

This observation helps explain why American Jews have such difficulty appreciating the virtual monopoly the Orthodox exercise over the meaning of Judaism in Israel. It also explains why, for the most part, Israelis have such difficulty in taking the non-Orthodox denominations in the United States seriously. Israelis' disdain for non-Orthodox religious movements constitutes an obstacle to stronger links between Israeli and American Jews, although, in this case, the burden to change, we believe, is on the Israeli side.

3. **Personalism and individualism** is reflected in the observation that "the modern Jew selects from the vast storehouse of the past what is not only objectively possible for him to practice but subjectively possible for him to identify with" (Sklare and Greenblum 1979: 48). Personalism provides the basis for innovations, such as those undertaken by American Jews, which more Jewishly conventional Israelis would find outlandish or disturbing. The innovations can come in the form of individuals or communities inventing their own Jewish rites, ceremo-

nies, and symbols. This may be undertaken without the sanction of any religious movement and with little regard for the preservation of traditional forms or meanings. For example, an elaborate folder advertises a weekend retreat, "The Living Waters Weekend," under the direction of Rabbis Phillip and Shoni Labowitz, co-Rabbis of Temple Adath Or in Ft. Lauderdale and "creators of healing rituals in Jewish Renewal." The following is the Saturday program:

> Optional Sunrise Walk and Meditation. Musical Worship Service at the Ocean. Guided Conscious Eating at Breakfast. Water Exercises for Body Toning. Yoga with Kabbalah. Relaxation Time. Luncheon Recalling Our Heroes. Outdoor Games, Informal Talk, Time for Massage. Sacred Gatherings for Men and Women. Poetry Reading and Pre-dinner Music. Sunset Barbecue with Folk Dancing. Havdalah Ritual on the Beach. Kabbalistic Meditation.

The Sunday program is:

> Sunrise Co-ed Mikvah Ritual in the Ocean. Breakfast Celebration with new Affirmation. Sacred Sharing and Closing Ceremony.

This kind of program is extreme in its departure from conventional mores, but hardly unique in American Judaism.

Personalism emerges clearly in the repeated reference to the self in these remarks by a California woman, interviewed for a study of contemporary American Jewish identity (Cohen and Eisen forthcoming). When questioned about what it would take for her to become more involved as a Jew, the woman's answer used the first person singular ("I" or "me") seven times in two sentences:

> It's [my becoming more Jewishly involved] really about me coming to terms with what I want and whether I decide whether there is something important for me about being involved [in a Jewish community]. I guess I would say that I can't really see anything because it's really something that has to come from the inside and not the outside.

The shift of authority from the outside to the inside, from God or the group to the individual, subtly—or not so subtly—undermines a central assumption of Zionism. To a personalist audience, it is difficult to speak of peoplehood and one's obligation to Israel. Large numbers of American Jews are unlikely to relate seriously to Israel unless they can

construct and maintain a personally significant meaning to that relationship or unless that meaning is provided for them.

Personalism and individualism, as we already suggested, detach the
individual from the larger group. Some observers attribute these and
related changes to the impact of television viewing, pointing to a flight
from organizations into individual activities. In the last two decades,
one researcher notes, the number of American bowlers has doubled,
but the number affiliated with bowling leagues has dropped by half.
Even ethnic identities are sustained, albeit in a most superficial manner, without ongoing contact with a particular group. Sociologist Richard Alba writes:

> Ethnic identities are not typically anchored in strongly ethnic so-
> cial structures. Such structures still do exist, although they have
> been weakened by powerful currents of assimilation. Intermar-
> riage is widespread; friendship circles are typically quite diverse
> in ethnic terms; membership in ethnic organizations is quite rare;
> and so forth. As a consequence, many whites who identify in eth-
> nic terms, even intensely so, have only limited contact with per-
> sons of the same ethnic background. (1990: 301)

4. **Voluntarism** is closely related to personalism. It refers to the voluntary nature of Jewish identity and the manner in which it is expressed.
Jews in the United States are free to identify or not to identify as Jews;
there is no fixed national registry of the population by religion
or ethnicity. Writing about white ethnic groups, Alba notes:

> For Americans of European background in general, ethnic iden-
> tity is a choice. In contrast to many parts of the world where eth-
> nic origins are recorded in passports, no governmental recogni-
> tion is accorded the ethnic identities of American-born whites.
> (1990: 295)

Indeed, evidence from the recently conducted National Jewish Population Study indicates that a significant number of respondents who
identified as Jewish in 1990 denied such an identity when resurveyed
in 1993. Research on members of other ethnic groups, especially those
with multiple ancestries, demonstrates that group identity in the
United States is fluid and situational (Waters 1992). Ethnic identity
changes from one time to the next, in part dependent upon the needs
of the moment, the social context within which one finds oneself, or
the holiday calendar.

Not only are individuals free to decide whether to be Jewish, they are free to choose the intensity of their Jewishness, generally with little social sanction attached to their choice. Moreover, they can vary the intensity over the course of the year, or over the course of their lives.

Diversification, Not Decline, in American Jews' Group Identity

To succeed, any policy aimed at strengthening American Jews' relationship with Israel needs not only to contend with the values of American Jews but with a complex variety of American Jews.

Seen from afar, American Jews may appear undifferentiated and uniform. As a result, many policy makers—both in Israel and in the United States itself—formulate policies under the implicit assumption that there is only one type of American Jew. But common sense alone would suggest that the nearly six million Jews who are scattered throughout the country constitute a heterogeneous population likely to respond in diverse ways to the challenges facing Jewish life. The proportion of American Jews who intermarry, for example, may be on the rise because it has increased dramatically among one set of Jews, but not among another. Indeed, there may even be an increase in commitment to Jewish norms and values in one segment of the community.

To be clear, we reject that image of American Jewry widely shared by American Jewish leaders, and, perhaps, even more widely shared by influential Israelis—the image that projects a uniform American Jewish population whose Jewish loyalties and commitments are steadily eroding. Rather, we believe American Jewry is becoming increasingly fragmented as it responds in diverse ways to the temptations and the challenges posed by contemporary American culture and society to Jewish identity, Jewish family formation, and the sense of Jewish peoplehood. These temptations and challenges, in turn, are expressed in increased intermarriage, but also increased day school enrollments; the adoption of patrilineal descent by the Reform, but increased Orthodox militancy (and increased ritualism among the Reform); the trivializing of Judaism, but also spiritual search; institutional disaffiliation, but the growth of Jewish studies courses at the college level; residential dispersion, but an explosion in the number of Jewish discussion groups on the Internet, etc. The contradictory trends in Jewish demographics and institutional behavior both reflect and provoke contradictory trends in patterns of Jewish identification on the individual and local levels. We believe that virtually all American Jews have absorbed the values of universalism, moralism, personalism, and voluntarism, but they have done so in different measures, and interpreted them in different ways.

Our analysis of the 1990 National Jewish Population Survey identified four groups of American Jews. We label them: the actively engaged, the moderately engaged, the loosely engaged, and the disengaged (Cohen 1985; Wertheimer, Liebman, and Cohen 1996). Each group contains about a quarter of American Jews. The cumulative intermarriage rates for the four run from 4 percent (for the active) to 10 percent, to 19 percent, and to 49 percent, respectively.

We have argued that Jewish continuity and outreach efforts should focus on strengthening the most active group, and enlarging it by focusing on moderately or loosely engaged Jews. By extension, proposals for strengthening relations between Israel, Israeli Jews, and American Jews require the formulation of targeted policies rather than general ones meant for an entire, undifferentiated mass of American Jews.

Jews who have remained actively engaged in Jewish life are resisting, unconsciously if not consciously, many of the values to which we have alluded. One reason, we suspect, that Israel is important in the lives of some Jews is precisely because, almost by definition, relationships with Israel run contrary to the values that the majority of American Jews espouse. With respect to the remaining Jews, policies that explicitly contradict values of universalism, personalism, and voluntarism are unlikely to attract more than a tiny constituency. At the same time, however, these values diminish ties between American Jews and the Jewish people, and the stronger they become, the more trivial Israel becomes. What we are suggesting is that, to the extent that one can formulate policy in these spheres, and this itself is a most delicate task, Israel must project itself as a source of resistance to these prevailing values (moralism aside), while at the same time appreciating that head-on confrontation is counterproductive.

We cannot dismiss the possibility that the relationship of American Jews to Israel will be increasingly characterized by irrelevance. In point of fact, contrary to the assumptions of Israelis who believe an Israel-orientation is essential to an active Jewish life in the Diaspora, more than a few active and involved American Jews conduct their Jewish lives in ways in which Israel is largely divorced from their Jewish concerns.

About a third of American Jews now find Israel clearly irrelevant (and they say so, almost in so many words). Israel is not all that important for their sense of being a Jew. They don't even express an interest in visiting there.

Among other American Jews, Israel is little more than a country whose places of historical interest evoke some romantic and even nostalgic associations, but little else. About half of American Jews find Israel an exciting tourist attraction—a minority of this group has actually been there already and the remainder report that they would like to do so when they have the time and money. To the extent that Israel projects itself only as an interesting place to visit, it serves to strengthen a model that undermines meaningful relationships between Israel, Israeli Jews, and American Jews.

• In contrast, the models that strengthen such relationships are the Mobilized one to which we have already referred, and the Source of Personal Meaning model, upon which we elaborate below.

Although in decline, the Mobilized model still characterizes the manner in which most actively engaged Jews relate to Israel. Israel is seen as a needy country and American Jews are obligated to come to its defense—though they need not relate to it in any depth in religious, educational, cultural, or social terms. While our introductory pages dismissed this model as poorly suited to the changing complexion of American Jewish life—especially the strengthening of the private sphere and the weakening of the public sphere—it is appropriate to say a few words on its behalf.

First of all, it is foolish to believe that, because Israel is no longer as dependent on the financial and political support of Diaspora Jewry as it once was, this dependency will not recur or that it is of no value today. Israeli leaders who deny the importance of philanthropic and political support from American Jews realize in most instances that their remarks are exaggerated and are uttered mostly to score political points with their domestic constituencies. Although philanthropic contributions represent a declining proportion of Israel's total national income, when for specific needs—for example, education—the Diaspora contributions may represent a major source of income. It is a mistake to believe that the government of Israel picks up the slack represented by diminished contributions. In reality, the programs underwritten by the contributions suffer.

Secondly, the Mobilized model still characterizes tens of thousands of highly active albeit generally older American Jews. It has not only served the interests of Israel, but of American Jews as well. It provides many American Jews whose ties to Judaism are primarily ethnic rather than religious and who, when they open their daily newspapers, turn first to stories about Israel. As early as twenty years ago, we recall attending a meeting between American Jews and Israelis in which the Israelis told the Americans that their philanthropic contributions were increasingly marginal to the Israeli economy. An American Jewish leader replied, "We don't care if you burn the money we send you, but we have to keep on raising money if we are to involve American Jews with Judaism." The Mobilized model may appeal to fewer and fewer Jews but it has by no means disappeared.

The Mobilized model also has served as a path into personal meaning. In other words, many American Jews, especially the elite group of contributors and political activists, first became involved with Israel through their public-ethnic concerns, but later found personal, even spiritual, meaning in this effort. As a result, they built richer Jewish lives at the personal and family level. If we were forced to choose between the Mobilized and the Personal Meaning models, we would prefer the latter, but it is best to avoid the choice.

The Source of Personal Meaning model envisions a community of American Jews with strong personal ties to Israel and Israelis. They visit, call, and write their friends and family members. They follow news of Israel in the Jewish as well as the general press. They probably have some knowledge of Hebrew, and they are familiar with Israeli society and culture, not only with Israel–Arab relations. They maintain direct relations with Israeli people and neighborhoods, and not just formal ties with institutions. They may have business relationships as well. Many of them envy American Jews who make aliyah, and would be satisfied, if not pleased, were their own children to do so. Such American Jews may be characterized as those who spend the major portion of their lives in the United States, but for whom a significant portion of their emotional lives takes place in Israel. While not unknown among Conservative and even Reform Jews, these sorts of relationships are more typical of many Orthodox communities where, for example, spending a year in Israel between high school and college is the norm, and where at least a few families in the synagogue have made aliyah.

Be that as it may, it is among the most committed Jews that we find the greatest number who see Israel as a source of personal meaning. What is striking, however, is that these Jews also are easily mobilized in the public support of Israel. In other words, the two models—one conducted in the public sphere, the other in the private sphere—are by no means mutually exclusive. For the most committed of Jews, the private and public spheres of Judaism reinforce one another.

This, in turn, implies that developing the private sphere of Zionist or pro-Israel identity will not come at the expense of the public sphere, where the Mobilized model is played out. It also suggests that currently Mobilized Jews may be the best candidates for new private sphere relationships.

About fifteen percent of American Jews fit these two models. About fifteen percent have visited Israel at least twice, a sign of a more than passing interest. Perhaps two thirds of this group—roughly ten percent of all American Jews—are, or have been, heavily involved in fund raising or political work on Israel's behalf, but only a third of this group—about five percent of all American Jews—can be classified as deeply personally attached to Israel in the manner we envisioned above.

In our view, given the relative strength in the private sphere of Jewish life, and given the cultural influences of American modernity upon contemporary Jewish identity, the most fruitful approach to enriching American Jews' relationship with Israel lies in attempts to expand the number who draw powerful, enduring, and compelling personal meaning from their relationship with Israel and Israelis. We endorse policies aimed at augmenting the meaning of Israel for those who are now in the Mobilized mode, and trying to elevate erstwhile mere "tourists" to a more serious and personal engagement with Israel.

Are such attempts feasible? The answer is "yes" if we concentrate our efforts on that segment of American Jews already engaged or involved in Jewish activity. This is the segment of Jews seeking a focus that can assist them in constructing a meaningful Judaism. It is the segment of Jews anxious about the threats to its Jewish roots and likely, therefore, to respond to a message that subtly and tactfully challenges the values of universalism, personalism and individualism.

Policy Directions

Projecting Israel in this manner is no simple task nor do we pretend to have many answers. If Israel is to become a focus of personal meaning, then American Jews will have to take serious interest in Israeli life. It follows that the image of Israel and Israelis will be more realistic than that which presently exists. And the question American Jews will ask themselves is whether Israelis are really interested in them as

American Jews rather than as potential contributors or political allies.

Recent work by Daniel Elazar points us in a useful direction. He notes that the Jewish people is now engaged in a world-wide struggle between what he calls "Judaizers" and "normalizers." The struggle is taking place in both Israel and the Diaspora. He calls upon the Judaizers in all countries to unite in efforts to assure the Judaic character of the Jewish people. Such an alliance would provide a common ground for Israeli–Diaspora interaction.

The Israeli Judaizers will need Diaspora support. Their constituency is predominantly the Orthodox, *edot ha-mizrah*, and ultra-nationalist secularists. This constituency suffers because it is not anchored in the academic, cultural, industrial or bureaucratic establishment, and because it is situated in one part of the political spectrum (the right; those who identify with the Meimad movement represent a clear exception to this generalization, as do the small numbers of Masorti and Reform movement members). It needs support of politically moderate and Ashkenazi Jews who have yet to involve themselves in the conflict. Mobilizing Diaspora Jews, American Jews in particular, will be helpful in attracting them. Israelis, on the other hand, have a vital stake in assuring that Jewish life in the United States is not eroded through the conquest of the community by the normalizers and minimalists.

In addition, the Judaizers in both the United States and Israel need one another's help in establishing models of Jewish vitality (Modern Orthodox, Conservative/Masorti, Reform, or even secular Judaism) that are attractive and coherent. The battle for modern Judaism must be waged against the normalizers in Israel who seek to de-Judaize the State of Israel, and the normalizers in the United States who would universalize and personalize Judaism by ridding it of its ethnic components and its ritual traditions.

Relationships built around this struggle necessarily mean engagement in the private as well as the public arena. The struggle would render Israel and the Diaspora relevant to one's private identity as well as one's public commitments. Such a common struggle would provide the conceptual framework for all sorts of common activities and joint relationships tying Israeli and Diaspora Jews to one another.

There may be other bases for action as well. We need to identify other struggles where the moral, symbolic, political, and financial support of Jews from one country can be utilized on behalf of Jews in the other country. Environmentalism, feminism, civil liberties, democracy, and consumers' rights suggest themselves as causes that might draw small, but culturally significant, numbers of Jews from both societies together. Israeli and American Jews should welcome one another's participation in their own struggles.

Orthodox Jews throughout the world are pioneers in advocating their particular vision of Israel, and in advancing the interests of their own communities, institutions, and programs. They also exhibit, as we suggested, the highest rates of personal involvement in Israel. The two phenomena are connected. Other Diaspora Jews and Israelis would do well to adopt the Orthodox model, not in substance, of course, but in form (a position first argued in Cohen 1990b). That is, they should feel free to advance their particular, ideologically driven visions of Judaism and of Israel regardless of where they live.

The endeavor to forge meaningful and enduring cultural relationships between Israel and American Jewry, and more broadly, Israel and the Diaspora, is a daunting one. Yet, we remain convinced that the construction of such relationships, or perhaps just the search for effective ways to do so, constitutes a national priority for the State of Israel in the twenty-first century, and an essential feature of the contemporary Zionist movement.

References

Alba, Richard D. 1990. *Ethnic Identity: The Transformation of White America* (New Haven: Yale University Press).

Auron, Yair. 1994. "The Ignorance of the Israeli Teacher," *Yahadut Hofshit No. 2* (May): 20–22.

Cohen, Steven M. 1985a. "From Romantic Idealists to Loving Realists: The Changing Place of Israel in the Consciousness of American Jews," in William Frankel, ed. *Survey of Jewish Affairs:* 169–82.

Cohen, Steven M. 1985b. "Outreach to the Marginally Affiliated: Evidence and Implications for Policymakers in Jewish Education," *Journal of Jewish Communal Service* 62, 2 (Winter): 147–57.

Cohen, Steven M. 1987. "Ties and Tensions: The 1986 Survey of American Jewish Attitudes Toward Israel and Israeli." (N.Y.: American Jewish Committee).

Cohen, Steven M. 1989a. "Ties and Tensions: An Update – The 1989 Survey of American Jewish Attitudes Toward Israel and Israelis" (N.Y.: American Jewish Committee).

Cohen, Steven M. 1989b. "Are American and Israeli Jews Drifting Apart?" (N.Y.: American Jewish Committee).

Cohen, Steven M. 1990a. "Israel in the Jewish Identity of American Jews: A Study in Dualities and Contrasts," *Shofar: An Interdisclipinary Journal of Jewish Studies* 8, 3 (Spring): 1–15.

Cohen, Steven M. 1990b. "To Strengthen Weak Ties: The Conservative Movement and the Country of Israel," in John S. Ruskay and David Szonyi, eds., *Zionism and the Conservative/Masorti Movement* (N.Y.: The Jewish Theological Seminary), pp. 59–66

Cohen, Steven M. 1992. "Are American and Israeli Jews Drifting Apart?" in David Teutsch, ed., *Imagining the Jewish Future* (Albany: State University of New York Press), pp. 119–33 .

Cohen, Steven M. 1996. "Did American Jews Really Grow More Distant from Israel (1983–1993)? — A Re-Consideration," in Allon Gal, ed., *Envisioning Israel.*

Cohen, Steven M. Forthcoming. "Conservative Jews in American Synagogues: Contrasts and Variations," in Jack Wertheimer, ed., [no title yet].

Cohen, Steven M. and Arnold Eisen. Forthcoming. *In Search of Jewish Meaning* (Tentative title) (New York: Routledge, 2000).

Cohen, Steven M. & Leonard Fein. 1985. "From Integration to Survival: American Jewish Anxieties in Transition," *Annals of the American Academy of Political and Social Science* (July): 75–88.

Cohen, Steven M. and Charles S. Liebman. Forthcoming. "Understanding American Jewish Liberalism." Ms.

Lasch, Christopher. 1995. *The Revolt of the Elites and the Betrayal of Democracy* (New York: W.W. Norton).

Liebman, Charles S. 1977. "Jewish Accommodation to America: A Reappraisal." *Commentary* 64 (August): 57–60.

Liebman, Charles S., and Steven M. Cohen. 1990. *Two Worlds of Judaism: The Israeli and American Experiences* (New Haven: Yale University Press).

Sklare, Marshall, and Joseph Greenblum. 1979. *Jewish Identity on the Suburban Frontier.* (Chicago: University of Chicago Press).

Waters, Mary. 1992. *Ethnic Options* (Berkeley: University of California Press).

Wertheimer, Jack; Charles S. Liebman, and Steven M. Cohen. 1996. "How to Save American Jews." *Commentary* 101, 1 (January): 47–51.

Steven Bayme

Response

Steven M. Cohen and Charles Liebman suggest a new direction and agenda for building relations between American Jewry and Israel. More specifically, they perceive the Mobilization model as receding, although by no means disappearing, in favor of a Source of Personal Meaning model. Essentially this means that we have heretofore focused our energies primarily upon the public spheres of politics and philanthropy. They urge us, correctly I believe, to focus more now on the private sphere of personal meaning—family and friendship patterns, shared culture, and spiritual-religious values.

Particularly perceptive is the argument on behalf of a segmented rather than monolithic model of American Jewry. All too often the agenda of Israel–Diaspora relations focuses on the questions of the disappearance, survival, or renewal of American Jewry. The authors argue, instead, that no monolithic analysis suffices to describe the diversity of American Jewry. Some Jews indeed are disappearing. Other sectors of the community are becoming far more identified Jewishly than their parents or grandparents, let alone Israelis, might ever have thought possible. Still others are just holding on. For Israel to become a source of personal meaning for American Jews, traditional stereotypes and assumptions concerning American Jewry as a whole must be abandoned in favor of specific constituencies within American Jewry that have varied degrees of attachment to Israel.

Given my broad agreement with this argument, I would like to offer a number of *caveats* and qualifications to the analysis and prescriptions. First, under the best of circumstances, it is far too premature to be proclaiming the end of the Mobilization model. The future of the peace process itself is very uncertain, and even if one projects a final agreement, serious questions will remain as to the nature of the peace between Israel and her Arab neighbors. Moreover, beyond the context of the peace agreements loom the larger threats of Islamic fundamentalism and the introduction of nuclear weaponry within radical

Moslem states. For these reasons, whatever our level of optimism concerning Israel–Arab relations, it seems somewhat naive to suggest that
Israel will no longer require American political support. Therefore, the
most important agenda item for American Jews continues to be political advocacy on behalf of Israel within American society and government. To proclaim that model as eclipsed, which, to be fair, the authors
do not, bespeaks an all too sunny optimism concerning the conduct of
international relations and diplomacy.

Secondly, the authors' argument for a shift in emphasis from the
public to the private spheres has great significance. One caution, however, in speaking about American Jewry, with all its diversity and plurality, is whether the same degree of passion, commitment, and energy
may be harnessed on behalf of an agenda devoted to personal meaning
as has been mobilized on behalf of the more public agendas of politics
and philanthropy.

What I find most attractive in the Source of Personal Meaning model
is the conclusion of building a united front of Judaizers vs. normalizers.
Indeed, to some extent that is the parallel struggle taking place within
American Jewry between those who perceive continued salience and
spiritual sustenance in Jewish heritage and communal life and those for
whom being Jewish has no applicability or meaning in contemporary
American society. In that context, the real struggle for American Jewry
is not between the respective religious movements, but rather between
the "Judaizers" found within all of the movements and those for whom
being Jewish has little or no value, with large numbers of "middles"
standing between these two poles.

Cohen and Liebman see a similar struggle taking place in Israel, to
some extent inviting comparison with Zionists vs. "post-Zionists," and
urge a broad-based alliance among all committed to the Jewish historical enterprise. I appreciate the analysis and share the vision. However,
I think if we go down this road, some real fissures within the "Judaizers"
camp must be acknowledged.

First, taking this model seriously, it does suggest an image of continued mutual need. In this model, American Jewry is certainly in need,
for the challenges of assimilation and the toll it will take on American
Jewry are likely to be quite serious. Therefore, American Jewry clearly
needs Israel as a source of energy and sustenance. Yet the model suggests a view of Israel as also in need—particularly in that large numbers
of Israelis also have been unable to find meaning in the power of Jewish
tradition and heritage. The coalition of Judaizers would have us

combat currents within Israeli society that perceive Judaism as at best an anachronism and at worst reactionary. In other words, if we accept this model, we ought to acknowledge the shared need between us on the issues of Jewish continuity. Indeed, if I may be so bold to suggest it, the diversity of American Jewish religious and cultural experiences may have much to contribute to the Jewishness of Israeli society.

But even more questionable, and I say this as a friend of the non-Orthodox religious movements, has been the route taken by the American religious movements in advocating religious pluralism within Israel. First, their focus continues to be the public agenda of politics and human rights rather than the private agenda of finding spiritual meaning and personal enrichment within Jewish tradition broadly perceived and understood. More specifically, the alliance of these religious movements in Israel with the Meretz Party suggests that civil liberties and freedom from religious coercion are far more significant issues than the fundamental messages of Jewish tradition that characterize the ideologies of Conservative and Reform Judaism. To be sure, in the public sphere, I do not believe that the coercive powers of the state should be invoked to enforce religious behaviors. What I question, however, is the image projected of the non-Orthodox movements in focusing their agenda on civil liberties and human rights rather than on the existential questions of what it means to be a Jew in a Jewish state. Precisely because I share the agenda for a Personal Meaning model, and precisely because I welcome the coalition of Judaizers, I suggest that the direction taken by the religious movements in their well-intentioned quest to promote religious pluralism has been fundamentally flawed. It is almost as if the religious movements have welcomed the monopoly of the Chief Rabbinate, for it provides them with a lever by which they can oppose Orthodoxy rather than promote a true religious diversity.

American Jewish organizations have aggressively advocated government recognition of non-Orthodox forms of Judaism in Israel, but their efforts have not resonated with the Israeli public. In Israel, where the American notion of strict separation of religion and state has little backing, even most secular Jews are ready to accept Orthodoxy as the only authentic version of the religion they do not practice. In fact, many Israelis impute ulterior motives to the American Jewish groups that press for pluralism. Some claim that the non-Orthodox bodies in America are simply looking to legitimize their status in their own communities against Orthodox attacks. Others suggest that non-Orthodox American Jews, stung by Israeli criticism of their high rates of

intermarriage and assimilation, have seized upon the religious pluralism issue as a way to feel comfortable about themselves by pointing out
a weakness in Israeli religion.

In light of the very different perceptions of Israeli and American
Jews about religious pluralism in the Jewish state, what can American
Jews do to nurture greater pluralism in Israel?

To begin with, we must distinguish between diversity, tolerance, and
pluralism.

Religious diversity is a fact of Israeli society. There are many different types of Jews who espouse different ideologies. This is acknowledged by all, including the most extreme Orthodox.

Tolerance is something that most Jews would agree we need more
of. It implies the recognition that we must live side-by-side in peace
and harmony, even if we do not necessarily validate the views held by
others.

Pluralism, however, is much more controversial. True pluralism implies that diversity of views is not only a reality that must be tolerated
but a virtue that strengthens Jews as a people. Pluralism suggests that
each mode of Jewish expression has its place in the Jewish mosaic.
There are many Jews—primarily but not exclusively among the
Orthodox—who resist pluralism.

Jewish religious pluralism encompasses four elements.

First, pluralism recognizes that different Jews require different avenues of Jewish expression; no single formulation will work for all Jews.
By welcoming a variety of expressions, then, we strengthen the Jewish
people.

Second, pluralism entails intellectual humility, the recognition that
there is much to be learned from those who disagree with us. In the
words of the Ethics of the Fathers, "Who is wise? One who learns from
everyone." The Orthodox and the non-Orthodox can and should learn
from each other.

Third, pluralism rejects relativism. We cannot validate everything
that Jews happen to do. As Rabbi Norman Lamm has put it, "If everything is kosher, nothing is kosher."[1] This suggests that Judaism has no
boundaries. Simply to "let a thousand flowers bloom" without asking
what limits our tradition places on beliefs and practices misuses pluralism to justify relativism. It is, in fact, the confusion with relativism that
makes Orthodox Jews so suspicious of pluralism, since it suggests that
all Jewish expressions are equally legitimate. But for that matter, no
passionate Conservative or Reform Jew ought to espouse relativism

either, since these non-Orthodox forms also entail ideological convictions. In short, defining pluralism as relativism must be avoided since it requires the surrender of any claim to ultimate truth.

Fourth and last, pluralism functions as a means to correct excesses. Thus non-Orthodox formulations help counter tendencies to extremism within Orthodoxy, while Orthodoxy may counter tendencies toward religious indifference. For example, since the Rabin assassination, Reform and Conservative leaders have performed a service in pointing out the Orthodox failure to marginalize Kahanism. At the same time, Orthodoxy stands as a corrective to those within the non-Orthodox movements who align themselves with post-Zionist forces in Israel that seek to diminish the Jewish identity of the state.

In Israel, the struggle over religious pluralism is played out on three issues: laws regarding personal status, the coercive powers of the Chief Rabbinate, and the absence of religious alternatives to the legally recognized Orthodoxy.

Primary among the laws of personal status is the Law of Return, the bedrock of Zionist ideology, which grants every Jew who comes to the country the right to immediate citizenship. "Jew," for the purpose of this law, is defined in accordance with tradition—having a Jewish mother or being a convert to Judaism. Efforts to amend the law to insist on conversion "in accordance with Jewish religious law" have so far been resisted, largely due to the influence of Diaspora Jewry, which contains many who have converted to Judaism under non-Orthodox auspices. Recent proposals officially to limit conversions within Israel itself to Orthodox rabbis (a situation that has been the de facto reality up to now) have aroused similar dismay in the Diaspora. While the number of people actually affected by such a law is small (though an unknown number of immigrants from the former Soviet Union may be affected), the issue is symbolically significant for religious pluralists.

Complicating matters is the reality of the Chief Rabbinate's power in Israel. Dismissive statements about non-Orthodox Judaism emanating from the Chief Rabbinate have caused a backlash against Orthodoxy. In fact, according to the noted Israeli journalist David Landau, the Chief Rabbinate has been quite flexible in adjudicating questions about personal status on a case-by-case basis.[2] Nevertheless, the Rabbinate has come to represent the coercive powers of the state, and many of its public statements and actions have stimulated complaints about religious coercion.

However justified, such complaints obscure the need for serious

religious alternatives to Orthodoxy in Israel. Although it is a Jewish
state, Israel faces its own problems of Jewish identity. An earlier generation of Israeli secularists were familiar with the Judaism that they
were rejecting, but today's secular Jews receive inadequate Jewish
education. The recent Shenhar Commission, set up by the Israeli government, recognized this problem and recommended more Jewish
studies in the secular public schools, to be taught from non-Orthodox
perspectives.[3]

To be sure, as secular Israelis correctly note, the Guttman Report on
the Jewishness of Israelis documents a continuing Jewish consensus
within Israel. Most Israelis feel themselves part of the Jewish people
and wish to preserve some modicum of Jewish tradition in both public
and private spheres. In this context, one should not invoke the lexicon
of problems confronting American Jewry—assimilation, intermarriage, etc.—to describe the Jewishness of Israel. Religious indifference
is a serious issue within Israel, but it by no means necessarily leads to
assimilation a la the American model.

Moreover, as Charles Liebman has recently argued, the Guttman
Report does appropriately signal future concerns for the Jewishness of
Israel. In a new analysis of the Guttman Report, Liebman demonstrates that the "totally nonobservant" represent only twenty percent
of Israel's population. However, the group is disproportionately Ashkenazi, represents the best educated sectors of the population, and thus
exercises great influence in elite media and higher education. And
whereas eighty percent of Israelis feel themselves to be part of the Jewish people worldwide, only forty percent of the "totally nonobservant"
do so. Similarly, this group attributed greater importance to individual
self-fulfillment and less importance to living in Israel than did Israelis
generally. Ironically, this group mimics Israeli Ultra-Orthodoxy in
downgrading the importance of serving in the army.

From the broad perspective of Israel's general Jewish population,
there appears to be little danger of assimilation. However, given the
influence of this "totally nonobservant" group, its prestige within the
media and educational institutions, and, perhaps above all, its prominence within American Jewish intellectual circles on questions of politics and the peace process, this group is likely to enhance its standing
in the years ahead.[4] Perhaps in reaction to the influence of this group,
as many as 250,000 secular Israelis voted for the religious parties in the
last elections in an effort to affirm unwavering commitment to the Jewishness of Israel.

A positive religious pluralism, then, must constitute a corrective to Israeli religious indifference. Such a pluralism must not just combat the extremism of the Orthodox right and the monopoly of the Chief Rabbinate, but it must also be a force for strengthening the role of Judaism in society, broadening Jewish education, and enhancing the Jewish nature of the state.

Some who fight for religious pluralism in Israel—the Reform Movement's Israel Religious Action Center and HEMDAT come to mind—couch the struggle in the language of civil rights—the right to perform marriages, the right to conduct conversions. This approach is popular in the U.S. because it resonates with the American commitment to religious freedom. Thus Leonard Fein has argued that the struggle should be articulated not in terms of religious pluralism but of freedom of religion, since that will energize American Jewry.

Yet there are reasons to avoid such a strategy. Calling for religious freedom in Israel suggests that Israel is less than a democratic state, that it is even a hotbed of religious persecution. Indeed, some Reform rabbis are so offended by these implications that they criticize their own movement for seemingly reverting to its old anti-Zionist stance.[5]

More fundamentally, the language of civil liberties misses the essential thrust of religious pluralism, the enhancement of Israel's Judaic ethos. In this connection, the alliance with the Meretz party in Israel was especially misguided. Analysts of the 1996 Israeli election noted that the increases in support for the religious parties did not go to the ultra-Orthodox Agudat Israel, but to Shas and the National Religious Party (NRP). Sixty percent of Shas voters were not Orthodox, and the NRP, in this election, muted its nationalist ideology and stressed the preservation of the Jewishness of Israel. Thus the increase in votes for the religious sector owed far more to concerns over a perceived erosion of Jewishness in the country than to a desire to enhance the Orthodox monopoly or to hold onto territories. Soon after the election, MK Ephraim Sneh, who served as Minister of Health in the previous Labor government, criticized his party for its alliance with Meretz and its insensitivity to legitimate concerns about the future Jewishness of the State of Israel. He recognized that campaigns for religious pluralism that stress civil liberties without a concomitant Judaic thrust alienate a substantial segment of the Israeli electorate.

Pluralism remains a problematic concept in the Orthodox world. The sectarian Orthodox express nothing but scorn and contempt for the non-Orthodox movements. The Modern Orthodox are more civil and respectful, but no more willing to espouse pluralism, claiming that allowing non-Orthodox conversions in Israel would transfer to the Jewish State the same confusion that reigns in the U.S. over who is a Jew. They add that nothing prevents Conservative and Reform Judaism from growing in Israel except the low level of interest on the part of Israelis. There is considerable truth to this claim. While the non-Orthodox forms of Judaism evoke some support in Israel among the opponents of the Orthodox monopoly, little of this stems from a religious desire for an alternative to Orthodoxy. As one Israeli intellectual recently put it, "I joined a Reform synagogue so I would be able to say that the synagogue I did not go to is a non-Orthodox one.[6] In fact, a study of the adult children of members of Conservative and Reform synagogues in Israel indicated that only 42 percent of the children of Conservative congregants, and 27 percent of the children of the Reform, identify with the Jewish denomination in which they were raised.[7]

On the American Jewish scene, where there is religious pluralism, the future of Judaism is tightly bound up with the future of the non-Orthodox movements: to the extent that they retain their adherents, we will have a Jewish community. It is for this reason that statements emanating from Israel that denigrate the non-Orthodox movements undermine American Jewish continuity. These expressions of Judaism need and deserve validation, not scorn, from the official bodies of the State of Israel.

On the other hand, the debate over religious pluralism in Israel all too easily spills over into Orthodox-bashing there and in the U.S. An extreme example of this on the Israeli scene was the suggestion by Zeev Chafets that the country be partitioned into two states, one theocratic and the other secular, since the Orthodox would not live by the rules of democracy. This obscene proposal unfortunately received some consideration in the mainstream Israeli press, further poisoning the relationship between Orthodox and non-Orthodox Jews.[8]

The Jewishness of Israel is of enormous concern to Diaspora Jews, since our ties to the Jewish State are based on a common heritage and peoplehood. This commonality may become endangered by post-Zionist trends in Israeli culture—which, thankfully, are still confined to the margins of the society, but whose advocates see the country's future in integration with the Middle East, a scenario that would surely erode Israel's links to world Jewry. Positive religious pluralism in Israel, which would counter the excesses of post-Zionism by bolstering the Jewishness of the state, would therefore strengthen Israel–Diaspora relations.

What, then, ought we do?

Our message to the Orthodox must be that the primary threat to the Jewish future comes not from religious pluralism but from religious indifference. A truly religious pluralism would combat assimilation and Jewish apathy.

To the non-Orthodox movements, we must underscore the need to broaden their message from one of civil liberties to one that encourages serious Jewish commitment. There are already elements on the Israeli scene that seek to expand and deepen Judaic expression, ranging from the secular intellectuals trying to reclaim their heritage to the bridge-building Modern Orthodox groups.

American Jewish involvement can help. For example, the American Jewish Committee joined forces recently with the Jerusalem Municipality to co-sponsor a seminar for Jerusalem school principals—secular and religious—in the U.S. for the purpose of learning about Jewish pluralism. It addressed not questions of civil liberties, but the broader existential issue of how to transmit Jewish identity today. Based on the success of that project, the Israeli Ministry of Education, headed by an Orthodox minister, entered into an agreement with the AJC for a similar seminar. Through such programs involving religious and secular Israelis, and Orthodox and non-Orthodox American Jews, true pluralism can help strengthen the Jewish people.

We must, however, acknowledge the real division within the Jewish body politic over who is a Jew. To solve the problem of diverse conversion procedures, we require a uniform procedure acceptable to all the major Jewish movements. Prime Minister Shamir, to his credit, did launch such a initiative in the late 1980s involving the heads of the major American rabbinical seminaries. Unfortunately, the opposition of the ultra-Orthodox Agudat Israel to any proposal that seemed to recognize non-Orthodox rabbis, and the insistence of Reform on maintaining patrilineal descent as a criterion for Jewish identity doomed the proposal. Thus both the hostility of extreme Orthodoxy to pluralism and the unilateral Reform rejection of Judaism's traditional matrilineal principle worked against harmonious Israel–Diaspora relations, further polarizing them instead.

A true pluralism would acknowledge that the conflicts over personal status are serious, would uphold the need to preserve the marriageability of Jews with each other, and would find ways to solve the difficulties. Such a pluralism would strengthen the Jewish people and merit the support of all Jews.

Lastly, while I welcome the analysis of American Jewry as segmented, I believe it requires us to rethink some of the assumptions that characterized Israel–American Jewish relations in the 1980s. The rhetoric of bicentralism, common at that time, is deeply challenged by the findings of the National Jewish Population Study. Steven Cohen, in particular, is correct to remind us that American Jewry is far from disappearing. However, given the severe toll of assimilation in America, which carries with it the prospect of Jews disappearing as Jews, we should have the honesty to admit that as important as the North American Jewish community is, it cannot be co-equal with Israel. North American Jewry requires strengthening and will doubtless continue to play a major role on the world Jewish agenda. To speak, however, of bicentralism, given the reality of assimilation and the prospect of serious losses in the fairly near future, appears increasingly apologetic and misleading. As the probably irreversible toll of assimilation continues, the importance of Israel in the world Jewish polity will only increase. Given the place of Israel in American Jewish consciousness and its role in Jewish history, Zionist proclamations concerning the centrality of Israel ought be welcomed rather than resented by American Jews, so long as they are not articulated in the traditional language of "negation of the Diaspora."

In this context, the terminology adopted by Professors Cohen and Liebman of "Judaizers vs. Normalizers" may be misleading. Zionism itself began as an effort to normalize the Jews as a people. There is nothing pernicious in acknowledging the center of Jewish life as the historical homeland of the Jews and launching efforts to improve the quality of life in that homeland. That type of normalization should be welcomed. Recently, however, the desire for "normalization" has led some Israeli intellectuals to articulate a radical post-Zionist vision that can only undermine the Jewishness of Israeli society and its links with other Jewish communities around the world. To the extent that Israel-Diaspora relations are based upon a shared Judaic heritage, radical post-Zionism, with its vision of Israel as a democratic state of its citizens in which the majority of its citizens just happen to be Jews, raises legitimate fears for the Jewishness of Israeli society. This can only reinforce those elements of Diaspora Jewry that seek to distance themselves from Israel.[9]

Notes

1. Norman Lamm, "Unity and Integrity," Critical Issues Conference: "Will There Be One Jewish People by the Year 2000?," CLAL: National Jewish Center for Learning and Leadership, 1986, p. 56.

2. Joint Advisory Board meeting, Institute of American Jewish–Israeli Relations, American Jewish Committee, March, 1996.

3. Nuret Altuvia, "The Shenhar Commission's Report on Jewish Education in Israeli Schools," *Avar ve-atid*, vol. 2, no. 1 (September 1995), pp. 63–75, especially pp. 68–69, and discussion *ibid.*, vol. 3, no. 1 (September 1996), pp. 124–28.

4. *The Jewishness of Israelis: Responses to the Guttman Report*, edited by Charles Liebman and Elihu Katz, SUNY Series in Israeli Studies, 1997, especially pp. 94–97.

5. Stanley Ringler, "Reform Judaism in Israel—Why is the Movement Marginal?", *CCAR Journal*, Winter, 1996: 5–7 and Ringler, "Reform Judaism in Israel: Debating the Future," *ibid.* Fall, 1996: 92.

6. Mordecai Bar-On, Joint Advisory Board Meeting, Institute on American Jewish–Israeli Relations, American Jewish Committee, March, 1996.

7. Ephraim Tabory, "Reform and Conservative Judaism in Israel: A Social and Religious Profile," *American Jewish Yearbook*, Vol. 83 (1983): 55.

8. *Jerusalem Report*, November 28, 1996, p. 22, December 12, 1996, p. 22, December 26, 1996, p. 29. The fact that Chafets chose to delineate his suggestions in a 3-part series spanning six weeks underscores the seriousness with which the proposal was advanced.

9. See Rochelle Furstenberg, *Post-Zionism: A Challenge to Israel*, Institute on American Jewish–Israeli Relations, AJC, and Argov Center for the Study of the Jewish People, Bar-Ilan University, 1997.

Sheldon Zimmerman

Response

Demographers tell us that within the next quarter century and perhaps far more quickly, the Jewish population of the State of Israel will equal and possibly transcend the number of Jews in North America. Soon, one half of all of world Jewry will live in Israel. In terms of numbers alone, the balance between Diaspora and Israeli Jewry will shift. As we couple this with Israel's growing economic, military, and human strength, the balance has shifted radically. No longer is Israel the weaker brother and sister totally or in great measure dependent on the philanthropic and political benevolence and beneficence of Diaspora Jewry.

It would be a great error on our part, however, to dismiss the significance and necessity of the support both political and diplomatic of Diaspora Jewry, in particular the Jews of the United States. The millions of dollars that flow annually through philanthropic contributions and foreign aid, the political support facilitated and made possible by American Jewry are necessary to Israel's future security and viability.

As Israeli political leadership redefines itself against the perceived paternalism of American Jewry in the past, we cannot shy away from the ties that North American Jewry have made possible, nurtured, and built. American political support, congressional and presidential, did not just happen. Further, it will not continue unless the mobilization model works. (With all the Israeli politicians' protestations, they still run to North America to raise money for their political campaigns.) Israel's security depends on the viability of the mobilization model.

Nonetheless, there exists a growing alienation of Diaspora Jews from Israel. The personal meaning model therefore assumes greater importance. An essential part of making this happen will be the social and religious character of Israel. If Israel remains closed to religious pluralism and diversity and indifferent to Jewish religious values, in the broadest sense, fewer and fewer Diaspora Jews will feel a connection or the need to build connections and bridges.

Therefore, a new form of the mobilization model must emerge—mobilization to fight for equal religious rights and recognition for all Jewish religious streams, mobilization to reach out to Israeli Jewish society and educate them, mobilization to battle the growing assimilation and what some call the "Canaanization" among Israeli Jews. The new mobilization model moves us beyond the political, diplomatic, and philanthropic areas alone to a battle not just for the soil of Israel but for the soul of Israel. In order for the personal meaning model to work, we must build bridges of religious understanding as well. The personal meaning model works both ways—for Israeli Jews as well as for Diaspora Jews.

Diaspora Jewry has much to learn from the Jews in Israel, where very act and every moment possesses Jewish meaning and consequences. Israeli Jewry has much to learn from the creativity, openness, religious diversity, and Jewish values that are the hallmark of Diaspora Jewry. We do not wish to transplant Diaspora Judaism into Israel. We wish to open Israeli society to an encounter between the enrichment of diversity and religious creativity and the spiritual life of Israelis. Let new forms, exciting and meaningful ones, emerge.

We resonate to the old pioneer song, *Anu banu artza livnot u-lehibanot bah*: "We have come to Israel to build and to be rebuilt in it." The new era of Diaspora–Israel relationships will be one of mutuality, interdependence, shared endeavors, and the willingness to learn from each other. Thus we shall build and be rebuilt.

NEGATION
OF THE EXILE?

Yosef Gorny

Shlilat Ha-Galut: Past and Present

It seems to me that since the Balfour Declaration, and particularly since the end of World War Two, after the Holocaust of European Jewry and the establishment of the State of Israel, relations between American Jewry and Israel have not been limited to "survival" and "philanthropy," each of which seems to express total dependence on the other, in a sort of catastrophic mutuality, with American Jewry dependent upon Israel for its spiritual existence and Israel dependent upon American Jewry for its material existence. Such a definition of the relationship, very subjective for each of the collectives, does not characterize the dynamics between the two, either in the past or in the future—even if there were periods when it was true, and even if it has always been so.

It would be more correct to see them, for the past fifty years, in a partnership in which each has had a certain advantage and function of its own, and the dependence between them has been mutually satisfying, even when the contributions of the parties were not equal in every area, particularly in all that relates to the continued existence of *klal yisrael*. Based on Israeli reality, these relations are analogous to an army that has fighting forces stationed on the front and supporting forces stationed in the rear. Both are dependent on one another. It is important to note that those standing at the "front" are mobilized, by virtue of their being citizens of their sovereign country, while those standing in the "rear" are volunteers, by virtue of their being citizens of other countries. And this distinction highlights both the difference and the mutual relationship that exists between them.

If the network of relationships between Israel and American Jewry is based on mutuality, as I have tried to define it, then the term *shlilat ha-galut* (negation of the exile) deserves renewed study and evaluation.

For the sake of clarity, I would like first off to distinguish between three terms that relate to the term *galut:* the *state of exile,* the *sense of exile,* and the *recognition of exile.*

The *state of exile* refers to the complex of discriminatory political, legal, economic, and social conditions in which a particular group finds itself at a particular time in history and in a certain place because it has been exiled from its country. Of course, this situation can change according to the conditions of the place, the passage of time, and the character of the majority rule in the place. What does not change is the dependence of the Diaspora or the exiles on the ruling majority.

The *sense of exile* expresses the sense of *golah* and *nekhar*, as defined by Yehezkel Kaufmann. But whereas he was referring to the formal and informal legal status of the Jews, I am referring to their emotional and spiritual attitude toward their places of residence—the sense of foreignness or strangeness vis-à-vis their surroundings that was so characteristic of the majority of Jews in Eastern Europe and the Islamic countries.

The *recognition of exile* refers to the recognition that in the historical and existential sense, the Jewish people outside its land is in a minority position, with all the ramifications of this situation on the form and continuation of its existence.

From this I come to *shlilat ha-galut*—a very emotionally and intellectually loaded expression in the Zionist outlook past and present, in all references to the relations between Israel and the Diaspora, and in relation to the internal reality in Israel and in each of the Diaspora countries. It is worth mentioning that Zionism received from the tradition the dialectic connection between *galut* and *ge'ulah,* but shifted it from the metaphysical level to the earthly level; from religious belief to national recognition; from the messianic expectation to the political activity of settlement. Moreover, Zionism, like the religious Judaism that opposed it, did not assume the abolition of the *galut* within the given historical time. Even the radical political Zionism that inherited Herzl's tradition did not believe in the physical abolition of the *galut.* At the same time, the Zionist *shlilat ha-galut* differed from the traditional form in that Jewish reality in the Diaspora was evaluated from the political, social, cultural, and moral points of view and defined by principles and values that were foreign to traditional Judaism. In this sense Zionism constituted an existential revolution, by proposing an alternative to *galut* without abolishing it.

At this point it is worthwhile to examine three distinct perceptions of *shlilat ha-galut* in Zionism in the past. Together they express the tension between acceptance of the existence of the *galut* and the recognition of the need to change its essence. I am referring to the views of Ahad Ha-Am, of Yehezkel Kaufmann, and of David Ben-Gurion.

Ahad Ha-Am, Yehezkel Kaufmann, and David Ben-Gurion

From 1907 to 1909, Ahad Ha-Am and Simon Dubnow publicly debated Dubnow's idea of national autonomy. Although Ahad Ha-Am did not oppose the idea itself, and even supported it, he did not consider it sufficient, in itself, to justify the existence of a national Jewish framework in the Diaspora. From his point of view, as we know, the condition for existence of the national autonomous framework was the presence of a central focus, and that was the Jewish national community in *eretz yisrael*. In the course of the debate, Ahad Ha-Am explained the way in which he understood the concept of *shlilat ha-galut*. According to him, "We can relate negatively to something in two ways; either by subjective rejection or by objective rejection." In the wake of this distinction, Ahad Ha-Am explained, "When we speak, therefore, of *shlilat ha-galut,* we must first remember that in the subjective sense the entire Jewish People are 'rejecters of the galut'—all of them, with the exception of individuals who set themselves apart from the community."

In his opinion, the vast and determining majority of the Jews, among them also those that did not support the Jewish national movement, would be happy to change their exilic condition and to live as a sovereign people in its historic land. Not so in the case of "objective rejection," that rejection that, according to him, "rejects the *possibility* of our national existence in the Diaspora in the coming generation, once the spiritual barrier that protected our forefathers in past generations has been destroyed, and we have no refuge from the stream of foreign cultures that surround us—a stream that washes over our national qualities and in this way slowly draws nearer the end of our existence as a nation."

This objective rejection leads those who live by it to two conflicting conclusions, both rooted in a sense of total despair in the exilic life. One, abandonment of the Jewish people through assimilation, and the other, separation of the Jewish people from the nations among which it lives and gathering it together in the fatherland, or at least in some territory where it will be able to develop and maintain a Jewish national society. But in Ahad Ha-Am's opinion, neither of these two opposing conclusions would be acceptable to the majority of the nation that, in his words, retains "its ancient faith that maintained it throughout all the generations: rejection of the *galut* in the subjective sense and confirmation of the *galut* in the objective sense."

Indeed, in his words, "the exile is a very evil and bitter matter, but we must and also can live in the Exile, with all its evil and bitterness. Leaving the Exile always was and will be a shining national hope for 'the end of days,' but the timing of the 'end' is 'a secret of God' that is hidden and unknown to us, and our national existence is not dependent on it." And the historical solution that he proposed to the question of national existence in a state of constant exile is well known: "The creation of a permanent center for our nationalism in its natural habitat."[1]

Twenty years later, in 1929, another Zionist intellectual, the historian and philosopher Yehezkel Kaufmann, developed a different outlook, in which the *galut* also does not disappear. Kaufmann, as is known, created a conceptual connection between *galut* and *nekhar*. He defined *galut* "as a complex of historical-social processes: destruction, enslavement, wandering, settlement in the ghetto, assimilation, and natural development in the direction of ethnic disappearance." *Nekhar,* on the other hand, he saw as the essential being of the Jewish exile, as a term for a persisting legal-popular (if not always legal-formal) condition, in which the Jewish people has existed in its countries of dispersion for generations: "This condition of a unique 'strangeness' that hundreds of years of permanent residence cannot bring to an end."[2]

Kaufmann, like Ahad Ha-Am, did not believe in the actual abolition of the *galut* as the place of residence of the Jews outside the Land of Israel. Both considered the Land of Israel as a national center, for as Kaufmann stated, "*Eretz yisrael* will remain inscribed forever in the soul of the nation... but the solution to the problem of exile will nonetheless not be found here..."

At this point, Kaufmann differed with Ahad Ha-Am. Instead of the *galut* as a form of national existence in its historical location in an autonomous cultural framework around the national center in *eretz yisrael,* as Ahad Ha-Am believed, Kaufmann proposed searching for a territorial solution to the exile outside of *eretz yisrael,* since that country would not be able to hold the entire people. Only by establishing a national Jewish territorial society could the nation free itself from the status of stranger among the peoples of the world. And so Kaufmann arrived at the paradoxical conclusion that, in fact, "it is in the very idea of the persistence of *galut,* in the recognition that the Jewish tribe is not going to end by assimilation, that *the most drastic and most energetic shlilat ha-galut is embodied,"*—the meaning being *"shlilat ha-galut* as a trend of the national will, as an absolute commandment to the nation to free itself of the curse of foreignness by means of a national enterprise." And the dialectic result of this stance is that "this rejection, despite its inclusion of the absolute commandment to struggle against the *galut,* still calls for the obligation to strive for *shlilat ha-galut* revival in the *galut.*"[3]

In other words, the *shlilat ha-galut* in Kaufmann's Zionist version is the political act directed at the creation of a national Jewish territorial center in the Diaspora.

Almost thirty years later, in 1957, David Ben-Gurion, Prime Minister of Israel, presented his own interpretation of the concept. It is worth noting that at that time Ben-Gurion did not delude himself: he did not anticipate that there would be mass immigration by American Jewry. In 1950 he signed an agreement with Jacob Blaustein, President of the American Jewish Committee, in which he granted, to all intents and purposes, "Zionist recognition" to the Jewish Diaspora in the United States, and acknowledged the qualitative level of this Diaspora, to which he turned for the assistance of experts and pioneers.

In 1951, after his first official visit to the United States, he told his listeners that while he indeed viewed the ingathering of the exiles as a possible vision, he was doubtful as to whether it was really an "historical necessity."[4] Yet, with all that, he remained in the classic Zionist sense a moral rejecter of the exile.

At the World Ideological Conference in Jerusalem in 1957, a debate developed between Ben-Gurion and Nahum Goldmann about the substance of *galut.* Whereas Goldmann considered it to be an historical fate—undesirable, of course, but also having some value in its own right, Ben-Gurion strongly disagreed. His words deserve to be presented because of their ideological and psychological importance from the Zionist perspecive:

"I am not partner to the glorification of the Diaspora that we have heard from the mouth of Dr. Goldmann. Each of us stands in awe and deep admiration before the tremendous emotional power revealed by the Jews in their wanderings and sufferings in the Diaspora...I will admire any man who is sick and in pain who struggles for his survival, who does not bow to his bitter fate, but I will not consider his to be an ideal condition... In contrast, the builders of the State of Israel rebelled against the lack of Jewish independence and freedom that character-ized Jewish history in exile."

At that point Ben-Gurion reached the height of his rhetoric, turning Shylock into a metaphor for the exilic condition. "I do not despise Shylock for making a living from usury. He had no other choice in the place of his exile, and in his quality of morality, he stood far above the grand lords who humiliated him; but I will not turn Shylock into an ideal and a man of stature whom I seek to emulate. The Jews of the Diaspora are not Shylocks—but it is difficult to accommodate the glo-rification of life in the Diaspora with the ideal that seventy years ago was given the name 'Zionism.' As a rejecter of the *galut*, I reject the glorification of the *galut*."[5]

Ben-Gurion's extreme words need to be understood in the context of his special relationship with Goldmann, in which opposition and mutual admiration walked hand in hand, but they are the essence of the radical Zionist *shlilat ha-galut*, which at that time had already be-come passé. This was the same moral aesthetic rejection of life in the Diaspora—i.e. Eastern Europe—that had had its beginnings in the works of Yosef Haim Brenner, who swore that he would never again look upon the humiliation of his father by a wild mob; in the pioneer-ing youth movements that dreamed of the new working and fighting Hebrew person; and in Ze'ev Jabotinsky, who created the formula for the Jewish gentleman and nobleman, bearer of the culture of Hadar. And that same *shlilat ha-galut* was what led the poet Abba Kovner and the historian Yitzhak Ringelblum to exhort the Jews who were being destroyed to oppose their murderers and not to go "like sheep to the slaughter."

This value-oriented *shlilat ha-galut* had a valid rationale in its place and time. And all who criticize or deny it seem to me not to understand how historically and mentally correct it was, in reference to the total and objective Jewish reality in Eastern Europe. Ben-Gurion was, there-fore, the last to give utterance to the spirit of the past, and undoubtedly he himself was aware of this, because already at that time he stressed that American Jewry was not similar to East European Jewry, and therefore its Zionist perception was also different. In his opinion, Zion-ism in Eastern Europe had personal value, whereas this was not the case among the American Jews. In the past it was "egoistic," the legacy of Jews struggling for their own rights and their own status, whereas in the present, in the free Diaspora, where the population already has rights, it is "altruistic."[6] From this we learn that the radical Ben-Gurion was also a realist. And it was the realist who pointed out this important "generational change" between the pre-Holocaust and the State, and between the Holocaust and the *tekumah* (all-embracing national revival).

Shlilat Ha-Galut Today

And now it is time for us to move from the past to the present and ask ourselves: Does *shlilat ha-galut* still have a legitimate place in the Zionist idea and in Jewish being? It is not my intention to explain how different the experience and position of the Jews in America is from that of the Jews in Eastern Europe, from whence sprang the idea of *shlilat ha-galut*. As a historian who tends to compare historical situations in order to evaluate the changes that have taken place in them, I only wish to point to three characteristics unique to American Jewry: its economic power, unparalleled in Jewish history; its intellectual and cultural contribution to the general society, which surpasses that of German Jewry in its time; and its political status, to which the Zionist leaders of Polish Jewry between the two world wars, Yitzchak Greenbaum and Moshe Sneh, aspired, but which they failed to achieve because of the special national structure of that country, and because of the ideological and political antisemitism of the Polish majority that ruled it between the two world wars.

Undoubtedly, the two foundations of the moral and subjective *shlilat ha-galut*, formerly held by all streams of Zionism, radical and moderate alike, no longer exist. The "Shylock condition," which Ben-Gurion turned into a metaphor for Diaspora existence, has almost entirely disappeared. The professions practiced by Jews and the economic spheres in which they lead are among the most respected in the modern, and even in the post-modern, Western world. As a result of the Holocaust, against the background of the existence of the state and with the consolidation of the Jews' civil status, they have become an active political force that stands strongly and quite successfully on guard to protect the rights of Jews, wherever they may be. Witness the struggles of Diaspora Jewish leaders and organizations for the right of Soviet Jews to emigrate, and their watchfulness for any antisemitic attacks against Jews anywhere in the world. And, may I add, their steady and important politicial support for the State of Israel.

In view of this reality, the "subjective" *shlilat ha-galut* of Ahad Ha-Am gradually disappeared, as did the sense of "foreignness" emphasized by Yehezkel Kaufmann. But precisely because, in terms of social and cultural-psychological processes, American Jewry is becoming more and more an integral part of the dominant white majority of that country, I am "taking a chance" with a paradoxical thought and claiming that it is necessary to nurture the "objective *shlilat ha-galut.*"

With this claim I follow in the footsteps of Ahad Ha-Am, but at the same time I am also deviating from him in light of the different reality. Ahad Ha-Am opposed the "objective" *shlilat ha-galut* of the assimilationists on the one hand, and of the radical "Palestinocentric" Zionists on the other, because he believed that the desire for national existence would overcome all difficulties, even when the nation was in the Diaspora—and a large part of it will continue, always, to live in that Diaspora. But we all know that Ahad Ha-Am lived in the "ghetto" Jewish reality. Despite the processes of modernization and assimilation occurring in that "ghetto," it remained for the most part Jewish, religious, and national, with all the internal and external components that this entailed. In our time, Jewish reality is at the opposite polarity and changing at an accelerated pace through universal and normalistic trends whose consequences are centrifugal for the existence of *klal yisrael.* In this sense, the concern expressed by Ahad Ha-Am about the separatist trends in the Jewish people ought to be even more prominent on our Jewish agenda today than it was in the past.

Here we have to note that we are living in a state of national paradox. Particularly on the political level, we have never been so united. On the existential and cultural level, we have never been so divided. The truth is, we are separated into a number of categories: politically, some of us are living in a national territory as a sovereign people, while the majority of us live as free citizens with equal rights in other countries; religiously, most of us are secular, and a minority religious; among the secular there is a distinction between those of us with a passive awareness of our Jewish sources and those who are actively Jewish and express it in affiliations of national or religious Jewish character. In religious Jewish society, there are also at least four main streams that together constitute a sort of "Jewish Protestantism": the Haredi (ultra-Orthodox) stream; the Orthodox—modern and nationalist; the Conservative; and the Reform. Linguistically, the Jews are living in and contributing to the enrichment of five cultures: the Hebrew, English, French, Spanish, and Russian.

Their accelerated integration into the various cultures leads to two phenomena: a demographic one and an ideological one. I will not discuss the first, which relates to the rate of intermarriage among Western Jews in general and United States Jews in particular, which is increasing, and the percentage of Jews organized in the Jewish institutions, which is decreasing. What I will spend some time on is the second phenomenon, an ideological one.

The Jewish people is presently in the midst of a process of normalization. In Israel, the process manifests itself in the adaptation to national life in a sovereign national state that, with all its difficulties, is becoming more and more unlike Jewish existence in the Diaspora. In contrast, Jews in the Diaspora are integrating themselves into global ethnic trends, as an expression of their normal status in the countries where they are citizens. This normalization is taking on what I call a "Canaanite" quality.

In other words, the territorial-cultural base is increasingly becoming the determiner of one's Jewish identity. It can be assumed that as the peace process progresses, a rapprochement between some Jewish and Palestinian groups based on mutual interests and shared intellectual interests is likely to create a special version of Mediterranean culture. Similarly, we are witnessing how Jewish intellectuals in the United States are trying to turn the Holocaust into an issue that belongs to the entire American people. The "Americanization of the Holocaust," as its philosophers define it, is nothing but a further attempt to reinforce Jewish integration into pluralistic American society. In this case, having become an inseparable part of the economic and intellectual elite of the ruling white majority, the Jews are now attempting, with the aid of the moral mission that emerges from the lesson of the Holocaust, also to create a connection with America's deprived minorities.

Separation vs. Disintegration

In light of the above, a question arises: Are all of us as Jews, wherever we may be, in the Diaspora and in Israel, actually in the *galut*? Not a *galut* of persecutions and prejudices, not a *galut* of strangeness and foreignness, not a *galut* of absence of territory and sovereignty, but a *galut* of separation—internal separation from one another within each of the Jewish communities, including the State of Israel, and on a larger scale, separation from one another between the various national

communities. First, between the state and the Diaspora, and then between the different countries of the Diaspora.

This diagnosis, despite the truth within it, requires an essential and
determinative limitation that touches on the distinction between the
situation in the State of Israel and that in the Diaspora. Israel's Jewish
society today, much more than in the past, is fragmented along religious, political, and ethnic lines, while Jewish society in the Diaspora
is disintegrating. The critical difference allowing for fragmentation
rather than disintegration is the framework provided by the State of
Israel: the existence of a Jewish majority; the supremacy of Hebrew;
the state institutionalization of the Jewish religion; and the agreement
of the great majority of the Jewish citizens of the State of Israel to accept
the burden of enforcement of Jewish interests that the State represents.
I refer to the non-separation of state and religion, and to the existence
of the "Law of Return," notwithstanding the difficult essential and practical questions that these two constitutional regulations raise in the
minds of many, including those who oppose their nullification.

In other words, the *separation* in Israel, although impossible to bridge
in some areas, such as the relations between the religious and the secular populations, will not lead to disintegration of the society, because
of the existing framework of Jewish statehood, built by Zionism.

In the Diaspora, however, since the individual's sense of belonging
to the various Jewish frameworks is voluntary, the rate of membership
in those frameworks is less than fifty percent. The personal voluntary
decision of a Jew as an individual to belong to a Jewish framework of
any sort is worthy of much admiration—perhaps even more praise-
worthy than the act of living in the State of Israel, where Judaism is
"forced" upon him by the statehood. However, our concern here is not
with the merit of choices made by the individual, but rather with the
ability of the society as a whole to cohere and not disintegrate. It is
what the late Ben Halpern called "the difference between the Jew's
interest and the Jewish interest."

The State of Israel is the only Jewish organization capable of representing the comprehensive Jewish interest, while Jewish organizations
in the Diaspora can represent it only in partial form. Therefore, we
should not forget that in the sense of belonging to a Jewish institutional
framework, most of the Jews who are organized in some such framework live in the State of Israel. True, there is no general consensus in
Israel and there is little likelihood of it in the future. But the Jewish
State, the great and almost unbelievable achievement of Zionism, is

like the cover of a book that contains a collection of articles by persons with different opinions. Without the cover, the book will fall apart. With the cover, it will remain whole, despite the opposing opinions within it.

Yet, despite the dividing line between the danger of separation in Israel and the danger of disintegration in the Diaspora, and precisely because of it, I am convinced of the mutual existential interest shared by both. And the interest lies in the shared need for the existence of both and in the reinforcement of the ties between them. Therefore, it is important to return to the paradoxical formula of Yehezekel Kaufmann, that the strengthening of national Jewish existence in the Diaspora "holds the key to the most decisive and most energetic *shlilat ha-galut.*"[7] In other words, the "national enterprise" of Jewish territorialism, in his opinion, will free the Jewish people from the strangeness of exile that exists in the Diaspora.

There is no need to emphasize that the issue is not Kaufmann's practical program, but the very principle of the need for a national enterprise. At the same time, of course, it is the objective *shlilat ha-galut* that leads to separation between Israel and the Diaspora, to internal disintegration within the Diaspora, and to deep rifts within Israeli Jewish society. The objective and unavoidable rifts in Israel that are a result of the great waves of immigration that continue to arrive have recently received the ideological approval of groups of intellectuals coming to terms with the fragmentation that has occurred within the State and are even welcoming it. And this position, with its basically post-Zionist foundations, bears the taste and the spirit of the negative *galut.*

It is against this background, and out of a shared distress and concern, that the mutual dependence of American Jewry and Israeli Jewry emerges. In speaking of a community with a shared interest, the reference is not to all the Jews of the United States, but only to those who belong to Jewish institutions and identify themselves with Israel as a secular and traditional national center. According to the evaluation of Wertheimer, Liebman, and Cohen, we are talking about forty-four percent of American Jewry.[8] And in Israel, with the exception of the ultraradical liberals, with their post-Canaanite tendencies, and the ultra-Orthodox, who have to all intents and purposes dissociated themselves from the Jewish body, we are talking about approximately eighty percent of the Jewish population, a group drawn from all shades of the Israeli political and cultural spectrum.[9]

These populations in Israel and in the Diaspora, seeking community existence based on Jewish identity, must take upon themselves the enterprise of the maintenance of *klal yisrael*. The mutuality of which I speak is first and foremeost theoretical, value-oriented, and moral in motivation. Economic assistance is decreasing and political support, so important in the past, will also decrease in importance in the future. Those in the United States who wish to live in an organizational Jewish framework can do so, and the opportunities will be even greater in the future, with no need to rely on Israel. The intoxication with the Jewish State, so important to them in the past, no longer carries the same weight today and certainly will not in the future.

Thus mutuality, although not devoid of various political interest, must rest on the principles of Jewish fraternity and mutual commitment; on the recognition that a historic people not only has the right to collective existence, but that its existence is its obligation; and on the belief and the feeling that being together has existential meaning. In this scenario, *shlilat ha-galut* changes from objective understanding into subjective feeling, in the sense that those Jews who wish to maintain their national "togetherness" will stand up against the objective exilic process that separates them from one another and disintegrates them.

The desire for an existence of national togetherness requires an ideological and organizational framework, in which the idea or ethos that bears the aspiration for the existence of *klal yisrael* precedes the organization and shapes it. In Jewish history during the past one hundred years, there is no idea more inclusive of the cultural and ideological variety among the Jewish people than that of Zionism.

From its inception—from the days of Hibbat Zion and up to our own time—Zionism has been and continues to be a pluralistic, ideological, and social movement operating on the basis of continual compromise to move it towards its national political goal and yet preserve its wholeness, despite its being a voluntary movement. In our time, when each ideological stream in the Jewish world represents only a section of the community, only Zionism can provide the lowest common denominator that will suit all. The only exceptions are, of course, the universalistic radicals and the ultra-Orthodox *haredim,* who have, in fact, removed themselves from *klal yisrael.*

What is necessary, then, for those Jews, wherever they may be, who want to preserve their collective identity, despite the differences between them, is the establishment of a New Hibbat Zion to serve as an ideological framework for all sections of the nation, acknowledging a Jewish nationalism that includes within it traditional and modern religious Jewish foundations, as well as nonreligious outlooks. Despite its internal difficulties, the historic Old Hibbat Zion was able to accommodate Jewish pluralism because it offered a common and clearly defined goal: the revival of Jewish life in *eretz yisrael.*

Today there is also a common goal—the continued existence of Jewish life in the Diaspora and in the State of Israel. For a public awakening of this kind to take place, a consensus is required on a number of essential and practical issues.

There is need for a recognition of the objective *shlilat ha-galut,* not because the *galut* endangers the lives of Jews; not because they are discriminated against in their host societies and demeaned by them as individuals; not because of their economic distress; and not because they are victims of antisemitism. Exactly the opposite is true. Their situation has changed completely and therefore they are in danger of shrinkage and disintegration.

What is required is a consensus regarding the central position of the State of Israel within the comprehensive Jewish framework. Not because the quality of Jewish life of a person in Israel surpasses that of his partner in the Diaspora; not even because the moral values of Israeli society surpass those of the partners in the Diaspora. In other words, not because in Israel there are better Jews, but because the State of Israel in its essence and in its existence embodies and represents the Jewish totality; and because the Jews that live in it bear, objectively, a special Jewish responsibility for the existence of a Jewish state, with all the internal and external, personal and public difficulties that this situation entails.

Moreover, the centrality of Israel is not due just to what the state is, but also to what the Diaspora requires in order to maintain its special existence. For as the objective split within the Jewish world grows, it needs, for its wholeness, a focal point that can be shared by all. From this point of view, New York, with all its wealth and intellectual vitality in the Jewish sense, cannot replace Jerusalem—as the focus for a loving, supportive, and even critical relationship—for the Jews of Buenos Aires, Moscow, Paris, and London. Israel's position at the center of the collective Jewish existence lies, therefore, in both the positive and negative attitudes of a Diaspora Jewry that cannot remain apathetic to what is happening there.

Israel's central position derives not only from the subjective feelings and emotions of part of the Jews, but also from its objective postion as a sovereign Jewish state. Although not without limitations, as with all countries of the world, whether large and powerful or small and weak, its sovereignty in regard to internal Jewish matters is absolute. The state serves, on the basis of its own resolution and by means of the Law of Return, as a sort of open shelter for any Jew who needs it; it maintains a national Jewish public face in all that relates to Jewish religion and Hebrew culture.

The Jewish Diasporas—in spite of their great wealth and powerful political clout even in the international arena, through the World Jewish Congress—do not possess such sovereign authority. And this does not minimize their Jewish institutions and personalities, who have conducted important and successful battles, such as the one for the freedom of Soviet Jews to emigrate. But the Diaspora's political power has significance only as long as it coincides with, or at least does not oppose, the interests of the host countries. A good example is the debate surrounding the visit of President Reagan in the military cemetery at Bitburg, Germany. In that instance, the courageous outcry of Jewish organizations and personalities was to no avail, because it contradicted the interests of the United States, as understood by its policy makers. Therefore, when the issue is a comprehensive Jewish interest and not the interests of individual Jews, the state plays the central role.

I think I will not be in error if I say that the secure position of Jewry in America and in other Western countries is a manifestation of the individual success of the Jew, a success the likes of which has never been seen in the history of the Jewish People in the Diaspora, whereas the State of Israel is the greatest collective achievement of the Jewish People since the final exile from its country.

The difference between the two is that in the United States there is a loose community of Jews, while in Israel, a Jewish society has been established. A community is ruled by the principle of voluntarism, while the dominant factor in a society is the generally-shared foundation. In the United States the achievement of the individual Jew in economics or in academia is first and foremost entirely his own, while in Israel it is significant for the whole society. Here I am disputing the ideological, political, and even academic trends, both latent and visible, that seek to compare the status of the State of Israel with that of the Diaspora, particularly the American Diaspora.

This comparison of separate areas, such as organization on a voluntary basis, academic level in the field of Jewish Studies, or intellectual quality of scholars—in some of which Israel does not surpass the Diaspora, and is even inferior to it—is not relevant to our discussion. For we are talking about the *comprehensive* Jewish interest, and in this sphere the birthright belongs to Israel. And there is nothing in this balanced and comprehensive view to diminish the honor of the Diaspora or to add artificially to Israel's status.

In conclusion, in the present situation the *galut* at its various levels of fragmentation and disintegration is present both in Israel and in the Diaspora, despite the essential differences between them. From this we learn that *klal yisrael* is today in a condition of negative mutuality—that is, it is in danger of splitting. Therefore it is incumbent upon us, its trustees, to put our heads together and think of ways to transform it into positive mutuality.

The Mutual System

The term *mutuality,* when used in reference to two entities, one official and the other voluntary, requires study and clarification. The roles of Zionism and the State of Israel that this mutual system offers are clear to all: the economic assistance and the constant political support of the State were crucial at certain times and are important to this very day. However, the non-economic role of American Jewry in the mutual system is less clear, though no less significant. It seems to me that one could say that since the days of Louis Brandeis, Zionism in the past and the State of Israel in the present have provided American Jewry with the ethos that unifies *klal yisrael,* and also, paradoxically, strengthened its status within American society. This has happened in two ways, whether, according to Brandeis's formulation, the support of the Jew for the Zionist enterprise turns him, because of the altruism of that act, into a better American; or, as is the opinion of the majority of Jews today, the political support for Israel, the democratic state, strengthens the position of the United States in an area of vital importance for its national and global interests. Moreover, as discussed by Charles Liebman and Steven Cohen above, support for Israel is, after all, an emotional and spiritual need for many American Jews.

All I have said up to now is in the realm of historical analysis and ideological clarification. But in fact the questions that face us will be tested on the practical level. Three areas of mutual relations between

Israel and the Diaspora can be distinguished: the political, the economic, and the cultural-spiritual. In all three areas, the Jews have varied degrees of freedom to act in the Jewish interest. The political area is limited by the global interests of the United States, while the determining factors in the economic realm are profit and loss. Only the cultural-spiritual realm is totally under Jewish sovereign authority—in Israel certainly, but in the Diaspora as well. And therefore, in principle, activity in that sphere can be directed totally or mostly to the benefit of the Jewish interest. Within the framework of the sovereign authority and on the bais of mutual interest, then, I propose the following:

1. To turn the study of the Hebrew language into a national enterprise through the community centers and the women's organizations.
2. To create a network of relationships between young and old families and singles by means of the Internet.
3. To hold joint summer camps for students from the Diaspora and from Israel.
4. To establish a traveling Jewish university that combines trips on land and sea to places connected with Jewish history and culture.
5. To promote theoretical-ideological seminars in universities through the Hillel Foundation network and the Israeli Student Union. Lecturers from Israel and from the Diaspora would participate together in these seminars.
6. To establish an enterprise to compose a canonical book of the works that will represent the Jewish world of thought and faith. For this it would be necessary to bring together joint teams of personalities from the fields of education and philosophy.
7. To establish direct contact between schools in Israel and schools in the United States and in other countries. Through this contact students could advance to shared study subjects.
8. To establish a joint Jewish foundation for education purposes. This foundation would subsidize tuition in the Diaspora Jewish education system and assist schools in Israel in the poorer areas on a differential basis.
9. To establish a pattern whereby every academic Jewish Studies conference in the Diaspora would hold at least one session in Hebrew. In similar conferences held in Israel, the discussions would be held in Hebrew and also in languages of the Diaspora.

10. To promote joint study circles in the fields of Jewish Thought and History that would meet at least twice yearly.
11. To publish a joint Jewish quarterly devoted to translations of the best papers in Jewish Thought and Jewish Society. The publication would appear in Hebrew, English, Spanish, French, and Russian.
12. To establish a public apolitical council of intellectuals and public personalities for public discussion of issues of principle that relate to the State of Israel, but also to Diaspora Jewry. Issues such as Israel as a Jewish state or as the state of all its citizens; religion and state; Judaism and democracy; etc. would be discussed.

Considering the lack of democratic institutions representing *klal yisrael,* perhaps it is worth considering a sort of "confederate" organization of national, public, and private foundations, which would coordinate its activities on the basis of "voluntary mutuality." The operational method would be similar to that of academic research foundations, but in this case the fields would be Jewish and community education. I think that, in addition to the private foundations, a foundation should be jointly established by the government of Israel, the World Zionist Organization, the World Jewish Congress, the American Jewish Committee, etc., that would be managed independently by a public academic committee. Continuous and institutionalized cooperation between the two types of foundations, private and public, would likely promote mutual activity between the Diaspora and the State of Israel. Perhaps with this suggestion I am stepping into a shoe that is already filled, because, if I am not mistaken, there is already such a committee with big contributors in the United States. But I am thinking of a much broader framework— one that would include private and public foundations from Israel and from all the Diaspora countries.

I will stop at this point because of the danger of crossing the line between realpolitik and fantastic utopia.

Notes

1. Ahad Ha-Am, "Shlilat ha-golah" (Sivan,[1909], in *Kol kitvei Ahad Ha-Am* (Tel Aviv, 1949), pp. 399–400, 403.

2. Yehezkel Kaufmann, *Golah ve-nekhar*, vol. 1 (Tel Aviv, 1930), p. 200.

3. Ibid., vol. 2, pp. 475–76.

4. See Yosef Gorny, *Ha-Ḥipus aḥar ha-zehut ha-le'umit,* (Tel Aviv, 1986) p. 82.

5. David Ben-Gurion, "Teshuvah le-mitvakhim," *Hazzut* 4(1958): 167.

6. See Yosef Gorny, loc. cit.

7. Yehezkel Kaufmann, *Golah ve-nekhar* vol. 2, p. 2176.

8. Jack Wertheimer, Charles Liebman, Steven Cohen, "How to Save American Jews," *Commentary* (January 1996): 47–51.

9. This is only an estimation, based on a study by the Guttman Institute in 1991. See Binyamin Neuberger, *Medinah u-politika* (Tel Aviv, 1994), p. 32.

Jonathan D. Sarna

Response
The Question of Shlilat Ha-Galut *in American Zionism*

Prof. Gorny provides in his paper a valuable survey of the concept of *shlilat ha-golah* (negation of the Diaspora) and its place in Zionist history and thought. He is an acknowledged expert in this area, and his thoughts on the relationship between Zionism and the Diaspora—past, present, and future—merit careful consideration.

In what follows, I want to focus more narrowly on the place of *shlilat ha-golah* in American Zionism—or more precisely, its lack of a place. Where negation of the Diaspora played a central role in European Zionist thought, American Zionists tended to dismiss it out of hand. Israel Friedlaender, for example, specifically disassociated himself from "those who champion 'the denial of the Golus.'" Instead, he believed that "given the unifying and inspiring influence of a Jewish center in our ancient homeland, Jewish life in the Diaspora may be so shaped as to harmonize both with the age-long traditions of our people and with the life of the nations in whose midst we dwell." His famous formula was "Zionism plus Diaspora, Palestine plus America." Negaters of the Diaspora, he charged, sought "to sacrifice the bulk of the Jewish people outside of Palestine for the sake of a small minority who are to form the Jewish nucleus in Palestine."[1]

Louis Brandeis was even less interested in negating the Diaspora. His Zionism demanded "loyalty to America" and was actually an extension of his Americanism. "The ideals which I ... set forth for America," he once wrote, "should prevail likewise in the Jewish State."[2] He famously argued that "every American Jew who aids in advancing the Jewish settlement in Palestine, *though he feels that neither he nor his descendants will ever live there,* will likewise be a better man and a better American for doing so."[3] [italics added]

Judah Magnes, heir to American Zionist thinking, maintained his opposition to *shlilat ha-golah* even after he himself made aliyah. In Jerusalem, in 1923, he spoke of "the spiritual significance of the Galut."

"My conception of Zionism," he reminded his largely unsympathetic audience, does "not at all provide for the Jews being taken out of their place in the struggling world."[4] Earlier he had written to Chaim Weizmann that "the despair theory of Zionism does not appeal to me."[5]

In short, the concept of *shlilat ha-golah* did not historically play an important role in American Zionist thinking. The reasons for this are complex, but they largely stem from the distinctive historical experience of American Jews. As Ben Halpern once explained, "Emancipation was never an issue" in the United States. "Because of this, the continuity of European Jewish ideologies is broken in America."[6] Negation of the Diaspora may have made sense to European Jews whose hopes for "normalization" had been dashed by brutal antisemitism. The situation in America, however, was different.

American exceptionalism, however, is only part of the explanation. To properly understand American Jewry's unique understanding of Zionism and of its larger role within the Jewish world requires us to appreciate that America, for many Jews, represented nothing less than an alternative to Zion. Even if Jews could not achieve full equality in the degenerate Old World, these Jews believed, their great goal might still be achieved in the blessed New World. Like so many of their Christian neighbors, they considered America to be an "almost promised land"—if not quite the equivalent of Zion, then surely the closest thing to it.

As early as the seventeenth century, the logic of mercantilism demanded that Jews in the New World be given freedoms undreamed of in the Old. "Treat and cause to be treated the Jewish nation on a basis of equality with all other residents and subjects in all treaties, negotiations and actions in and out of war without discrimination," the States General of the United Netherlands ordered, seeking to encourage Jewish settlement and trade in mid-seventeenth-century Recife Brazil.[7] Subsequently, liberty, democracy, church–state separation, *de facto* pluralism, abundant opportunity, and the fact that North America housed a variety of other out-groups, notably Blacks and Catholics, shaped a society that made it possible for Jews to obtain what they so rarely did in Europe: the chance to be treated as equals, to thrive economically, and at the same time to remain Jewish.

This, of course, constituted the dream of the *goldene medine* ("Golden Land"), and it represented an immensely powerful historical challenge. European Jews who looked upon emancipation as a failure, considered antisemitism inevitable, and saw no solution to the "Jewish Problem" except Zionism had regularly to contend with this daunting challenge. America offered an alternative refuge to persecuted Jews around the world. From the late nineteenth century onward (except when immigration to America was restricted), Jews seeking a land where they might live freely and prosper had two major options to choose from. Evidence that America was seen as an alternative "promised land" is easy to find. In 1912, a bestselling memoir by a Jewish immigrant to Boston named Mary Antin was actually entitled *The Promised Land.* "Next year—in America," she recalled hearing at the end of the Passover *seder* in her home town of Polotzk in 1891. "There was our promised land," she reported, "and many faces were turned towards the West."[8] An oft-reprinted greeting card from the same period uses a similar "promised land" image to depict East European Jewish immigrants arriving in America. "Open to me the gates of righteousness," the card declares in Hebrew, evoking the Psalmist (118:19). And then, quoting a phrase from Isaiah (26:2) that applies to Jerusalem, it cries "open the gates, and let a righteous nation enter."[9] The establishment of the State of Israel had little impact on such imagery. As recently as 1978, a history of American Jewry evoked in its title God's biblical command to Abraham to go forth to "the land that I show you." Another American Jewish history textbook, written by a leading scholar who is also a prominent Labor Zionist, bears the title *Zion in America.*[10]

The very idea that America could provide a "Zion" to persecuted Jews calls into question some of classical Zionism's central assumptions. Where Zionism argued that emancipation ideals could not be realized anywhere and that the Diaspora had thus to be "negated," the "golden land" of America seemed to prove just the opposite. It offered an alternative vision and an alternative solution to the problems faced by Jews throughout their history. To be sure, immigration restriction laws would often prevent persecuted Jews from finding refuge in the United States—a fact that helps explain both the growth of American Zionism and its embrace by such staunch American patriots as Louis Brandeis and (for a time) Mary Antin. But neither they nor most other American Zionists supported the "negation of the Diaspora." Instead, their Zion was very much an extension of the "American Zion." The Zion that they championed in Palestine was a projection of their fondest American ideals and values.

Whether this dream of "American Zion" was ever realistic is not the issue here. What is important for our purposes is that the dream enjoyed wide currency, and as such has played an enormously significant role in modern Jewish history. It undergirded the "On to America" movement that brought liberal-minded Central European Jews to America in 1848. It influenced masses of East European Jews to choose America over Palestine beginning in 1881. And it explains why hundreds of thousands of Jews (including many Israelis) have continued to immigrate to America since Israel's establishment in 1948. Indeed, a good case could be made that the dream of the "Golden Land" in America has been no less potent a factor in modern Jewish history than the dream of returning to the Promised Land in Israel. Even today, many of the tensions between American Jews and Israel—particularly those concerning "who is a Jew," religious pluralism, and free immigration—reflect the different assumptions harbored by proponents of these utterly different solutions to the problems that world Jewry faces.

In the final analysis, neither Israel nor the United States has proved to be utopia for Jews. Reality in both communities has turned out to be a good deal more sobering than starry-eyed advocates of "promised lands" expected. Prof. Gorny, recognizing this, proposes the establishment of a new Hibbat Zion (Lover of Zion) movement aimed at promoting Jewish continuity and revitalization among *all* sectors of Jewry both in Israel and in the Diaspora. This is surely a noble dream. My own suggestion, perhaps less Jerusalem-centered than his, is that we not only abandon *shlilat ha-golah*, but that we actually embrace, nurture, and encourage a spirit of friendly competition among the great contemporary centers of world Jewry so that each seeks to create a society where Jews and Judaism might flourish. Such competition, as we have seen, has long existed somewhat furtively, without official recognition or legitimation, between the Jewish communities of Israel and the United States. Now it is time to champion and expand such competition to include other communities, and to recognize it as a positive good, attendant with all of the benefits that general international and trade competition carry with them.

Shlilat ha-golah, in economic terms, is akin to a high protectionist tariff that rewards backwardness and waste. Even if once necessary for the development of the State of Israel, its time has long since passed. Competition among Jewish communities seeking to become the best place on earth for Jews to live, by contrast, promises to inspire Jews everywhere—in Israel, the United States, and smaller centers too—to exert their best efforts into making their community a model one.

Notes

1. Israel Friedlaender, *Past and Present: A Collection of Jewish Essays* (Cincinnati: Ark Publishing, 1919), pp. x–xi.

2. Jonathan D. Sarna, "'The Greatest Jew in the World Since Jesus Christ': The Jewish Legacy of Louis D. Brandeis," *American Jewish History* 81: 3-4 (Spring-Summer 1994), pp. 359–60.

3. Louis D. Brandeis, *The Jewish Problem: How To Solve It* (Cleveland: Joseph Saslaw, 1939), p. 22 [italics added].

4. Arthur A. Goren, *Dissenter in Zion: From the Writings of Judah L. Magnes* (Cambridge, MA: Harvard, 1982), p. 208.

5. Evyatar Friesel, "Magnes: Zionism in Jerusalem," in William M. Brinner and Moses Rischin, eds., *Like All the Nations? The Life and Legacy of Judah L. Magnes* (Albany: SUNY Press, 1987), p. 74.

6. Ben Halpern, *The American Jew: A Zionist Analysis* (New York: Schocken, 1983), p. 13.

7. *Publications of the American Jewish Historical Society* 33 (1934): 105.

8. Mary Antin, *The Promised Land* (Boston: Houghton Mifflin Company, 1969 [orig. ed.1912]), p. 141.

9. The image is depicted, among other places, on the cover of Jonathan D. Sarna, *The American Jewish Experience* (New York: Holmes & Meier, 1986).

10. Stanley Feldstein, *The Land That I Showed You: Three Centuries of Jewish Life in America* (Garden City: Anchor Press/Doubleday, 1978); Henry L. Feingold, *Zion in America: The Jewish Experience from Colonial Times to the Present* (New York: Hippocrene Books, 1974).

S. Ilan Troen

Response
Beyond Zionist Theory:
Coming to Terms with the American Jewish Experience

> We have now outside Israel I think
> two kinds of Jewry—in Hebrew I would
> call them people who are living in
> "Galuth" and people who are living in
> the "Diaspora." The difference may be
> subjective or objective. It does not matter.
> *[David Ben-Gurion to a closed forum*
> *of American Jewish leaders and key government*
> *officials, Prime Minister's Office, Jerusalem, July 31, 1950]*

America was beyond the pale of Zionist theoreticians. The further east one went in Europe, the greater the ignorance of what America was and what the experience of American Jews may have been. This was recognized by Ben-Gurion shortly after the establishment of the State of Israel and finds expression in public documents and private discussions. There is other evidence available, especially discussions over what Jewish children growing up in Israel ought to learn regarding Diaspora Jewry. Maintaining that Israel's leadership has fixed American Jewry within the classic Zionist categories that denied the validity or possibility of Jewish life outside the national homeland may have been appropriate prior to independence. It does not reflect the realities that the post-independence Israeli leadership have come to recognize and have acted upon.

The Zionist intellectual and political inheritance of the leaders of the Yishuv and Israel was European, particularly Eastern European. Insofar as Zionism was a response to the historical condition in which Jews found themselves in the modern period, it was the historical experience of Eastern European Jewry that was most relevant. It was logical and natural that the models employed for analyzing the historical possibilities of Jews were limited by the experience with which they were familiar and shaped by their personal histories. They perceived that assimilation or persecution were the options available to Europe's Jews, and their decision to make aliyah was based on this understanding. What they perceived in Europe in the first half of the twentieth century confirmed the theory that brought them to Palestine. Zionist thought in its most extreme, as formulated by Jacob Klatzkin, led to the "negation of the exile."

In Zionist formulations, the American Jewish experience has never found a significant place in Zionist theory. Despite ties of kinship and shared beginnings, deep knowledge of the experience of American Jewry was well beyond the ken and outside the concerns of Zionist leaders. One went to America to raise money and marshal political support. When necessary, one went there for temporary refuge. There was no consistent attempt to analyze what was taking place in the United States nor to assess the character and prospects of American Jewry as a possible alternative to re-establishing the national homeland in *eretz yisrael*.

Klatzkin's personal history well reflects the prospects and limits of the European Jewish imagination. He was born in 1882, when pogroms broke out in Eastern Europe and the BILU embarked for Palestine to realize Zionist ambitions. By the time he died, in 1948, Israel was established, and America had supplanted Europe as the prime locus of world Jewry. Like so many other Zionist thinkers, he was born in the Russian Pale of Settlement and migrated westward, making his home in Germany until the rise of Hitler. He became a Zionist publicist and man of letters. Together with Nahum Goldmann in the 1920s, he organized in Berlin the Eshkol Publishing Company, which published Hebrew literature and projected a new edition of the *Encyclopedia Judaica*. In 1933 both projects were suspended and Klatzkin fled to Switzerland. Although he spent the war years in the United States, he returned to Europe after the war and died in Switzerland. This limited contact with America did not change his ideas. The hostility of Europe to Jewish peoplehood was the overwhelming fact of his life experience. Convinced that only physical destruction or assimilation were inevitable, he was so negative abut Jewish possibilities in exile that, as Arthur Herzberg has written, "He is the most important Zionist thinker to affirm that a third-rate normal nation state and culture would be enough."

Klatzkin, as well as other Zionist writers, made no distinctions between Europe and America. Exile was the same everywhere. Apparently, there was to be no difference in the prospects of Jewish communities outside a Jewish state. This was not an entirely unreasonable position. At the beginning of the twentieth century, 83 percent of world Jewry was in Europe, mostly in Eastern Europe. At the end of the century most of the European Jews have been destroyed or fled their continent. Of those that remain, there is serious question whether they can successfully negotiate "a return to history." With the percentages almost exactly reversed now, most of world Jewry, nearly 80 percent, is divided between the two centers—America and Israel—that hardly existed when Klatzkin as well as Ben-Gurion and Israel's founders were growing to maturity.

The recognition that America might be different has come only haltingly and over a considerable period of time. My remarks began with a quote from Ben-Gurion, noting that there have developed "two kinds of Jewry" outside of Israel—those who live in "galuth" (exile) as opposed to those who are living in a Diaspora. This is a revolutionary idea for it suggests that Zionists embrace differential perspectives in assessing the possibilities of Jewish communities outside the homeland.[1]

Ben-Gurion's distinction is significant and revolutionary for it marks the recognition that American Jewry may be living in a condition unprecedented in the history of the Jewish people. The most direct way of appreciating this new departure is by examining the plain meaning of his terms. The *Oxford Dictionary of Etymologies* notes that "exile" is a religious term rooted in theology, denoting a condition of separation from homeland caused by Divine intervention as punishment for failure to obey Divine commandments. "Diaspora," deriving from a Greek word meaning "dispersal" and referring to the scattering of people, is a concept that describes a condition rooted in geography and sociology. There is no opprobrium or value judgment attached to it. Moreover, "exile" is properly written with a small "e," while "Diaspora" is capitalized, as if it were a territory similar to a sovereign state such as France, Belgium, or Italy. In employing "Diaspora" rather than "exile" to describe a Jewish community is to supplant a concept of traditional theology and its negative connotations with morally neutral sociology.

Ben-Gurion acted on this radical perception in agreeing to the formulations of an agreement with the leadership of American Jewry—the Ben-Gurion/Blaustein Agreement of 1950—that attempted to define the relationship between Israel and American Jewry. This document has been reaffirmed by every Prime Minister through Golda Meir, together with successive leaders of the American Jewish Committee. In this formulation, there is no hint of the "negation of exile" and an explicit avowal not to call on American Jews to make aliyah. Instead, admitting the special status of American Jewry as a viable, powerful, and creative community, it emphasizes its obligations to provide assistance to other Jews—including those in Israel and endangered communities throughout the world. It was in the context of formulating this agreement that Ben-Gurion and his advisors conducted a most extraordinary seminar that formulated, perhaps for the first time, the exceptional nature of the American Jewish experience.

In July 1950 Ben-Gurion created a closed two-day seminar of key leaders familiar with America to analyze the proper Israeli attitude toward American Jewry.[1] Among those in attendance were Moshe Sharett, Golda Myerson (Meir), Abba Eban, Eliahu Elath, Levi Eshkol, and Teddy Kollek. Ben-Gurion termed the meeting "*Gishateynu le-yahadut amerika:* Our Attitude towards American Jewry." Although the seminar confirmed the facts that America and its Jews did not fit Zionist stereotypes, that America did not threaten Jews, and that U.S. Jews would not make aliyah, it proved to be an unsuccessful attempt to discover an operative ideology for incorporating this anomaly into a traditional Zionist ideology rooted in the negative experience of European Jewry.

Teddy Kollek best articulated the novel situation by suggesting how a Zionist recruiter—the *shali'ah*—should and should not proceed:

Do not try to scare American Jews; there will be no pogroms in America.

Do not try to tell them they should not love and admire America. Never mention Marx; Berl Katznelson [the grand-teacher of Labor Zionism] is acceptable; the Bible and Hebrew language are better.

Only the misfits are likely to come; immigrants and perhaps their children who have not yet adjusted to the United States can be talked to in traditional terms; that is, as if one were in a *hakhsharah* or pioneering camp in Poland or Germany.

Do not try to inculcate the dream of the kibbutz; it is a romantic idea, but it does not have the same resonance in bourgeois, individualistic America.

Do not try to communicate to them the angry revolution some of us have undergone in relation to Jewish religion, Jewish ritual, and the synagogue. Treat Judaism and Jewish traditions with respect.

He concluded with an appeal for a new approach based on commonalities, particularly the notion of the "shared fate" and "common destiny" of the Jewish people.

Even had such advice been implemented, it is doubtful it would have had much impact. Few American Jews ever made aliyah and perhaps some of those who did could have been classified as "misfits"; others were often idealistic European immigrants less concerned with the possibilities of accommodation to America, which for them was a way-station, than with building a new society in Palestine. Still others emigrated for traditional religious reasons that were beyond Zionist imperatives. The net result was that emigrants from America were not conveyors of knowledge of that country, and America remained *terra incognita* to the Jews of the Yishuv.

It is important to add that knowledge of America at large did not fare much better. This has been a long-standing problem. Consider what was taught concerning America just after independence in 1948. There was very little American History. For example, the American Revolution was superficially explored as a precursor to a far more significant event, the French Revolution. The Civil War, slavery, and Lincoln were presented as historical fragments in the history of the nineteenth century; and something of the New Deal was imparted in the context of the interwar crisis in the West. The offerings on American culture rarely extended beyond *The Devil and Daniel Webster*, a bit of Poe and Whitman, and little else. Thus Israeli schools imparted a modest amount of information without moral or ideological moment.

Knowledge of America entered Israel only after World War II. Before then, America hardly existed in Hebrew: only a few works of fiction and one history text had been translated. During the 1950s, a flood of translations from American literature, history, and the American academy appeared, and America was "discovered" by practitioners of "high culture" as well as the general public. The reasons are conveniently stated in the geography textbook expressly written for Israeli schools in 1959. Its introduction states:

[This is] the first full-fledged text on the United States [in Hebrew]—the great nation on the other side of the Atlantic ocean.... It is remarkable that there have not yet appeared amongst us comprehensive monographs on the United States; there are many ties that bind the State of Israel with this Power, whether economic or political and even national. In America about half of our nation [i.e. the Jewish people] is concentrated. The Jews of America take a very active part in the building of this country and are involved in all that transpires here. The Israeli public is also interested in all that is done in the United States; witness the many articles and essays published in our press...[2]

The message is clear. With European power diminished by the destruction of war and its long-admired civilization exposed as the scene of one of the greatest tragedies in Jewish history, America emerged as the great and benevolent world power. Moreover, half the Jews remaining in the world lived there. The primary point is that a fundamental paradigm shift has taken place. America replaced Europe as the society against which Israel measured itself and on which, in many ways, it consciously tried to model itself. This has occurred both among Israeli intellectuals, especially academics, and among the general public.

The "discovery" of America usually brought recognition that America was different. The United States was and has come to be recognized as an historical anomaly in terms of European civilization. Americans themselves employ the term "exceptionalism" to describe their experience and this has been transported to Israel as it has elsewhere. Goethe had long ago remarked that "Amerika, du hast es besser." De Tocqueville and those that followed have found in America a particular genus of democratic society with a unique form of individualism rooted in the exceptional nature of American development. Such perceptions have become common to Israelis.

Reliable markers for change can be found in the evolution of the curriculum for Israeli children. By the mid-1950s, the teaching of the experience of Diaspora Jewry began to undergo reform. Those responsible for schooling the first generation of Israeli children, whether officials in government or educators, were European-born and well versed in classical Zionism. When confronting the products of post-independence Israeli schools, they became alarmed by the lack of connection that Israel's children felt for Jews abroad. Zalman Aranne, Minister of Education and Culture for most of the period between 1955 and 1970, formulated the problem in as concise and lucid a fashion as exists anywhere in the vast educational literature of that generation at a session of the Knesset in 1959.

The national school in this country has had to contend with a number of educational contradictions since its very beginning. How to educate youngsters here for loyalty to the Jewish people when the overwhelming majority of the Jews are in other places? How to implant in youngsters here a feeling of being part of Jewish history when half of that history took place outside the land of Israel? How to inculcate Jewish consciousness in Israeli youth when Israeli consciousness and the revolution it demanded denies the legitimacy of exile and dispersion?[3]

This perception generated a search for new teaching materials, which became institutionalized in the Ministry of Education under the rubric "Jewish Consciousness." The most recent example of the search to enhance knowledge of life in the Diaspora and stimulate sympathy for it is found in the proposals for educational reform presented in the Shenhar Report of 1994.

This activity did not bring unreserved success. Rather, there have been difficulties in inculcating a sense of connection with Diaspora Jewry as well as reconciling an appreciation of Jewish life abroad with the echoes of earlier Zionist teachings. Still there is a strong and consistent line among Israel's educators, beginning with independence and continuing through the present, that points to the recognition of the necessity for teaching a common destiny for Jews who live in Israel and those in the Western Diaspora.

Such a recognition is possible at the close of the twentieth century even as it was not plausible at its beginning. After the horrors of the Second World War, the course of Jewish history has witnessed the progressive improvement in the condition of the overwhelming majority of world Jewry. Threats to their physical existence have virtually disappeared through mass migrations to Israel or to other venues of safety. Indeed, there are very few Jews anywhere in the world who are today exposed to physical danger. This is a revolutionary change and one that was totally unanticipated by Zionism during its formative years.

In the face of such a radical change, an unchanging Zionism would mean irrelevance. Ben-Gurion recognized that Zionism's primary goal was fulfilled by the creation of Israel. He also appreciated that the conditions of American Jewry did not fit classic Zionist stereotypes. This appreciation has grown and can be extended to the smaller Diasporas where Jews live in Western-type democracies. In sum, nearly fifty years after Ben-Gurion's agreement with the American Jewish Committee and the seminar with Israel's American experts, there is little to be gained by posing questions framed in contexts that were not relevant then and certainly are not now. To do so is to engage in an anachronistic and unproductive exercise that can only aggravate tensions between American Jewry and Israel. After nearly fifty years of interaction and cooperation, there is a far more realistic base on which to conduct a vital dialogue between Israel and the American Diaspora.

Bibliographic Note

My understanding on this topic is the consequence of working on a diverse but related set of problems. An extended and detailed analysis on the idea of the "discovery" of America can be found in S. Ilan Troen, "The Discovery of America in the Israeli University: Historical, Cultural and Methodological Perspectives," *Journal of American History* 81,1 (June 1994): 164-82. The discussion of educational materials can be found in an essay, "'Europe' and 'America' in the Education of Israelis," prepared for a forthcoming book, *Divergent Centers: American and Israeli Jewry after the Holocaust,* co-edited with Deborah Dash Moore for Yale University Press. My appreciation of the role of America and its relationship to Israel can be found in the introductory chapter of S. Ilan Troen, ed., *Jewish Centers and Peripheries: European Jewry Between America and Israel after World War II* (New Brunswick, NJ: Transaction, 1998), as well as the introductory chapter to S. Ilan Troen and Benjamin Pinkus, eds., *Organizing Rescue: National Jewish Solidarity in the Modern Period* (London: Frank Cass, 1992). For a brief introduction to Jacob Klatzkin, see the still classic study by Arthur Hertzberg, *The Zionist Idea: A Historical Analysis and Reader* (Philadelphia: Jewish Publication Society, 1997), pp. 314–27.

Notes

1. *Gishateynu le-yahadut amerika* [Our Attitude Towards American Jewry], July 31, 1950. Ben-Gurion Archives, Sede Boker. [Hebrew] This is the source of the ensuing discussion.

2. Y. Paporich, *The United States: Physical, Economic, and Settlement Geography* (Tel-Aviv, 1959), p. 1 [Hebrew]

3. The Aranne quote is found in *Deepening Jewish Consciousness* (Jerusalem, Government Printing Office, 1959), p. 40 [Hebrew]. This paragraph was originally presented in a speech to the Knesset in a discussion on Jewish Consciousness on June 15, 1959. See, too, *Speech to the Knesset by the Minister of Education and Culture Zalman Aranne concerning the Ministry's Budget for the Fiscal Year 1965/66,* Jerusalem: Ministry of Education and Culture, March 22, 1965. [Hebrew]

THE MODERN JEWISH
KULTURKAMPF

Leonard Fein

American Jewry and Israel
The Ways of Peace

1

For the lover of democracy, there is much to be said in praise of ambiguity. In established totalitarian societies, the attitudes and aspirations, the instincts and ideologies of the citizenry may be nearly uniform. Elsewhere, and especially in a democratic society that encourages pluralism, diversity is the norm. Management of that diversity is the very purpose of democracy, and one key to its successful management is to avoid building walls around the inevitably contending camps. Such walls, or even sharply demarcated boundaries, impede a politics of accommodation and compromise. Yet a politics of accommodation and compromise is the only politics that can sustain democracy.

Ideological zealots and compulsive intellectuals alike will find the muddled politics of the successful democracy annoying, and may war against it. But the measure of the successful internalization of the democratic instinct is whether the citizen, no matter how persuaded he or she is of the truth of his or her beliefs, is capable of behaving publicly *as if* the other might be right—hence of making room for the other in the public square. Democracy is, after all, both purpose and method, both end and means. Its end is the accommodation of diversity. The plural democracy is based on the view that the process by which a free nation arrives at a usable truth is more important than the consensual truth itself. In such a state, process is substance. We will not live to see the end of the game, to learn the final and absolute truth, so all there is for us is the way in which the game is played.

The problem arises, of course, when significant numbers of citizens assert that truth has already been revealed to them, and not just their truth, but the comprehensive truth, The Truth for all time and for all people. Those who think themselves graced by such revelation are understandably impatient with the lumbering processes of a pluralistic

75

democracy. Their sense of entitlement arises neither from the guarantees of the constitution nor from their success in the inevitable competition among interest groups; it has, for them, a sacred, hence a supra-political status.

The great surprise of contemporary Jewish history is, of course, the staying power of Orthodoxy—more particularly, of pre-modern, non-accommodationist Orthodoxy. Ben-Gurion entered into the famous status quo compromise with the Orthodox convinced, as were most all observers, that the last half the twentieth century would mark the last gasps of an Orthodoxy that had been battered throughout the West by the forces of reason for at least two hundred years. In the heady aftermath of the Second World War, the conventional consensus was that history was on the side of the laboratory, and that religion, together with all the other opiates of traditional society, would soon enough be swept into the dustbin of history.

We are gathered today at a time when no one would any longer dare confidently predict an early end to religious conviction—indeed, at a time when the most rigid and cultic religious understandings are in the ascendent all around the globe. And we are gathered today in a city where that ascent is virtually palpable.

At the same time, the forward trajectory of modernity has plainly been interrupted. The forces of modernity are everywhere in disarray. Here in Israel, as against the crystal conviction of the religious camp, there is only the appetite for bourgeoisification. Here and there outside the Orthodox camp, perhaps, a snippet of a vision; more often, a dollop of nostalgia for the certainties of an earlier day. Sing the old songs a few times a year, perhaps even send your children for a summer week on a kibbutz to open a window on the past, but not at all because it is a door to the future. In the meantime, what news of the market today, and where shall we spend our Sukkot vacation, and are there casinos there?

The consequence is painfully evident, and I shall not dwell on it at length. The unequal competition between a zealous minority and a muddled majority, aided and abetted by a curious electoral system, has led to the hijacking of Judaism by a coalition of true believers and false witnesses. It has rendered Judaism inaccessible—indeed, offensive—to large numbers of people who, forced to choose between the benighted, corrupt, and anti-democratic official Judaism that is subsidized by the state and no Judaism at all, have elected to turn away from Judaism altogether. For those among them who, disillusioned with modernity, are in search of spiritual meaning, Judaism does not present itself as a fertile ground for exploration; better Buddhism, or any of the cultic outcroppings that now quite likely score victorious seductions two or three times more often than does the *ba'al t'shuvah* movement.

Not that the difference matters very much. A cultic Judaism has more in common with non-Jewish cults than it does with a more open, midrashic Judaism, a Judaism that proudly goes to Nineveh instead of retreating behind the walls of Jerusalem.

2

I begin in this fashion because I have been invited to speak to the issue of *Kulturkampf* in the context of Israel–Diaspora relations and because it is not possible to speak to that issue without remarking and lamenting that the religious sensibility that one might have supposed would connect our far-flung people is today a source of separation rather than connection.

I say this in full recognition that I speak from a particular vantage point. Within the American Orthodox community, there is a very different perception of the religious reality. There, the wayward rest of us are seen as doomed; we intermarry at an alarming rate, we are profoundly ignorant of even the most basic Jewish precepts, and, perhaps most important, we reproduce at below the replacement level. As Lord Jacobovitz once said to me, "We have no need to fight with you. History, in the form of fertility, is on our side, and we need merely outwait you." And if the Lubavitch Hasidim can build here in Israel an exact reproduction of their headquarters on Eastern Parkway in Brooklyn, why should they not believe that the future belongs to them?

And, obviously, from the Orthodox perspective it is we, the non-Orthodox, who rend Jewish unity. As Rabbi Avi Shafran, spokesman for Agudath Israel of America, said recently in response to the formation of a coalition of twenty American Jewish organizations come together to urge Israel's polity to resist Orthodox political demands, "It is the ongoing promotion of the myth of 'multiple Judaisms' that is tragically fracturing the American Jewish community. The last thing Israel needs at this sensitive, crucial time is to import the seeds of American Jewish disunity, ignorance, and intermarriage."

If I express distress at this aspect of our current condition, it is not simply because I see things so very differently, nor is it because I lament—though I do—the fact that the cultic Orthodox are a tiny minority rendered powerful by the idiosyncracies of Israel's electoral system. Nor, I should like to think, is it that I am myself a helpless prisoner of modernity, unable to see past or future alternatives except through the narrow window of my cell.

It is, instead, or so I believe, that I am the enchanted prisoner of a radically different reading of the Jewish tradition and experience, a reading that is at its heart aggadic and midrashic rather than halakhic, and, more important still, a reading that understands the Jewish people—the institutions they build, the stories they tell, the choices they make—as an unfolding commentary on the early texts. I speak as a heretic who regards the meter of Judaism as a path towards the melody of Judaism, who therefore refuses to be hypnotized by the meter, and as one who desires to be—nay, insists on being—a player of our ever-unfinished symphony, our ongoing improvisation on ancient themes.

Which is to say that I begin my Jewish wandering at the base of the mountain, where the people are assembled, and not at its mysterious peak.

3

If understandings religious divide us, what is left to connect us? Obviously, Jewish peoplehood, that immensely difficult concept, is the other tie that binds, or might, one Jew to another.

Go explain how this multilingual scattered people has sustained its sense of fellowship one with the other. To be a Jew is, among the many other things it is, to know that you have safe houses all over the world, that when you're in trouble, you need only look for the door with the mezuzah on it and they will take you in. Indeed, no small part of the shock of the Rabin assassination was the spectacular fracture of that axiom. We had, perhaps naively, believed that in extremis, being Jewish trumps everything else, and we learned from Yigal Amir that it does not—at least not always.

Still, when Israeli Jews and American Jews give expression to their kinship, they do so in the main not as "co-religionists," but as members of the Jewish people. And I want now to call attention to the dangerous attenuation of the concept of our peoplehood that we in the American Diaspora now witness.

The most serious of our communal responses to the perceived crisis in Jewish continuity is the proliferation of opportunities for the study of text. I am not aware that we have reliable numbers that describe the phenomenon, but the growing pile of anecdotal information suggests that there is a genuine return to Jewish learning, and, specifically, to immersion in our sacred texts.

Who can, who would dare, deny the value of such immersion, of such study? A people seeks to cast off its profound illiteracy, to turn away from trivial and sentimental renderings and to grapple with the word itself. Is this not cause for celebration?

It is, no doubt. But a close examination of what we in America are coming to define as Judaic literacy suggests a disturbing downside to this new development. Over and over, the courses we offer deal with "what the Jews believe" rather than with "where the Jews have been." And much of the sociological research on the Jewishness of America's Jews has concentrated on "mitzvah counting," on measuring Jewish identity in terms of rituals observed by the respondent. We depict a Judaism that is doctrinal rather than historical; we promulgate Judaism-as-faith rather than the Jews as a peoplehood.

There are diverse reasons for this turn:

First, this is a time of religious revival in America, and America is in any case more comfortable with assertions of faith than with assertions of "peoplehood," a concept that is essentially alien to our country, suggesting, as it does, something different from and even more threatening than "simple" ethnicity.

Second, our own community embraces a growing number of Jews by choice, people who have entered Judaism through a religious doorway.

Third, the synagogue is plainly the central institution of our community. When, recently, I asked a group of unaffiliated secular Jews to tell me about themselves as Jews, almost all understood the question to be about their relationship to the synagogue and to the faith.

Fourth, our rabbis are not, by and large, well-trained in history, still less in literature—even though our literature is, in a sense, an ongoing exploration of how the metaphors of our faith play out in the "real" worlds they portray.

Fifth, antique as faith seems to some, it is still more "modern" than "peoplehood," for faith is, presumably, something you choose, whereas membership in a people is biologically determined. And perhaps, in any case, the disillusionment with modernity leads to a preference for the antique.

Sixth, given the widespread ignorance of Jewish history, to impose historical fluency as yet another requirement on "the good Jew" would be to raise the bar uncomfortably high.

And, finally, no matter how many of us are *de facto* secular, "secularism" as a coherent ideological option has essentially disappeared.

This turn away from peoplehood and from history is an important development, and lamentable. It is not just that Santayana was probably right that those who forget history are condemned to repeat it. (Or the Ba'al Shem Tov, whose formulation was that "remembering is the path to redemption.") If and as one seeks to locate oneself in a living tradition, if one seeks "roots" and also branches, then the folkways and the debates and the stories and songs of our progenitors become, if not a template for our efforts, then at least a set of signposts along the way. That is why, for example, Irving Howe could write, in *World of Our Fathers*, "We cannot be our fathers, we cannot live like our mothers, but we may look at their experience for images of rectitude and purities of devotion."

If we ignore that template, we arrive at the anomalous complaint put to me just weeks ago by a devoted leader of his synagogue who was eager to have his social action committee take a stand on sweat shops in America but who could not find a text to warrant a stand as a Jew. I offered him two texts: One, the Triangle Shirtwaist fire; the second, the story of what happened when Rabbi Israel Salanter, the founder of the Musar movement in the nineteenth century, who was punctilious in his supervision of matzo-baking, was one year too sick to perform his usual task. His disciples volunteered to take over for him, if he would simply instruct them as to what precautions they should take to assure the purity of the product. "See that the women who bake the matzos are well-paid," Rabbi Salanter instructed them, and said nothing more.

In what sense are these texts? Salanter's is a text because it tells us how a Jew steeped in the ancient texts applied them a mere hundred or so years ago. The Triangle Shirtwaist fire, examined in its amplitude, is a window on a chapter of American Jewish history, which is to say, on the history of how a community of Jews, heirs to a sacred instruction of justice, came to struggle for justice in the early decades of this century. In 1902, for example, the women of the Lower East Side organized a boycott of the kosher butchers of the area. Meat prices had soared from 12 cents a pound to 18 cents a pound, and so the women organized themselves as the Ladies Anti-Beef Trust Association, and their three week-long boycott was a roaring success, imitated soon after in Cleveland and in Detroit. And then, in 1909, in a strike that would have major implications for trade unionism in general, 20,000 shirtwaist makers, mostly Jewish women between the ages of 16 and 25, went out on strike, the largest strike by women up to that time in American history, and the strike that made the International Ladies Garment Workers Union into a major force in the labor movement. Energized by the shirtwaist makers strike, a year later 65,000 men, chiefly from the cloak and suit workers, left their jobs and went on strike, demanding, among other things, a closed shop.

The uptown Jews sought to intervene, for they were horrified at the spectacle of Jewish workers striking against Jewish employers. Their efforts at mediation were finally successful when they invited a Boston lawyer by the name of Louis Brandeis to handle the matter, and when Brandeis successfully negotiated what was called the "Protocol of Peace." And again, a pattern was set: Three weeks after the New York strike was settled, the workers at Chicago's Hart, Shaffner, and Marx went out on strike, to be joined very soon by another 35,000 Chicago workers in the garment trades, striking 50 different manufacturers, and out of that strike was born the Amalgamated Clothing Workers of America. By the time of the Triangle Shirtwaist fire in 1911, a fire in which 140 women were killed and which became a landmark in the history of the American labor movement, the United Hebrew Trades, an umbrella union of New York Jews, had 250,000 members.

Is that saga not a text? True, it comes to us not through the grace of revelation, but through human effort and error. One can, I suppose, regard the role of the Jews in the creation of the American labor movement as a coincidence, therefore as Jewishly irrelevant. But I think it a mistake, a shrivelling mistake, to suppose that we can or we should separate out the story of Judaism from the story of the Jews. From its inception, our story is not contained in a set of injunctions; it is the story of how a tribe that was soon to become a people has understood, shaped, and been shaped by its injunctions. Such a living Judaism—or, as Mordecai Kaplan called it, "an evolving religious civilization"— does not ask, for example, "How shall we relate the doctrines of our faith or, for that matter, the story of our people, to the pursuit of social justice?" Such a living Judaism *is*, among the other things it is, a pursuit of social justice. It does not ask for a foundational text; justice is its purpose, the pursuit of justice its ritual and its way of ensuring that the story is not finished.

Or, to put the matter a bit differently, a bit more broadly: If, as we are fond of asserting, Judaism as faith is about ethical monotheism, then it follows that ours is an earth-bound faith, for only in such a faith do ethics have meaning. The ethical choices each generation makes become the midrash of that generation, its wrenching of revelation into history.

4

But if religion is corrupted in Israel and Jewish peoplehood is neglected in America, what is left us? In what shared understanding and in what shared experience shall our ethics be anchored? What song will we together sing? What then, beyond biological accident, will the word "Jew" mean, and who, then, will be a Jew?

I do not ask these questions rhetorically. I believe there are answers to them, and it is one kind of answer that I propose here.

For a scattered people to sustain a genuinely intimate relationship, protocols and manifestos are inadequate; seminars and symposia will not suffice.

What then? As we have learned these past decades, crisis is a powerful cement. But as Israel now moves from a climate of chronic crisis into more ordinary time, we are coming to realize, however belatedly, that crisis, for all its power and for all its tedious familiarity, may not be our destiny, hence cannot be relied upon as our basic bond.

No, if we are to refresh and extend the connection, at a time when our religious understandings diverge and our sense of common history is dulled, we must turn to the sharing of experience. Until now, the bulk of that sharing has been vicarious. We in America could agonize with you and celebrate with you, but no matter the peaks and the valleys, it was not, as we have so often been reminded, our homes or our children who were at risk. And I believe we are in any case these days witness to a marked fatigue in the capacity of American Jewry to sustain its historic level of emotional involvement with Israel.

In the immediate aftermath of the Rabin assassination, together with many other observers, I had thought we had experienced a watershed event in the life of America's Jews. Specifically, I thought that a new generation was now having its own equivalent to the Six Day War, to Entebbe. But my sense today is that the response was ephemeral, a spurt rather than a new stream. And I wonder whether the fact that the assassination was so manifestly an event in world history—the fact that CNN chose to cut away from all other coverage for three whole days and that President Clinton responded as he did—did not somehow make the assassination less Jewish an event, hence less potent as a framer of Jewish consciousness.

No, the kind of experience that is required if a refreshed partnership, a renewed vitality to the idea of Jewish peoplehood, is our goal, is one truly and fully shared. It does not depend on trauma or on crisis; it goes beyond the vicarious; it goes, as well, beyond our dispatching our young people to Israel for a summer tour.

I offer several illustrations of the kind of thing I have here in mind, illustrations that draw on the particular strengths of our people:

Might we not, in celebration of the triumph of Zionism in the century since Basel, create a Jewish people's version of the distinguished French organization known as Doctors Without Borders? We are, both in Israel and in America, as also in other Diaspora communities, blessed with a very large number of physicians. Israel also has the experience with field hospitals, and the means to transport them. We have access to a generous tradition of contributing pharmaceuticals in times of emergency. Could we not combine these resources and respond thereby to the diverse emergencies around the world?

I know that the Israeli government has from time to time participated in international relief operations. And I imagine that the Israeli government and the Israeli people are entirely capable of stepping up such participation without help from America's Jews. But there are at least two reasons to think in rather broader terms, to think in terms of the coherent participation of the Jews as a people.

The first of these reasons is that there ought to be a way to express the idea of Jewish peoplehood independent of the decisions and capabilities of the Israeli government. I say that not only because I come from a country where so much of this kind of work is carried out by the voluntary sector, but also because experience teaches that the government of Israel may, from time to time, for entirely plausible *raisons d'etat*, come to a decision regarding its participation that is different from the decision a representative body of the Jewish people would reach. Think, for example, of how differently the issue of Soviet Jewry would have played itself out had there not been such intense pressure, essentially from the Jewish street, for action well beyond the action thought appropriate by Israel's government.

And the second reason to think in international terms rather than in strictly Israeli terms is that we ought to take every opportunity we can to strengthen the fabric of Jewish peoplehood, which means to multiply the opportunities for collective action in the name of the Jewish people.

A second illustration: We approach, quite rapidly, a time when bioethical questions will emerge as the most vexing on humankind's agenda. Abortion and euthanasia, difficult as they may be, will seem like child's play when we will have the capacity, rapidly approaching, to engage in genetic engineering, hence in genetic selection. And that is only one of the problem areas to which our dazzling technological and scientific advances give imminent rise.

Plainly, none of us, individually or collectively, is well-prepared to deal with the kind of problems we shall soon all be facing. How, then, shall we prepare for tomorrow?

The people whose skills will be called upon to advise the political echelon are lawyers and biologists and doctors and philosophers and ethicists. And it turns out that in each of these professions, we are disproportionately represented. Why not, then, an international institute of bioethics sponsored by the Jewish people?

There's more: Given what the United States has contributed to Israel, might Israel not consider working with America's Jews to establish health care facilities in some of our inner cities? Given the huge number of Jews in the academies of America, ought we not consider the feasibility of establishing in Israel a University of the Jewish People, staffed not only by local academics but by American professors on sabbatical, a university that might well attract thousands of American Jewish students if the tuition fees were substantially below those in America? And what of an idea Shimon Peres once had, the possibility of establishing a university that would draw for its students on the peoples of the Mediterranean basin, and would also be staffed largely by Americans?

In short, can we not think of a dozen and more projects that draw on our talents and capabilities, that provide a genuine service, and that offer the opportunity for genuine partnership along the way? Surely we do not intend that the only partners-in-experience that will emerge in the coming decades will be in the business sector.

The general point is that if you want to have a relationship, that relationship is best attained if it is about something, best of all about a shared agenda. And the core agenda of the Jewish people remains what it has always been, to mend this fractured world. However we together go about trying to do that, it is out of such an effort that a genuinely intimate relationship can blossom.

5

What are my responsibilities to an Israel that abandons the peace process, whether explicitly or through its actions? What happens to the relationship, what is my responsibility to the relationship, and how do I encourage a relationship, if the values that the governors of Israel pursue are indecent, life-denying, and hope-denying values? How then can I claim that we are connected by shared values?

I put the question in so provocative a manner because the possibility of a noxious government in Israel is inherent in Israel's commitment to democracy. I come, after all, from a country that has had its share of noxious governors, and nothing we have learned these past years permits us to suppose that the Jewish people is immune from the angers and the errors that others have experienced and acted on.

Yet what kind of Zionism is it that asks to be suspended each time its adherents oppose, even sharply, the policies of the Jewish State? Such a Zionism of ideological convenience is inadequate as a vessel for the love of Zion we seek to express.

Which is why I lament the confusion of boundaries between state and society that has thus far, under governments of both the right and the left, characterized our relationship. However central the state in the experience of Israel, Israel is more than a state. I suspect that because the fact of statehood was for the Jewish people so startling, so revolutionary a fact, we have made more of it than we should have. We have chosen to forget that statehood alone is a vehicle and not a value. The prime minister of the State of Israel is not, whether his name is David Ben-Gurion or Binyamin Netanyahu, the prime minister of the Jewish people. The Jewish people has no prime minister. What it does have is a wide variety of contending groups, each asserting its own values and its own vision. That is precisely as it should be.

And that is what enables us to weather the political storms.

Some years ago, I wrote a piece in which I asserted that it is wrong for our American Jewish federations to invite Israel's political leaders to their meetings. I proposed that we ought instead invite teachers and artists, scholars and activists in the public interest sector. No one listened. On the contrary, my proposal was regarded as bizarre: How could federations give up the glamorous opportunity to show off to their constituents a prime minister or a foreign minister?

But I was right in making my proposal, and it is time to revive it. There is no consensus in our community on the fateful choices the citizens of this state must make, and the consensus organizations of our community, the organizations that are founded on the basis of a generalized love of and loyalty to Zion ought not be converted into battlegrounds where such consensus is pursued.

More generally, and over and over again, our task is to create and support every opportunity we have or can develop for association between American Jewry and the citizens of the State of Israel, between us and the non-governmental agencies and institutions that increasingly characterize Israeli society.

The prospect of such association depends heavily on the choices Israel makes in the coming years—specifically, on whether it chooses fear or hope as its leitmotif.

In Israel, a politics of fear has the character of a self-fulfilling prophecy; in America, such a politics is a path towards the alienation of considerable Jewish affection for and involvement with the Jewish State. While I do not doubt that some number of American Jews are themselves prisoners of fear, a vastly larger number will accelerate their distancing of self from an Israel governed by fear.

And we, for whom *ahavat tziyon* is an axiom, where do we turn now, from what sources do we draw renewed strength, or even just the stubbornness to remain engaged as, once again, a politics of fear leads to a government by fist, a government that draws on and nourishes the traumatic stress disorder to which our people is tragically so prone?

We must seek out alliances with those many people in that nation who refuse to dull their efforts to connect this place and its people to the timeless story we take as our guiding text. For some on both sides of the oceans, the story is told, and its newest chapters are written, in a language wholly secular. For others—I count myself among them—the story is an authentic expression of the religious conviction and sensibility of our people. And if I have any one plea of both, it is that we come together in understanding now, insist in a manner that befits our pluralistic conviction that Judaism is, as all complex sagas are, a story that may be variously interpreted, variously lived, and that the path we have chosen to walk and to live is not one whit less authentic than the path of chest-thumping others—and that our path, unlike theirs, leads to a better place, a place whose paths are paths of pleasantness, whose ways are ways of peace.

Bibliography

Biale, David. *Power and Powerlessness in Jewish History.* New York: Shocken, 1986.

Eisen, Arnold. *Galut: Modern Jewish Reflection on Homelessness and Homecoming.* Bloomington: Indiana Univeristy Press, 1986.

Ezrahi, Yaron. *Rubber Bullets: Power and Conscience in Modern Israel.* New York: Farrar, Strauss and Giroux, 1997.

Fein, Leonard. *Where Are We? The Inner Life of American Jews.* New York: Harper and Row, 1987.

Segre, Dan V. *A Crisis of Identity: Israel and Zionism.* Oxford: Oxford University Press, 1980.

Aviezer Ravitzky

Religious and Secular Jews in Israel
A Cultural War?

In recent years, Israeli society has been driven by the tensions between religion and state, the sacred and the profane, halakhic rulings and individual liberty, and particularism and universalism. According to widely held public opinion, these tensions reflect a definite tendency towards a cultural fragmentation that may undermine the nation's collective identity and threaten to rip apart the very foundation of the classic Zionist synthesis and the Israeli ethos derived from it. Have the values and consensus that once provided the basis for Israeli society given way to a post-modern, post-Zionist disintegration? In this essay, I will outline a somewhat different way of looking at these very same developments. I will attempt to show that the current confrontation between religious and secular Israelis does not necessarily represent a process of alienation and disintegration. Rather, it can be seen as an expression of social liberation and cultural plurality.

I will argue first that the political and social status quo that has governed relations between the secular and religious communities since the establishment of the State was the product of a mistaken assumption—shared by both—that its rival was bound to diminish, shrivel, and maybe even disappear. The current confrontation is in part a function of a new recognition by each contending group that its rival represents an enduring and vital reality that will continue to reproduce and flourish. Second, the current struggle reflects dissatisfaction with the dominant and monolithic model/prototypes, long considered to represent the "authentic" Israeli. And it is thanks to this challenge that previously marginalized groups (Sephardim, the religious, Revisionists) have been able to gravitate towards the center of society. Third, the many controversies swirling around the question of religion and state stem from the fact that Zionism's historical foes—the ultra-Orthodox on one side and the Reform on the other—have been integrated into the fold. They too are deeply involved in the debate regarding the image of the Zionist state and argue bitterly for the state to endorse their respective conceptions of Jewish identity. As a result, the State of Israel no longer reflects the victory of a particular (Nationalist) Jewish faction, but has become a broad and decisive forum, where the struggle for the Jewish future is played out. And that struggle has consequences not only for the Jews of Israel, but for Jews everywhere.

All this is not to deny that amidst all the rumblings, there lurks a real danger of disintegration. In fact, it is my intention to expose the roots of this social conflict in all their fierce tenacity. Nevertheless, it is my belief that these developments are creating new focal points of collective identity and granting a substantive "home" to formerly neglected groups. They contain within them the potential seeds of a multi-faceted society, which represents more accurately the complexities of the contemporary Jewish experience.

Contending Predictions

In 1949, Arthur Koestler published *Promise and Fulfillment: Palestine 1917–1949,* in which he analyzed the historical developments that had led to the creation of the State, depicted Israeli ways of life and experiences, and attempted to predict what the future held in store for the new society taking shape. While conceding that it was difficult to forsee at such an early juncture the direction of the new Hebrew civilization, he believed that one thing was "fairly clear: within a generation or two Israel will have become an essentially 'un-Jewish' country."[1] Koestler thought that, already, youths born in Israel showed definite signs of becoming a breed apart from their cousins in the Diaspora, "and with each generation this contract," he said, "was bound to increase." In due time, a Hebrew identity and culture would emerge that were altogether foreign to the Jewish experience.[2]

But what of the prediction uttered some thirty years earlier by the famed American sociologist Thorstein Veblen regarding the likely destiny of the hypothetical Jewish community that the Zionists proposed to establish in Palestine? In the event that the Zionists managed somehow to realize their hopes of returning the Jews to their ancient homeland, it was Veblen's contention that the ingathered people would withdraw into themselves and concentrate exclusively on their own particular heritage—on "studies of a Talmudic nature." Integration with modern European culture would cease, and the special circumstances that had enabled the leading lights among the Jewish nation to turn outwards, and to make seminal contributions to Western science and culture, would no longer obtain.[3]

These contradictory predictions, of course, were both talking about Jews living in modern-day Israel. In Koestler's opinion, they were not supposed to be Jews at all. In contrast, Veblen believed that they would be "too" Jewish—Jews untouched by world culture. Koestler imagined them concerned only with the present and future, whereas Veblen presumed they would be preoccupied with things past.

Which, if either, of the two had it right? How we answer that question depends on which Israeli social circle, cultural group, or ideological camp we examine. At one end of the social spectrum, several segments of the population seem to be completely alienated from the Jewish historical consciousness—devoid not only of religious belief or ritual observance, but divorced from Jewish cultural identity and collective memory as well. Meanwhile, at the other pole of Israeli society, a definite segment of the population is endeavoring with all its might to fulfill Veblen's diametrically opposite prophecy. These people aim to effect a complete break with everything external, Western, universal, modern—a list that includes Zionism and its role as the initiator of a modern, nationalist revolution among the Jewish people.[4]

Let me illustrate the point with an anecdote. A few years ago, around Passover time, the daily newspaper *Yedi'ot aharonot* published an interesting interview with a matzah baker from Tel Aviv. In the article, the man stated that each year the volume of sales tallied by him and his fellow bakers across the country consistently registered a two percent drop. His explanation for the trend is revealing. Non-observant young couples who discontinued their parents' practice of eating matzah during Passover—something that was done not so much out of religious obligation, but as an expression of cultural and national identity—accounted, he thought, for half of the decline. Responsibility for the other half lay with young religious couples who had grown up in households where regular matzah was deemed acceptable, but who now insisted on consuming hand-baked *shmurah* matzah throughout the holiday. Thus, he concluded, the poor bakers get pinched on one side and squeezed on the other.

Regardless of whether the baker's analysis stands up to rigorous statistical standards, it contains insight into the cultural dynamic at work in Israel today. This dynamic, interestingly, has placed professors of Judaic Studies at Israeli universities in the same boat as matzah bakers, at least until recently. For more than a decade student interest in subjects such as Bible, Talmud, Jewish philosophy, Jewish history, and Hebrew literature was steadily on the wane. While the trend seems to have been arrested as of late,[5] it did reflect a process analogous to that perceived by the matzah baker. Twenty or thirty years ago, a sizable number of secular students sought to learn about the history of their nation, its creativity and thought. The next generation of secular students appears, however, to be much less interested in classical Jewish sources and texts. (It sometimes seems as if a kind of fear arises in this group, lest the classical Jewish sources be used to deny them their spiritual and political liberty.) A parallel development took effect at the other end of the spectrum, where many religious youths who had formerly sought to learn about classical Jewish texts in an academic setting turned away from the university and devoted themselves to yeshiva studies only. Whichever way you turn, therefore, there were fewer students to be found.

This polarization, to be sure, is nothing new and has characterized the Israeli experience from the very beginning. However, whereas formerly the split was manifested only on the margins of society, today it is threatening to move into the center and to set the contemporary social and political agenda. And as this demarginalization progresses, it appears that the old public arrangements and agreements between secular and religious Jews are beginning to lose both effectiveness and acceptance among members of both communities.

Should this surprise us? In my opinion, no, and in due course, I shall attempt to analyze some of the factors involved in this trend. First, however, I should like to call attention to the internal tensions that characterize the Israeli experience, the inherent duality at the core of the Zionist idea and project. To my mind, the polarization process reflects, in large measure, the unwillingness of large segments of the Israeli population to continue to endure this tension; they are striving, both covertly and openly, to resolve the long-standing conflict between past and present, between normality and uniqueness, between living in a Homeland and living in a Holyland.

Zionism incorporated many of the characteristics of both revolutionary and renaissance movements. And in both aspects, the revolutionary and the revivalistic, it revealed radical tendencies.

On the one hand, it set out to effect a sweeping reform, more far-reaching and comprehensive than those attempted by other modern revolutions.[6] Take, for example, the French Revolution, or even the Bolshevik Revolution. In both, the insurrectionists addressed members of existing nations, who spoke established tongues, and who lived within defined territorial and cultural boundaries. As revolutionaries, they aimed to transform certain aspects of the social reality, such as the political or the economic system. On occasion, they were even depicted as changes that would lead to salvation. But whatever the program, it was contained within the bounds of an existing territorial and historical framework, and did not extend to every imaginable sphere of existence. In the Zionist movement, however, it was necessary to generate a far-reaching, almost total revolution. The sons and daughters of the Jewish people had to be transported from their countries of residence, change the language of their conversation, adopt new modes of life, and take on new professions. Zionism had to wage its battle on all fronts: the social, the cultural, the political, the legal, and the economic. And the movement operated within a historical context that offered very little in the way of continuity. For example, not only did the Zionists, like other revolutionaries, have to reform a political system and expel a foreign power. They had to create a new political entity out of nothing after 1900 years of the absence of Jewish sovereignty.

In addition to seeking a radical, almost total, transformation of the conditions of Jewish life, the main Zionist groups advocated a radical departure from Jewish religious practices and traditional beliefs.[7] And yet, at the very same time, Zionism was a renaissance movement aspiring to restore a bygone reality. Whereas other modern revolutions forged a future-oriented mythos and a forward-looking ethos with symbols suggestive of a better tomorrow, Zionism drew its symbols primarily from the past. While not entirely free of utopian visions, the main building blocks of Zion's radical myths and ethos were culled from materials preserved in the historical and collective memory: ancient landscapes, old proverbs, kings, heroes, and prophets. Like a boomerang describing a circle, the movement burst forth in quest of a radical revolution, while turning its face towards ancient memories and images.

Admittedly, Zionism was not very different in this from some other nationalist movements that utilized historical memory and traditional symbols to build the national awareness and the collective consciousness. Even the use of religious symbols is not unique to Zionism; it can be found in the Polish, Irish, and Czech national movements, and for that matter in most related movements in Europe.[8] Nevertheless, even as the revolutionary elements of the Zionist movement extend further than those of other revolutions, its retrospective gaze towards revival penetrates deeper and demands more.

This was all to be expected. Unlike other revival movements, Zionism is the product of a nation whose ethnic and religious identities were for countless generations fused into a single whole. The Jewish religion is particular to one nation, and in the present era (as opposed to the messianic one), it does not pursue a universal constituency but focuses its messages and meanings in a specific nation, its "Chosen People." Similarly, the Jewish people, throughout its history, has seldom operated within any other than a religious context: its memories have, for the most part, been filtered through the prism constructed by classical Jewish texts. Its collective national identity and its religious identity were essentially interchangeable. ("Your people are my people, your God is my God";[9] "I am a Hebrew, and I revere God, the Lord in Heaven."[10]) Its laws, culture, language, politics, and social norms were rooted in a joint religious and ethnic heritage.[11] Any attempt to resurrect symbols from the nation's past will perforce disinter certain religious claims. For it is the nature of the religious consciousness to see the past not only as the source of history and existence, but as a source of obligation. It is a spring from which, in addition to memories, beliefs and commandments flow.

Consider the dualistic nature of Israel as a *Homeland* and as a *Holyland.* Whereas the birthplace and the home bring to mind a sense of intimacy, of comfort, and of naturalness, providing protection and shelter to its children, the Holy conjures up feelings of reverence and transcendence, awe and fear. The Homeland is a distinctly national category. The Holyland is a distinctly religious category. Birth is an existential term, while Holiness is metaphysical and laden with demand. Throughout Jewish history, the two have always gone hand-in-hand—with all the internal tension inherent in the coupling.[12] When Zionism reawakened the desire for a concrete Homeland, it also aroused from its slumber the yearning for the Holyland. And the latter has now risen and is staking its claim.

This dualistic intertwining of nationhood and religion expresses itself in any number of ways: in the relationship between modern Hebrew and the holy tongue,[13] between Herzl's State of the Jews and the classic visions of redemption, or even in the contrast between Tel-Aviv and its liveliness and Jerusalem and its symbols.[14] It is no wonder, then, that a number of Israelis are attempting to escape this immanent strain; they wish for a hard and fast resolution and are no longer prepared—on either side of the fence—to live with the cultural duality. Paradoxically, the more extreme elements seem to have reached a kind of hidden understanding. Both the ultra-Orthodox and the ultra-secularist despise the contradiction and are surging towards a decisive and unequivocal resolution of the debate between past and present. Each in his own way reviles the ongoing clash between life in the Homeland and life in the Holyland.[15]

Normalization

The dualistic tension here in question is not simply the result of conflict between sacred and profane or between the religious and the national spheres. It is woven into modern Zionism's fabric, and built into the national revolution itself. One of the central themes of Zionist rhetoric was the "Normalization" of the Jewish people.[16] To wit: a normal people should reside in its own land, speak its own language, control its own destiny, be free of political subservience, and establish for itself a healthy social order. So the nationalist movements preached. But what kind of a process did the Jewish people have to go through in order to attain such normality? A singular and "abnormal" process, apparently without precedence in world history.

A short illustration from the annals of academic history will, I think, help to illustrate my point. In 1911, the great linguist Theodor Noeldeke published a survey of ancient Semitic languages in the *Encyclopedia Britannica*. There were sections in the article about Akkadian, Canaanite, Phoenician, and the like, and next to them, a special examination of the Hebrew language and its history from biblical times and onward. As the modern Zionist movement was just then beginning to grow, the author saw fit to comment on the call of contemporary Zionists to revive the Hebrew language as the everyday spoken tongue of the Jewish people. "The dream," wrote Noeldeke, "of some Zionists that Hebrew—a 'would be Hebrew,' that is to say, [17]will again become a living popular language in Palestine, has still less prospect of realization than their vision of a restored Jewish empire in the Holy Land."[18] An objective scholar without any particular biases, Noeldeke deemed the attempt to revive Hebrew and to establish a political entity in Palestine far-fetched, even fantastic. The historical record, of course, has shown him to be mistaken. Is it fair, however, to accuse him of error or poor judgment? One may argue, to be sure, that a scholar has no business making predictions of this sort. If, however, he decides to go ahead and speculate anyway, he must do his best to evaluate possibilities rationally and to anticipate developments using existing precedents and historical analogies. Noeldeke could find no precedent for the rebirth of a sacred tongue as an everyday spoken language or for the mass migration of people to an ancient homeland after an absence of many centuries. What alternative did he have, but to pronounce it unlikely?

Since Noeldeke, many rich studies of the revival of spoken Hebrew have been conducted.[19] And to this date, no accurate analogy has been identified. Take modern Greek, for instance. While it boasts many similarities to its ancestor, a speaker of the current language will struggle to read texts written in ancient Greek, whereas the modern Hebrew speaker progresses without difficulty through the Bible. Similarly, recent attempts to revive the use of Gaelic in Ireland have had only modest success, and the language is used today mostly in poetry.[20]

To repeat, the return to the homeland and the rebirth of the Hebrew language were described by Zionists as steps in the direction of normality, which was accorded a certain moral stature. To achieve normality, however, it was necessary to undergo a completely unprecedented historical process, unique in human history. What was considered routine, proper, and "normal" to other nations (a national territory and a spoken language) demanded the expenditure of incredible energy, and the playing out of a singular historical drama for the Jews.[21] Normality, as it were, was inextricably bound up with anomaly.[22]

Today, centrifugal social forces are seeking to resolve the dichotomies inherent in the Zionist enterprise: old or new, sacred or profane, particular or universal, "in favor of normalcy" or "in favor of singularity."[23] While Zionism did succeed in reshaping the Jewish public domain, there are movements and individuals who are now seeking to mold this domain in different and conflicting ways. Substantive ideological confrontation, dormant for many years, is now threatening to penetrate and infiltrate the general consciousness. There seems, for instance, to be growing likelihood of collisions between the state (secular) courts and the rabbinic courts and between military commands and rabbinical halakhic rulings. To be sure, the very possibility of such conflicts is not new. All we have to do is compare Herzl's Zionist expectation that in the new state rabbinical influence would extend no farther than the walls of the synagogue, with Rav Kook's Zionist expectation of the reconvening of the Sanhedrin in Jerusalem and the assumption by rabbis of the roles of judges and legislators for the Jewish people (When Kook established the chief rabbinate in Jerusalem in 1921, he intended it as the preparatory first phase of this Messianic project.)[24]

The practice so far has been to postpone these conflicts and neutralize them as much as possible. But now we see individuals attempting to bring these issues of state law vs. Torah law to a head and to expose all of the latent contradictions. In the past, the exponents of religious Zionism were particularly eager to find ways to mitigate such potential clashes, determined as they were to live and thrive in both worlds. Of late, however, leaders have risen among them who have sharpened the horns of this dilemma and who brandish them prominently before their students.

Status Quo

In light of all this, must we then conclude that Israeli society is doomed to experience *Kulturkampf,* civil war over cultural issues, and that the Zionist synthesis is marching ineluctably towards its undoing?[25] Before answering that question, let us rephrase it in more sober terms, and ask why the arrangements that seemed to work well enough in years past no longer are sufficient, and why they are now rejected by various factions within the Israeli public.

It is a matter of common knowledge that just after the establishment of the State of Israel, the secular and religious communities engineered a kind of compromise, which has been termed the "status quo."[26] More than just a political agreement, this was a kind of unwritten social charter designed to enable the two sides to live together, whatever their theological and ideological disagreements. And despite, or perhaps because of its internal inconsistencies, the arrangement worked well for some time. For example, according to the agreement, public buses were not to run on the Sabbath (except in "red-flag Haifa"), but travel was permitted in private cars and taxis. While difficult to justify on halakhic grounds or according to secular liberal doctrine, each side could claim in this arrangement a partial victory; thus, no one came away from the table feeling alienated and defeated. If anything, the (partial) disappointment and (partial) satisfaction that resulted from the deal were what guaranteed its (partial) success.

Another example: the Israeli "Declaration of Independence" concludes with the sentence, "Out of trust in the Rock of Israel, we sign our names..." Who or what is the "Rock of Israel"? Is it the God of Israel, the genius of the Jewish people? And what is the "trust" described in the declaration: In the religious tradition, it connotes a belief in God and suggests a passive nod towards the Redeemer of Israel.[27] In modern Hebrew, however, "trust" (the Hebrew word is *bitahon,* which also means "security") refers principally to physical and military power. The disputes regarding the phrasing of the Declaration drove its writers to settle for these intentionally ambiguous terms, which each individual and camp was free to interpret as it wished. At the time, one of Israel's leading thinkers derided this ambiguity and deemed it hypocrisy. In my opinion, however, that very ambiguity is what gives the document its advantage in that it provides points of identification for people of different factions and denominations.

An extremely important development in recent years is the politicization of the "religious" and "secular" divide, with the evolution of the "religious right" and the "secular left." In this separation we see a deepening of the two principal rifts that divide contemporary society: the question of peace (and territorial compromise) and issues of religion and state. Of the many and various events and developments that have contributed to the heightening of tensions, I should like to focus on three basic factors that have had an especially important influence on the Israeli consciousness.

First, in the nearly half-century since the old status quo agreement was reached, the Israeli reality has undergone great changes. Consequently, it is almost impossible today for any segment of society to recognize its own social and ideological stamp imprinted on the status quo. An example will serve to illustrate the current situation. Today's secular Jew will claim (and he will be supported in this by most religious Zionists) that when yeshiva students were granted exemption from military service, the exemption applied to somewhere between four hundred and nine hundred young men. Today it extends to tens of thousands, and the number is growing year by year. Who could have imagined in the late forties that the day would come when the vast majority of a significant segment of society would exempt itself from military service? Though the initial terms of the agreement continue to be honored, its spirit and intentions have been wholly distorted, or so the secular Jew claims. A member of the Orthodox community, on the other hand, might raise a counter objection: when it was agreed to permit private transportation on the Sabbath, how many Israelis had access to a vehicle? Not many. It was their right, therefore, to assume that the public domain would be almost free of open violations of the Sabbath. Who could have imagined that the day would dawn when the privately owned automobile would become the standard means of transportation? From this angle, too, a wide discrepancy has developed between the original agreement and its contemporary implications. As is the nature of things, each side pays less attention to what it has gained, inclining to harp on what it has lost over time. It follows, therefore, that each side feels that its rival has usurped control of the public domain.

Second, I would claim that the original political and social agreement was grounded on a mistake common to both sides. Each assumed, for reasons of its own, that the rival camp represented a fleeting historical phenomenon. Secular, religious, and the ultra-Orthodox all adhered to the belief that the "others" were fated to diminish in strength and numbers and eventually to disappear. Ben-Gurion and his secular disciples; the Lubavitcher Rebbe and his followers; Rav Kook and his Zionist students—all harbored the same conviction. And while they may not have believed that their forecasts would be realized in the immediate short term, all were sufficiently assured in their expectations that any agreement they reached was bound to have a temporary quality, the character of a tactical compromise rather than a fundamental reconciliation.

From the point of view of secularist leaders, it was inconceivable that the future held any promise for what they considered to be the antiquated world of Orthodoxy. Secularists believed that the sons of that world—observant Jews, yeshiva boys, Hasidim or Mitnagdim—would all be overwhelmed by the normalization process that was transforming the nation. In the Diaspora, such people had served as cultural guardians. But no longer. Their children and grandchildren would conform to the profile of the new Jew then being molded in the national homeland. And until that day, why not compromise with these anachronistic representatives of a fading epoch and even show them a degree of nostalgic empathy.

The Orthodox, however, far from imagining themselves on the brink of extinction, believed that it was the secular Jews who were doomed to disappear. In fact, to the ultra-Orthodox, the term "secular Jews" was an oxymoron. Some would assimilate and some would return to God and their faith, but they themselves were not a self-sustaining group. The religious Zionists from the school of Rav Kook, in their own way, subscribed to a similar assumption.[28] True, they said, the secular Zionists claimed that they were staging a revolt against their parents and grandparents and were abandoning the messianic faith. But what in fact did they do? They returned from the exile to the Holy Land; they adopted the holy tongue in preference to foreign languages; they abandoned the option of assimilation in favor of the congregation of Israel. One should expect, therefore, that once they accomplished their political and mundane goals, they would seek an even deeper return of a spiritual and religious nature. And who could withhold affection and good will from these potential returnees, who were already in the process of fulfilling an active part of the process that would ultimately lead to the redemption of Israel?

To my way of understanding, it was the very same sort of logic that was responsible for the failure to create a constitution for the State of Israel. A constitution is mandated for a long time and is liable to perpetuate prevailing conceptions and entrench the established balance of power. Thus each side preferred to hold out, waiting for more favorable conditions that would enable it to formulate a constitution in tune with its own heart and mind. Until then, the status quo and a provisional social truce would do.

But the "optimistic" expectations have failed to materialize. The fleeting phenomena have refused to disappear or to redefine their religious or secular identities. They even insist on asserting themselves as enduring and vital realities that will continue to reproduce and flourish. No longer, indeed, is it possible to imagine a future free of the "others," who seem as likely as one's own group to go on existing in this country, and to be fruitful and multiply. This realization has led naturally to an escalation of tensions. It was easy in the past to display tolerance and solidarity towards those who, one imagined, would soon be trading in their colors for our own. Today we are being asked to deal similarly with individuals and groups who seem determined and likely to preserve their own identities. This demands a kind of acknowledgment and acceptance much different from what was formerly required.[29]

The Jews of the Diaspora are exempt from these demands. An ultra-Orthodox Jew living in Williamsburg will not encounter a Reform Jew from Manhattan, not in a synagogue, not in a "Temple," and not in a community center. And if he runs into him on the street or in the subway, it will be a chance meeting between two Americans, not between two Jews. Zionist nationalism, however, assembled all of these Jews within a stone's throw of each other. It created a forum, a common public space for them. So long as each appeared to the other as an anachronistic vestige or an ephemeral historical accident, face-to-face contact did not occur. Today, it would seem, that meeting is finally taking place—out of rancor and anger, perhaps—but, it is taking place.

The Contested Area

The reevaluation to which the status quo has been subjected in recent years is related to a third change that has taken place in the Israeli reality and consciousness. Marginal social groups (Sephardim, the religious, Revisionists), as well as certain streams of thought (ultra-Orthodoxy and Reform) that were once opposed to political Zionism, have been brought into the mainstream of the Zionist enterprise. More and more the Jewish State has taken on the shape of an arena in which the contemporary debate about Jewish identity is played out. Less and less does the state reflect the outlook and principles of a single victorious group.

In the Israel of 1948, it was possible to point to a single prototype of the "authentic" Israeli. In those days it was easy to define what it meant to participate in the collective Israeli experience, and what it meant to deviate from it, to recognize who stood at its center and who on its margins. "The struggle over Israeli identity, synthetic a concept as that might be, was a search for a norm, a foothold and a point of departure, for a society that had lost its European and Jewish identity," Gershon Shaked wrote in 1983. He continued:

> It is possible for a *religious* Israeli, a *Sephardi* Israeli, an *Ashkenazi* Israeli [emphasis in original], and a "Western" Israeli to co-exist with a "Jewish Israeli. So long as they have a common identity, there is nothing as important as pluralism in a society as rich in human resources as our own; on condition that there is a nexus, a common foothold, a mutual point of departure... I will continue to speak out in defense of this Israeli nexus, which seems to have gone missing: we must go back and search it out. There is such a thing as an Israeli secular experience... Without Israeliness, it is difficult to be an Israeli.[30]

Therein lies the rub. The nexus that was supposed to bind all Israelis together was forged according to the mold of one elite Israeli group,[31] while other groups—Sephardim, the religious, Revisionists—were assessed according to their compatability with this model.[32] Only later did these groups arise and gravitate towards center stage, first by challenging the dominant ethos and its monolithic ideal, and then by penetrating the centers of national culture and government. There is no doubt that this challenge to the hegemony of the once prototypical "new Jew"[33] is exacting a toll. It has unleashed confrontations and conflicts that threaten to disturb the Israeli equilibrium. But if this cost appears sometimes to be great, it can also lead to social liberation and cultural plurality. It grants a "home" to "other" congregations, creating for them places of their own within the society, rather than on its margins.

This inclusionary process has not skipped over streams of Judaism that were initially inimical to the Zionist movement, but that have, over time, become integrated into its historic undertaking. Even those factions that formerly opted to stand to the side or even outside the national enterprise have joined the project. I will bring this point home by calling to mind the debate spawned by the Law of Return—namely, the "Who is a Jew?" question. Who are the principal combatants in this fierce debate, which has already brought down more than one Israeli government? On the one side stand the ultra-Orthodox, led by the *alte* Lubavitcher Rebbe, and on the other, the leaders of the Reform religious movement. That this should be the case is no wonder. The argument, after all, concerns the question of how one becomes a member of the Jewish people, that is, who possesses the authority to convert non-Jews to Judaism. (Most accurately put, the question is, Who is a rabbi?) This is, of course, an issue that inflames first and foremost the leaders of the competing Jewish streams in North America,[34] all of whom attach inordinate importance to the question of who will be recognized as a religious authority by the State of Israel, its citizens, and institutions.

Now consider: Who were the fiercest religious opponents of Zionism in its early days? None other than leaders of ultra-Orthodoxy and of Reform Judaism. The former worked themselves up in anger towards Zionism, seeing it as a rebellious, secularist movement with anti-messianic intentions. The reformers also greeted the movement with fury, viewing it as a backward nationalist reaction that denied the universal mission of the Jewish people. For example, Rabbi Shalom Duber Schneerson of Lubavitch was an implacable turn-of-the-century foe of Zionism.[35] He could never have imagined that the day would come when the monumental struggle between two opposed branches of Judaism would spread to the very core of a Jewish state. That is to say, these two movements, which once fought against the formation of a Jewish state, are today bitterly debating the question of the character of that very state, and how it should decide questions of Jewish identity and of religious authority. Are we to see in this evidence of the failure or the success of Zionism? Israel's founding fathers were indeed disposed to see their creation as a manifestation of the triumph of one Jewish outlook—theirs—as if a decisive verdict had been rendered in the debate concerning the future of the Jewish people. And yet, the Israel of today has become an arena for the continuation of that very struggle. The state has increasingly come to include the various opinions of diverse factions, who now argue their positions within the walls of the national home. Again, there is no denying that this inclusivity exacts a toll. And the price may, in fact, be deemed too steep by those who expect Zionism to revive Jewish nationalism and normalize the Israelis. The price, however, is not too steep for those who see the movement as a means of reviving the Jewish people in its entirety.

As it turns out, most of the internal tensions that have been stirring within Judaism throughout history have been carried over to the State of Israel and are reflected in the community that is coming together there. Zionism did not create the fragmentation. On the contrary, from a historical, dialectical point of view, it is possible to depict Zionism as a logical outcome of this division. The Jewish nation was able, until relatively recently, to exist without territorial concentration and in the absence of a solid political base. The *Shulḥan arukh* (the most widely accepted code of Jewish law) and the prayerbook were sufficient to bind the people together. In recent generations, however, halakhic principles and religious faith have become a source of contention. In this sense, it is possible to see the Zionist act as a heroic gesture, an almost desperate measure, to reestablish a common denominator in a non-virtual context, as a political and historical entity; to establish once again a national and existential center, despite theological rifts and ideological divides. If we adopt this point of view, it emerges that the attempt of the founders to shape the culture and identity of a new society using as their model a single, victorious image was itself contradictory. It was destined to alienate various segments of the community. But in fact, it was precisely those political and social compromises, the "gray areas," as it were, designed to foster mutuality, that most suited the internal logic of the Zionist entity and the complexities of the contemporary Jewish experience.[36]

With the reconstitution of a public forum for the Jewish people in the Land of Israel, an arena for contests and judgments was also created. Outside of Israel, there are almost limitless opportunities for individualistic and pluralistic Judaism. Every family and community can pitch its own tent. As it is possible to avoid contact, so is it possible to avoid collision. There is no need for public showdowns, or for legal or political verdicts. Not so in Israel, where such interaction occurs daily. And as it is impossible to avoid confrontation, it is necessary to agree on rules for dialogue and decision-making, although not necessarily on belief and life style. We must nurture "one language" but not necessarily a "single vocabulary." It is enough to encourage empathy and solidarity on an existential level ("a covenant of fate"),[37] and not necessarily on an ideological and theological one ("a covenant of faith").

Conclusion

In this article I have written about groups, factions, and camps on both sides of the "divide."This does not, of course, provide a comprehensive picture of the complex Israeli social construct, but only of the potential combatants for a *Kulturkampf.* As many studies have shown, there is great diversity of opinion in Israeli society, as well as a continuity of religious identification, which slopes gradually from one end of the spectrum to the other. Looking at the surveys, the extremes do not appear quite so stark. Using a statistical profile, the scholars at the Guttman Institute for Social Research concluded in a 1994 study that "there is no basis for the rehetoric that maintains that Israeli society is polarized between religious and secular Jews." Their authoritative and comprehensive study concludes that "there is a spectrum, from those who are extremely observant of the mitzvot to those who do not observe them at all, not a distinct separation between an observant minority and a secular majority."[38]

I do not dispute the validity of their findings. I beg to differ, however, with the optimistic reading that they have been given. Are polarization and alienation, after all, only the products of a society that is sharply divided into two warring camps? Is it not possible for there to be a social and cultural rift, despite the existence of a spectrum, and despite the existence of people and groups of intermediate persuasions? Consider a citizen of India who ventures forth from his home. As he proceeds, he will notice changes in the spoken dialect. Progressing further, he will begin to hear many words he does not understand. If he continues to put distance between himself and his point of origin, it will not be long before he no longer recognizes the language of his fellow citizens, despite the linguistic continuity linking the various villages that line the way. To put it in other words, social polarization does not depend only on the slope of the curve that connects one group to the other; it is also a function of the distance of the gap and the depth of the gulf between one extreme and the other—assuming that each extreme is populated by a significant segment of the population. And there is all the more reason to use this second measure when it becomes evident that it is actually on the ends of the spectrum that one is likely to find the society's leading groups—i.e., its educated elite, its moral and political spokespeople, and the individuals filled with ideological fervor.

That is the situation that prevails in Israeli society. Let us take a look at the sociological data. About one-quarter of the population claims to observe the Sabbath strictly,[39] and to put on phylacteries every day (25 percent of men, that is); more than 75 percent attest to fasting on Yom Kippur.[40] Quite surprisingly, 56 percent of Israeli Jews report that they "believe with all their hearts" in the giving of the Torah at Sinai; 15 percent "do not believe at all"; and the rest are "unsure" about the matter. According to these statistics, there appears to be a religious orthodoxy on the one hand, and a secular "orthodoxy" on the other, each of which claims a relatively equal following (20 to 25 percent of the population). The rest (i.e., the majority of the population) sits somewhere in the middle, expressing different degrees of affinity to and distance from the traditions and religious faith.

It is my impression, however, that in terms of both quality and quantity, Israeli society's cultural creativity—be it literary, artistic, philosophical, theological, polemical—derives overwhelmingly from both "orthodoxies," and not from the intermediate group. On the one hand, the volume of rabbinical literature being produced today exceeds that of any period in the history of the Jewish people. High level secular Hebrew literature is flourishing to a no less impressive degree. (The field has produced, in recent years, four legitimate candidates for the Nobel Prize in literature.) It is important, then, to differentiate between the realm of personal observance and religious emotions, and the realm of culture and creativity. In the first, there exists today a number of tempering factors that can bridge the gap between the two polarized groups. Here, without a doubt, the intermediate groups play an important role. The in between groups, however, have less to offer when it comes to dulling the edge of the divisions in the intellectual and cultural realm. And they have very little to do when it comes to bridging political differences. For that to happen, it is necessary for members of both "orthodox" elites to internalize the duality of which they have seized only one half, and to come to terms with the "otherness" of their fellow Jews and fellow Israelis.[41] I have attempted to explicate some of the current processes that may encourage such a development.

Notes

This article also appeared in Michael Brown and Bernard Lightman, eds., *Creating the Jewish Future* (Walnut Creek, London, and New Delhi: Altamira Press, 1999).

1. Arthur Koestler, *Promise and Fulfillment: Palestine 1917–1949* (London, 1949), pp. 330–31.

2. See also Georges Friedmann, *The End of the Jewish People?* (N.Y.: Doubleday, Anchor, 1968), pp. 26–37, 251–99; Ernst Simon, *Ha'im od yehudim anaḥnu?* (Tel Aviv, 1983), pp. 46–49; S.Z. Shragai, *Be-sugi'ot ha-dor* (Jerusalem, 1970), p. 110.

3. Thorstein Veblen, "The Intellectual Pre-eminence of Jews in Modern Europe," *Political Science Quarterly* 34 (1919). Reprinted in Leon Ardzrooni, ed., *Essays in our Changing Order* (N.Y., 1934); R. Ginge, ed., *American Social Thought* (N.Y., 1961), p. 40.

4. Aviezer Ravitzky, *Messianism, Zionism, and Jewish Religious Radicalism* (Chicago, 1996).

5. Interest in classical Jewish texts seems to have been recently rekindled among certain segments of secular Israeli society, an interest distinct from the return to religion. In fact, in many cases this intellectual involvement seems to stem from a feeling that the classical legacy should not be forfeited to the religious.

6. S.N. Eisenstadt, *Jewish Civilization* (N.Y., 1992), pp. 141–52.

7. David Vital, *The Origins of Zionism* (Oxford, 1975); idem, *Zionism* (Oxford, 1982).

8. Hedva Ben-Israel, "The Role of Religion in Nationalism: Some Comparative Remarks on Irish Nationalism and on Zionism," in Ben Israel et al., eds., *Religion, Identity and Nationalism in Europe and America* (Jerusalem, 1986), pp. 331–39; idem, "Nationalism in Historical Perspective," *Journal of International Affairs* 45 (1992): 79; idem, "From Ethnicity to Nationalism," *Contention* 55 (1996): 54–56.

9. Ruth 1:16. The biblical text is not necessarily used here with its original connotation.

10. Jonah 2:9.

11. Thus there is a basis to the portrayal of Judaism as an integral civilization that transcends the national or religious sphere in itself. This description was put forth, in different directions, by Rav Kook, Mordecai Kaplan, and Arnold Toynbee. See Yehezkel Dror, "Bi-ge'ut ha-normali'ut," *Kivunim* 12 (1995): 9.

12. I hope to discuss this unique phenomenon in a separate work

13. Gershon Scholem, *Od davar* (Tel Aviv, 1988), pp. 59–60.

14. Zali Gurevitch and Gideon Anaan, "Al ha-maqom: Anthropologiya yisra'elit," *Alpayim* 4 (1998) pp. 41–45; idem, "Never in Place: Eliade and Judaic Sacred Place," *Archives de Sciences Sociales des Religions,* 1994, pp. 4–14.

15. The religious side of this equation is discussed at length (see n. 4). For the secular side see A. B. Yehoshua, *Bizekhut ha-normali'ut* (Jerusalem and Tel Aviv, 1980); Gershom Weiler, *Theokratia yehudit* (Tel Aviv, 1977); Yosef Agassi, *Bein dat u-le'om: Likrat zehut le'umit yisra'elit* (Tel Aviv), 1984; Prat (Avigdor Levontin), *Boker ve-erev* (Jerusalem, 1991).

16. See, however, Shmuel Almog, *Le'umi'ut, tziyonut, antisheymiyut* (Jerusalem, 1992), pp. 126–36; Arik Carmon, *Mamlakhtiyut yehudit* (Tel Aviv, 1994), pp. 44–50.

17. It is worth noting that recently Eric Hobsbawm has claimed that modern Hebrew is nothing but a Zionist invention, bearing little resemblance to the original! This coheres with his general claim that nationalism is a fictive creation. See E.J. Hobsbawm, *Nations and Nationism since 1780* (Cambridge, 1980). Cf. idem, ed., *The Invention of Traditions* (Cambridge, 1983); Uri Ram, "Narration, Erziehung, und die Erfindung des jüdischen Nationalismus," *Ostreichische* 76, 5,2(1994): 175. See also Hedva Ben Yisrael, "He'arot hashvalatiyot al ha-tziyonut," *Kivunim* 10 (1977): 5.

18. Theodor Noeldeke, "Semitic Languages," *Encyclopedia Britannica* (N.Y., 1911) vol. 24, pp. 617–30.

19. Ze'ev ben Chaim, *Be-milhamtah shel lashon* (Jerusalem, 1992); Shlomo Morag, "Ha-iyut ha-hadashah be-hitgabshutah," *Cathedra* 56 (1970), pp. 70–92; Mordechai Mosho, "Tehiyat ha-lashon: ha-omnam nes?" *Leshonenu lo-am: Kovetz shnat ha-lashon* (Jerusalem, 1990); Moshe Bar-Asher, "Some Observations on the Revival of Hebrew," *European Regional Development Conference of Jewish Civilization Studies* (Jerusalem, 1992), pp. 2–30; Haim Blanc, "The Israeli Koine as an Emergent National Standard, in J.A. Fishman, ed., *Language Problems of Developing Nations,* (N.Y., 1968) p. 237; S.H. Herman, "Explorations in the Social Problems of Language Choice," in J. A, Fishman, ed., *Readings in the Social Problems of Languages* (Paris, 1968), pp. 494–508.

20. On the failure of governments, including the Irish Republic, to reestablish national languages, see Punga Slocka Ray, "Language Standardization," J.A. Fishman, ed., *Readings in the Social Problems of Languages,* p. 763.

21. Binyamin Harshav, "Tehiyata shel eretz yisra'el ve-ha-mahapekha ha-yehudit ha-modernit," in *Nekudat tatzpit: Tarbut ve-hevrah be-eretz yisra'el,* ed. Nurith Gertz (Tel Aviv, 1993), pp. 31–37; idem, "Masah al tehiyat ha-lashon ha-ivrit," *Alpayim* 2 (1990): 32–39.

22. A considerable number of Zionists described this anomaly as a continuation of the Jewish singularity throughout history. In the words of David Ben-Gurion: "Our very historical existence, nearly 4,000 years old, all of Jewish history up to and including the creation of the State of Israel, is essentially a singular occurrence for which it is difficult to find the like in all of human history." *The World Congress of Jewish Youth,* (Jerusalem, 1954, p. 187). See Ze'ev Tzahor, "Ben-Gurion kime'atsev mithos," in David Ohana and R.S. Wistrich, eds., *Mithos ve-zikkaron* (Jerusalem, 1997), p. 139.

23. Elsewhere I have dealt extensively with the tensions between the historical and messianic outlooks and between the search for partial and final solutions. See n. 4, above.

24. Rav Kook's successor as chief rabbi, Rabbi Y.A. Halevi Herzog, was vexed by the question of two hypothetical systems of justice in the future Jewish state and corresponded on the subject with Rabbi H. A. Grodzinski, the head of pre-Holocaust Europe's Council of Learned Scholars. See Y.A. Halevi Herzog, *Tehuka le-yisra'el al pi ha-torah* (Jerusalem, 1982), p. 25; idem, "Din ha-melekh," *Talpiyot* 7 (1948): 18–24;

Aviezer Ravitzky, *Al da'at ha-maqom* (Jerusalem, 1991), pp. 108–11, 124–25; idem, *History and Faith: Studies in Jewish Philosophy* (Amsterdam, 1996), pp. 50–58; 69–72.

25. Eliezer Schweid, *Ha-tziyonut she-aharei ha-tziyonut* (Jerusalem, 1996), pp. 100–109; Erik Cohen, "Yisra'el ke-hevrah post ziyonit," in Ohana and Wistrich, *Mithos ve-zikkaron,* pp. 156–66.

26. Menachem Friedman, "The Chronicle of the Status Quo: Religion and State in Israel," in *Transition from 'Yishuv' to State, 1947–1948: Continuity and Change,* ed. Varda Pilowsy (Haifa, 1990), pp. 47–80.

27. Moshe Greenberg, *Studies in the Bible and Jewish Thought* (N.Y., 1995), pp. 63–74.

28. Rav Kook developed a complex historiosophy with respect to the place for secular Zionism. I deal with this theory at length in my book cited above (see n. 4) pp. 86–110. Here I will address only one aspect of his theory, which was very popular among his students. See also Eliezer Schweid, *Ha-yahadut ve-ha-tarbut ha-hilonit* (Jerusalem, 1981), pp. 110–42. Binyamin Ish Shalom, "Sovlanut be-mishpat ha-Rav-Kook ve-shorasheihah ha-iuni'im," *Da'at* 20 (1988): 151–68.

29. Sometimes tolerance entails de facto acceptance and at other times de jour recognition. For examples of mutual recognition, see David Grossman, "Ani tzarikh etkhem, atem tzrikhim oti," *Yediot aharonot,* Nov. 23, 1995 for the secular perspective. For the religious perspective, see Uriel Simon, "Shutafut hilonit datit bevni'at medinah yehudit demokratit," *Alpayim* 13 (1997): 154–66.

30. Gershon Shaked, *Ein makom aher* (Tel Aviv, 1983), p. 29.

31. Yonatan Shapira, *Ilit le-lo mamshikhim* (Tel Aviv, 1984); Dan Horowitz and Moshe Lissak, *Me-yishuv li-medinah* (Tel aviv, 1987); Anita Shapira, "Dor ba-aretz," *Alpayim* 2 (1996): 179–203; Tzvi Tzameret, *Yemei kur ha-hitukh* (Beer Sheva, 1993), pp. 56–63.

32. Amnon Raz-Karkotzkin, "Galut be-tokh ribonut," *Theoriah u-bikoret* 5 (1994): 125–30.

33. Amnon Rubinshtin, *Me-Herzl ad Gush Emunim u-va-hazarah* (Tel Aviv, 1980), pp. 77–79.

34. David Landau, *Parashat 'mihu yehudi'* (Ramat Gan: Ha-va'ad Ha-yehudi ha-Amerika'i, 1996; Moshe Samet, *Mihu yehudi?* (Jerusalem, 1986).

35. Rabbi Schneerson predicted certain defeat for the nationalist Zionist initiative: "Their presumptuous goal of gathering [the exiles] together on their own will never come to pass." See Shalom Duber Schneerson, *Igrot kodesh* (N.Y., 1982), p. 110; Aviezer Ravitzky, "The Contemporary Lubavitch Hasidic Movement: Between Conservatism and Messianism," in *Accounting for Fundamentalisms,* M.E. Marty and R. S. Appleby, eds. (Chicago and London, 1964), p. 34.

36. Dafna Barak-Erez, ed., *Medinah yehudit ve-demokratit* (Tel Aviv, 1996).

37. Rabbi J. B. Soloveitchik, "Kol dodi dofek," in *Ish ha-emunah* (Jerusalem, 1971), pp. 86–99. Idem, *Hamesh derashot* (Jerusalem 1974), 94–95. See also Michael Mozenak, "Ha-Adam, ha-yehudi, ve-ha-medinah," in *Sefer Yovel, likhvod rabi Yosef Dov Halevi Soloveitchik,* eds. Shaul Yisraeli, Nahum Lamm, and Yitzhak Raphael (Jerusalem, 1984), pp. 163–69.

38. Shlomit Levi, Chana Levinson, Elihu Katz, *Emunot, shmirat mitzvot, vihasim hevratiyim be-kerev ha-yehudim be-yisrael* (Jerusalem, 1994), p. 1.

39. This seems trustworthy, as only 16 percent of the population, fewer than the Orthodox component, claimed to observe *niddah* and *tevillah* (laws of family purity).

40. This statistic was later supported in surveys conducted in 1995 and 1996.

41. This article has dealt exclusively with the cultural tensions present in Jewish society. The co-existence in Israel of Jews and non-Jews raises a different question, and requires recognition of a duality and otherness of a different nature.

David Twersky

Response

As usual Avi Ravitzky teaches me much. As always, Leonard Fein delights me with his command of language, and I find that I agree with many of his emphases—as on peoplehood and history—while parting company with him over several of his conclusions.

Nothing so underscores the growing differences between Diaspora— I mean, really, American—Jewry and Israeli Jews as their varying reactions to Israel's most recent elections and the long political trail of peace processes, terrorism, territorial compromise, and religion and state issues that led up to them. In this regard, Ravitzky is mostly right that the forms of Jewish life hammered out in Israel will shape the Judaism of the future. I also believe American modes of Jewishness will also exert an influence over the Jewish future, in large measure due to its unique historical circumstance as a post-emancipatory society, and the unusual voluntary nature of Jewish affiliation amidst a culture of fluid identities; still, it would be perverse to gainsay the powerful influence cast by Israel over the contemporary Jewish experience.

For example, the two bills promised in the basic guidelines of the Netanyahu government to overturn Supreme Court decisions that opened the door to a liberalization on the pluralism front frightened non-Orthodox American Jewry not because they represented a perceived denial of rights. The Knesset was not dismissed as a foreign parliament in a small country in which Orthodox and irreligious Jews and a few Arabs voted on the validity of alternative forms of Judaism. Rather, such a vote was seen as delegitimating non-Orthodox Diaspora Judaism. Thus the Knesset and government are endowed with a symbolic power over Jewish life inside *and* outside Israel.

Fein was not sufficiently kind to either the Orthodox or the security and ideological hawks. Their views—different from each other—are also lumped together, all different than his (and mine for that matter). But surely a plea for tolerance, pluralism, and appreciation for ambiguity should include some space to allow for the views of those who

are rather less flexible than Fein might like. I also think, Peres sup-
porter though I was, that the decision by centrist voters to break for
Netan- yahu (enough centrist voters to put him over the top), or the
vote of Orthodox Jews and ideological hawks for Netanyahu, cannot
be reduced to a triumph of "fear over hope." It could just as easily and
no less incorrectly be ascribed to the victory of realism and sobriety
over illusion.

Most importantly, and symptomatically, there is a failure to address
the cultural issues that helped drive what we in America would call
social conservatives into an alliance with what we'd refer to as the
foreign policy hawks. I am employing American lingo intentionally,
in order to underscore the similar lines of development among the
two electorates.

Since Ha-Rav Shach leaned right in his famous 1990 speech at Yad
Eliyahu, the *haredi* Orthodox world has joined the national religious
camp in favoring the political secular right. The combination has created a semi-permanent conservative Jewish majority.

Of course, the gap between American and Israeli Jews cuts through
both Jewries along theological/ideological lines and not just geographic
ones. Thus American Orthodox Jews—certainly in my community—
are more likely to send their children to Israel. And aliya, while never
high, is surely higher among them than among non-Orthodox American Jews. American Orthodox Jews share many of the religious, social,
and political attitudes and approaches of their Israeli coreligionists. Reform and Conservative and Reconstructionist have too few "coreligionists" in Israel for them to follow the same pattern.

In Israel, an Orthodox shul is the shul most people won't go to, and
while this is sorely regretted by most affiliated American Jews, it does
not appear likely to change soon. At the same time, while secular Israelis may be comfortable in the mix of Jewishness and modernity that
comprise their identities, Jewish secularism in America is decidedly
weaker and, as an ideological force, largely spent.

For decades, the relationship of secular Jews in America to secular
Jews in Israel was mediated through Zionist politics or socialist ideology. But that era is over and liberal American Jews in search of Israeli
partners no longer find them in the kibbutz—or certainly not to the
same degree, as the socialist component has so sharply declined on
both sides of the ocean. And surveying the landscape, they do not see
the same pattern of liberal religious Judaism with which they are familiar in America. What they can find are liberal Israeli Jews who are,

likely as not, to be Hebrew speaking versions of unaffiliated—what we once called *assimilated*—American Jews.

These Israelis may be patriots, without necessarily being Zionists. They love the modern West, which is seen as a bastion of free thinking liberalism into which Jews (or in their case, Israelis) can fit, equally— and profitably. This attitude is the equivalent in the nineties of the yearning by the Zionist left in the thirties, forties, and fifties for recognition by the socialist states. This reality underscores the significance of the collapse of the socialist, social democratic, and utopian modes of thought that dominated Zionism in Israel and held the allegiance of so many American Jews for most of the century. In America, this evolution has fed both liberal religious movements and the ranks of those opting out. In Israel, it has created a large body of liberals who don't see Jewish categories, whether ethnic or religious, as desirable or applicable to them.

The tendency to see "Jewish" as too small a category, or a shameful one linking a new national condition to the ghetto and the shackles of an obscurantist faith, has been called "post-Zionist," a term I identify with Bernard Avishai, who I believe coined it in the late seventies in his book *The Tragedy of Zionism,* and who considered himself one. In Israel during the fifties the same attitude was ascribed to the so-called "Canaanites," and its modern mantra is that Israel should become a state of all its citizens. This is appealing enough—Israel's Arab citizens should share more equally in the benefits—and the obligations—of citizenship. But behind the mantra is a desire to be rid of the limitations of Jewishness and of an extra-territorial peoplehood, a religious civilization that makes claims beyond those imposed by democracy and liberal values.

Although they may differ in many respects and even object to much of the post-Zionist mantra, voices from this part of Israel have increasingly called into question the philanthropic and political roles that have characterized American Jewish activism on behalf of Israel. Thus many "classical" Zionist voices (like President Ezer Weizman) decry the "pocketbook Zionism" of those whose dedication to Zion does not include immigration there. Combined with the disagreeable rejections of the most widespread forms of American Jewish religious practice and leadership, this has resulted in a pervasive cognitive dissonance among non-Orthodox American Jews keenly tuned to the twists and turns of the relationship with Israel.

I have in mind Yossi Beilin's famous, though to my mind misunderstood, call at a 1994 WIZO meeting for redirecting federation dollars, A. B. Yehoshua's widely reported comments at the World Jewish Congress meeting in the winter of 1996 that Israel did not need Diaspora philanthropy or *olim,* and the late Yitzhak Rabin's widely reported attacks in the summer of 1992 on the pro-Israel lobby in Washington, the American Israel Public Affairs Committee, for getting in the way of a direct Israel relationship with Congress and the executive branch (precisely the reason Israel helped invent AIPAC in the first place). Add to these widely noticed disorienting messages the success in getting many Jews out of the former Soviet Union, the progress in the peace process, and widely read reports of Israel's growing affluence. No wonder American Jews experienced a form of motion sickness.

There is a certain irony involved as liberal Israelis struggle over identity and religion, group responsibility and individual rights, and the competing claims of past and future. How uncannily like American Jews Israeli liberals seem. Fifty years after the Holocaust and the establishment of the State rendered obsolete most pre-war Jewish ideologies, the children of Zionism have found their way back to the other great postmodern stream of Jewish life, what we might call, after a recent book by Seymour Martin Lipset, "American exceptionalism." And with its almost obsessively great focus on how Israel works out, or fails to work out, its Jewish and land and religious issues, the American Jewish experiment comes to Zionism, after a fashion.

Zionism came about to rescue the Jewish people from the conditions prevailing in Eastern Europe at the turn of the last century and, to a lesser degree, from those barriers preventing assimilation in Western Europe (Herzl after all was forced to abandon assimilationist schemes during the Dreyfus trial). But as Ravitzky points out, Zionism was also a movement against—and simultaneously within—a Jewish tradition viewed as quietist and insufficiently activist.

History plays jokes on us all, as Zionism proved itself less than able to transform the lives of the entire Jewish people or to create a new Jewish culture transcending the old—in part because of the Holocaust and in part due to the long Arab siege, which imposed ghetto conditions, though not, praise be to Zionism, ghetto weakness on Israel. America, meanwhile, proved that Dreyfus was a metaphor with a short shelf life: half a century later the Rosenbergs were convicted of spying against America for Russia (Julius, at least, was guilty as charged) and no mass antisemitic uprising took place. Decades later Jonathan Pollard went to jail for spying for Israel, and no noticeable rise in antisemitism occurred.

In the peculiar conditions of the post-emancipation social contract, American Jews were able, through struggle and coalition, to create an environment in which the liberal thesis could at last be tested and deemed successful. We now stand on top of these accomplishments and their intended and unintended consequences. Many Israelis want America's voluntary, liberal social contract and bridle at the pre-enlightenment, Middle Eastern style compact of religion and state. Having eliminated social and legal barriers to success, rendering antisemitism unfashionable in the process (Pat Buchanan and Louis Farrakhan notwithstanding), American Jews now seek inner directed reasons for group continuity.

But it would appear wrong to me to suggest, as does Leonard Fein, that the steps forward should be along the path of liberal Jewish social action—American Jewish–Israeli Jewish joint ventures in the field of combating world hunger raises the question of why a specifically Jewish response is required. Last time I looked, while Israelis weren't going hungry, there remained large pockets of poverty there, as well as among the elderly and disadvantaged among American Jewry. The poor in our own town should take precedence, not to mention middle class cash-strapped day school parents, like me. How about a joint emergency drive to ensure Jewish literacy?

On the other hand, Fein is right to insist that Jewish history, and not only ritual and liturgy, should be taken seriously, and brought back into focus. An emphasis on history would naturally include the story of our common ancestry—at least the ancestry common to our elites—as well as the history of how we came to this moment in time with these attitudes and values. Fein argues that these values, the history of the way we lived, constitute support for his liberal politics. To a degree, he is right. But there is in Jewish history also a stubborn conservative streak he declines to acknowledge.

More specifically, we need each other's modern histories, which we have avoided because they were each seen as subversive to the other. Several years ago, I was lecturing to the students doing the *du shnati* (two year program) at Ramat Efal, kibbutzniks released from work for a non-degree college level course of study. Since many of the kibbutzniks had seen Barbara Streisand's "Yentl," I asked them where they thought Yentl, disillusioned with the possibilities of being a woman scholar in turn of the century Poland, was sailing away to at the end of the film, and they all answered, "Falastina." It never occurred to them that she would be sailing to America instead.

I fear though that a reminder of our common history isn't enough—we need to reconnect with the Jewish-modern dialectic of our earlier period. Rabbi Eric Yoffie, speaking at a Reform synagogue in my community a few months ago, reminded us that the early Reformers had an intimate knowledge of the tradition against which they were rebelling. This struck me as remarkably similar in its inner structure to the small but vital voice in the kibbutz movement, once grouped around the journal *Shdemot*, that sought to bring the secular (but not assimilationist) Zionist left back into a connection with the tradition from which all Jewish modern and post-modern existence derives.

Shmuel (Muki) Tsur once told me that when Berl Katznelson was a child, in White Russia I suppose, he burst into tears when he heard that Hebron was still a living community (the anecdote appears in Anita Shapira's biography of Katznelson, *Berl*). I do not mean to suggest that it follows that the IDF should not honor Oslo B and complete its withdrawal from Hebron; in fact, I did not think it wise for Jews to move into Hebron back in the seventies when the current community established itself. I am saying though that those who support withdrawal, as well as those who don't, can share basic Jewish feelings about land and history. True enough, there is a frighteningly radical hard right out of whose ranks sprang Goldstein and Amir, but to cite another essay by Muki Tsur (written shortly after the first "*mahapakh*" in 1977 as an editorial in the kibbutz movement publication, *Shdemot)*, as grown-ups Jews are good at playing a game we all played at summer camp as kids— capture the flag. In this game, each side had to make it through the protective lines of the other and steal their flag. Our political and cultural life, Tsur suggested, also involved stealing the other team's flags. Tsur was reacting to the large photo of Ben-Gurion that hung above the dais as the new Likud laid claim to all of the fathers of modern secular Zionism, and not only Jabotinsky.

Capturing the flag is precisely what the left has allowed the right to do. Reading *Ha'aretz* and listening to friends, one has the distinct impression that many of the "round glasses liberals" or "north Tel Aviv yuppies"—pick your cliché—are prepared to let Amir and Goldstein be the Jews. How different only a few years ago. During elections in the early eighties, Gush Emunim used to run ads anointing themselves the successors to Hanita, a kibbutz along the northern border. Hanita, filled with Labor voters, would promptly run an ad denying paternity. Nowadays, settlements of any sort, ours or theirs, are passé, Zionism deconstructed.

Katznelson also studied on many Shabbat afternoons with Agnon; secular Israelis broke records buying Anita Shapira's two volume biography of Katznelson. This suggests an appetite. But is it too late to reforge this connection? There is every reason to believe so. But what are the alternatives for those committed to a revival not of ritual or faith per se but of the peoplehood that has been the faithful and at times faithless carrier of the tradition?

It will depend on reestablishing the dialectical relationship between our reformers and modernizers, between our liberals and the tradition. Advocates of liberal Judaism and secular Jewishness must renew their covenant with Jewish knowledge. The richest, most fruitful period in our modern history came at points in which modernizers in the religious and secular political arenas were steeped in the tradition. They created something new out of the old. Properly understood, they were not a one way bridge out of the ghetto into modern society and assimilation, but a bridge in two directions (to borrow again from the title of an essay by Tsur that appeared in *Shdemot*). From the old to the new and back again.

According to a story I heard, when Ahad Ha-Am (Asher Ginzburg), the cultural Zionist, met Max Nordau, the political Zionist, at a Zionist Congress, Nordau asked, "But are you a Zionist?"

To which Ahad Ha-Am replied: "Yes, I am *the* Zionist."

Ahad Ha-Am stood his ground, insisting that his ground was *the* Zionist ground, refusing to let Nordau the political Zionist capture the flag. I don't know if Ahad Ha-Am was "right." Probably he and Nordau were both right. I am taken more by his method than the substance of his message—political Zionism in all its variations certainly has had strong historical vindication.

It is time to recapture the flag.

Bibliography

Avishai, Bernard. *The Tragedy of Zionism: Revolution and Democracy in the Land of Israel.* New York: Farrar, Straus, and Giroux, 1985.

Lipset, Seymour Martin. *American Exceptionalism: A Double-Edged Sword.* New York: Norton, 1997.

Shapira, Anita. *Berl: The Biography of a Socialist Zionist—Berl Katznelson, 1887–1944.* Cambridge: Cambridge University Press, 1984.

Tsur, Muki. Editorials in *Shdemot* [Hebrew], June–November, 1977.

Deborah Weissman

Response

We are meeting together towards the end of what I think has been the most traumatic year in Israel's history since the War of Independence. One has only to mention in this context the assassination of our Prime Minister, the suicide bombings in our major cities, the unending fighting in Lebanon, the roadside shootings, and, on the other hand, the human tragedy we have inflicted on innocents in Kfar Kana, or the long, difficult closure of the territories, to have a sense of the pain and agony of 5756. Many of us looked forward to the elections for some hopeful signs, and I suppose that about half of our population were at least partially satisfied with the outcome. Nevertheless, even dyed in the wool Likudnikim may be disturbed by some of the results—the rise of Jewish fundamentalism or the tremendous drop in the representation of women.

In our recent election, as you know, we employed a new system of voting, using two separate ballots, one for the Prime Minister and one for the leading party in the Knesset. "For the lover of democracy," in Leonard Fein's phrase, these elections presented a more accurate picture of the pluralism and of the sociological and ideological complexity that characterize Israeli society than had previously been the case. They showed that the long-term neglect of serious internal issues can be anything but benign in its consequences. The much-touted peace dividend has not been shared by vast segments of our population. And for too long social scientists have described a society in which the ultra-Orthodox played, at best, a marginal role. One wonders if it makes sense any longer to portray Israeli society in terms of a center-and-periphery paradigm.

As an Orthodox, or at least Orthoprax Jew, I am worried about the attitude of our government to non-Orthodox religious movements and to general questions of Judaism and Jewishness in the State of Israel. Paradoxically, perhaps, I have begun to be disturbed by many of the spokespeople (mostly of course spokesmen) for concepts I previously

116

espoused, such as "Jewish identity," "Jewish culture," and so on. This is especially true when to them, the more Jewish the state is, the less democratic it must be.

However, I believe we must choose our battles wisely—not for every issue is it worth going to the barricades. As long as alternate routes are available, I don't think the closing of Bar Ilan Street on Shabbat merits a major public struggle. But, for example, the right of archaeologists to excavate does, as well as the right of Conservative and Reform Jews to express their religious identity in a way that reflects their world view. The present predicament will only serve, I fear, to strengthen what I see as a self-defeating tendency on the part of these movements in Israel. Too often, their public stance is seen as primarily or even solely Orthodox establishment-bashing, without offering a positive and substantive Jewish spiritual alternative for the non-Orthodox population. Unfortunately, it appears unlikely that this situation will change in the near future.

I fail to see how we could have had an expectation that the murder of Rabin would be a "framer of Jewish consciousness." In the first few days after that awful event, it did seem that a "window of opportunity" had opened that might facilitate dialogue among the various segments of the population. But a number of factors contributed to a fairly rapid slamming shut of that window—first of all, as a friend of mine remarked, *ḥeshbon ha-nefesh*, soul searching and stock taking, became Israel's great spectator sport. It seemed that very few individuals or groups actually undertook to do such soul-searching for themselves, but they certainly enjoyed watching others engage in it. Several public figures tried to gain political capital out of the situation, and there were many public statements that simply shouldn't have been made. Secondly, I suppose the biggest enemies of a constructive dialogue in Israel were the Hamas and Hizbollah terrorists who set our national agenda for this spring and influenced the outcome of the elections. Third, the election campaign itself was uninspired and uninspiring. To quote Yossi Klein Halevi of the *Jerusalem Report*: "At times the election seemed a choice between Western materialism and Eastern superstition."

So in the future, can we expect to have a serious, meaningful dialogue (or "polylogue," if there is such a word) about Jewish culture in Israel? Will there be a "culture war" in which verbal violence might pave the way to physical violence? Rather than attempt to predict what will happen—I am, by training, a sociologist, and this year, the predictions of sociologists, especially in some of the pre-election polls, have been quite generally discredited. Instead, I would like to suggest certain conditions that I think must obtain if a meaningful dialogue is to take place:

1. There has to be a common cultural basis and a shared cultural language for discussion. And by this, I don't mean only that within the state-secular school system, Israelis should be taught more about traditional Jewish culture (although I mean that too). I also think that within the state-religious school system, there has to be a reevaluation and revision of the curriculum. Perhaps the Education Ministry can set up a parallel to the famous Shenhar Commission for the religious schools, exploring their teaching not only of democracy, but also of general humanities, secular Zionism, and contemporary Jewish thought and culture.

2. The Knesset and the media have to stop projecting the worst possible models of shouting matches in place of discussions. There's a popular television program—I wouldn't call it a "talk show," but a "shout show"—on which politicians, journalists, and other public figures try to outdo each other in yelling and not listening to what anyone else is saying. This cannot be our substitute for reasoned public debate. Moreover, a meaningful cultural expression cannot be developed through sound bites.

3. A reevaluation is long overdue of the classical Zionist attitude towards the Diaspora. We need to negate its negation. I've never understood why in Israel things that are American are in such great demand—like MacDonald's hamburgers—while those that are American Jewish—like non-Orthodox synagogues—are perceived as foreign and *galuti*. In what has been described by some as post-Zionist society, this last vestige of classical Zionist ideology somehow remains.

One of the fashionable subjects for discussion among a small intellectual elite in this country—which may simply serve to underscore their alienation from everyone else—is whether Israeli culture should be more oriented towards the Middle East—i.e., the Arab world, or toward the Mediterranean basin—Greece, Italy, Spain, and so on. It has always bothered me that no one ever suggests deepening our cultural connection with the Jewish Diaspora. Very few Israeli intellectuals have ever read Heschel or Kaplan or heard of the Havurah movement. But I'm not referring only to an ignorance of the North American

Diaspora. This year, when the great French Jewish philosopher Emanuel Levinas passed away, I organized a memorial evening at the Kerem Institute. To most of my Israeli colleagues, his name was unknown. If Israelis knew more about Diaspora Jewish thought and culture, perhaps the secularists among them could develop a less puerile, outmoded, and unsophisticated approach to religion as a cultural phenomenon. Similarly, perhaps the religious among them could learn about more models for integrating Jewish tradition with democratic and humanistic values.

I want to agree with Fein's point that Diaspora-Israeli relations should be shifted from the level of the fund-raisers and the politicians to that of the educational and cultural leaders. I believe that both sides have a good deal to learn from and with one another.

4. Lastly, I want to disagree with Professor Fein's approach to Halakhah. I do not dispute the importance, as well, of aggadic and midrashic categories, but I find that halakhic thinking and language can be very helpful. (In this, I suppose, I am a student of Professor David Hartman.) There is a set of concepts that can be particularly useful in communal dialogue. The concepts are *le-khathila,* "from the outset," "as a rule," and *be-di'avad,* "post factum." They roughly correspond to *de jure* and *de facto* or perhaps even the ideal and the real. These concepts can make it much easier for us to arrive at compromises and understandings.

One of the great teachers and leaders of our generation, the late Professor Eliezer Berkowitz, wrote on the issue of conversion:

> We know well what your *le-khathila* position on conversion is. But since this is a case of *et ha-zorekh* (a time of need) and *she'at hadhak* (urgency), what would be your *be-di'avad* position in view of the need for Jewish unity and for the sake of your love for your fellow Jews?[1]

I find this a most constructive approach to many issues that divide the Jewish community. There are many other halakhic and meta-halakhic categories—e.g., *et la'asot la-shem, pikuah nefesh, tikun ha-olam, mi-pnei darkhei shalom*—that might be brought to bear on some of our concerns. In 1967 anthropologist Joseph Gusfield wrote an important article called "Tradition and Modernity: A Case of Misplaced Polarities in the Study of Social Change."[2] As Jews, we know that early Christendom set up another case of misplaced polarities—"the God of love" versus "the God of law." Tradition and modernity need not be mutually exclusive; indeed they can be even mutually reinforcing. I want to conclude by stating that I personally would like to see an Israel that is both more Jewish and more democratic, and since unity doesn't mean uniformity, both more united and more pluralistic. Thank you.

Notes

1. Berkowitz, Eliezer, *Crisis and Faith*, (New York: Sanhedrin Press, 1976) p. 127.
2. *American Journal of Sociology*, January 1967, pp. 351–62.

TEACHING AND APPRECIATING THE OTHER

Barry Chazan

Through a Glass Darkly
Israel in the Mirror of American Jewish Education

The story of the place of Israel in American Jewish education is a microcosm of the overall issue of the relationship of Israel and contemporary American Jewish life, and the saga of teaching Israel is a mirror of the twentieth-century American Jewish gestalt towards Israel.

In this paper I shall look at the place of Israel in American Jewish education from the pre-State period until the 1990s. In analyzing this dynamic, I shall propose the thesis that the main (albeit not only) route taken in teaching Israel for much of this century has been rooted in religion and the humanitarian concern for fellow Jews. This direction has placed great emphasis on the meaning of Israel for the survival of Jews and Judaism. Concomitantly, it has meant that there has been much less focus on highlighting other aspects of contemporary Israel such as language, culture, and people.

It may well be that over the decades, teaching Israel in American Jewish education has played an important role in the creation of a culture in which the connection to Israel is based on philanthropy, humanitarianism, survivalism, and religiosity, while at the same time, legislating against the creation of a culture in which the relationship is rooted in language, the arts, and personal connections to the land and the people of Israel.

Locating the Roots: The Pre-State Period

The state of teaching Palestine and Zionism in the period from the beginning of the twentieth century until 1948 is reflected in a series of curricula and publications produced by a diverse cross-section of early twentieth-century schools, agencies, and individuals. These positions arrange themselves along a continuum encompassing five categories: Mainstream Traditional, Reform, Conservative, Cultural-Pluralist, and Zionist.

1. The Traditional position presented *eretz yisrael* as an inherently religious concept inseparable from Jewish tradition (Mizrachi, 1918; Jung and Kaminetsky, 1946; Frishberg, 1946). The modern Zionist Movement was presented as a continuation of the Jewish link to *eretz yisrael* and as a means for the restoration and ultimate redemption of the Holy Land (*reshit tzemihat ge'ulatenu*). At the same time, the humanitarian, social, and cultural creations of the Yishuv—especially the renaissance of Hebrew—were neither denied nor neglected. *Eretz yisrael* was taught in such schools in an integrated manner within the context of other subject areas. The notion of Israel as a living contemporary reality—and as an ideal to be aspired to—found its place in this school system from its earliest years.

2. The first curricula of the Reform Movement in this century reflect a conception of Jewish education as purely religious and hence devoid of any national or peoplehood dimensions (Joseph, 1908; Berkowitz, 1913). However, from the 1930s on, those curricula reflect an ever-growing concern for Palestine and Zionism within the context of Jewish peoplehood (Franzblau, 1935; Gittelsohn, 1935). By the 1940s, Palestine and Zionism were part of mainstream Reform curricula, which included the study of life in Palestine, contemporary heroes, and even Hebrew literature (Gamoran, 1942). Indeed, the educational wing of the movement appears to have been the vanguard of the gradual Reform move to a pro-Israel position ("Gamoran's main objective as educational director [for the UAHC] was to Judaize and Zionize the educational system of Reform Jews" [Wechman, 1970])

3. Between Alter Landsman's *Curriculum for Jewish Religious Schools* (1922) and Lou Katzoff's *Issues in Jewish Education* (1949), the Conservative Movement reflected a clear pro-Palestine position (Landsman, 1922; Cohen, 1932; Katzoff, 1949). Regarded as important aspects of the Jewish experience, Zionism and Palestine were viewed both historically and religiously. The emphases in teaching about these subjects were on religious dimensions of the link to Palestine; the heroic halutzic movement; the need for a Jewish state; Palestine's potential as a cultural and religious center for world Jewry; and the humanitarian responsibilities of American Jewry for rebuilding the land. In reviewing the state of teaching about Israel in 1946, Katzoff expresses the sentiments that later echo throughout much of this century: "Essentially Palestine evokes at most a sentimental attachment in the conscience of American Jewry today, but does not affect them in any intrinsic manner. Palestine is important but it is not real in the congregational school." (p.91)

4. The Cultural-Pluralist Movement in American Jewish education was rooted in the teachings of Ahad Ha-Am, Israel Friedlaender, Mordecai Kaplan, John Dewey, and William Kilpatrick. Its power base was the newly created Bureaus of Jewish Education that began to spring up across North America. The Cultural-Pluralist stance was avowedly pro-Palestine and pro-Zionist. It viewed Palestine as an integral part of the Jewish experience—past, present, and future. It focused on cultural, humanitarian, and religious dimensions of Palestine and Zionism, and it called for the integration of Palestine into all curricular and extra-curricular areas of schools and youth movements.

While clearly stating that Palestine was "a homeland" in a religious, cultural, and symbolic sense, however, this position affirmed that only America was Home. In 1936 the Zionist leader Enzio Sereni presented an impassioned classical Zionist *shlilat ha-galut* (negation of the Diaspora) speech at the Eleventh Annual Conference of the North American National Council for Jewish Education. In responding to Sereni's remarks, Golub, Chipkin, Honor, and Gamoran, all prominent Jewish educational leaders, heartily agreed with his cultural historical and pro-Zionist remarks, but firmly rejected his *shlilat ha-golah* stance, arguing instead for the possibility of a viable American Jewish civilization (Jewish Education, 1936).

5. An American Zionist curricular stance found its place in Jewish education, mainly in the youth movements (Sampter, 1915; Grand, 1947). Calling for a thorough "Zionization" of Jewish life, this approach focused on knowledge about the rise of the Zionist Movement and modern Palestine, appreciation of the legitimacy of Palestine and its vital link to American Jewish life and to the individual Jew, personal involvement with the rebuilding of Palestine; the role of Hebrew and Hebrew culture; encouraging personal pilgrimages to *eretz yisrael* for pioneering purposes; and Zionism as the ideal response to the Jewish problem and as a morally desirable Jewish lifestyle (Honor, 1939).

The Legacy of the First Half Century

I have analyzed these pre-State perspectives in some detail because I believe they set a pattern that was to continue for the next fifty years. First, a consensus position emerged that postulated concern and love for Israel as an important goal of American Jewish education. Second, Israel almost unanimously came to be regarded pedagogically as connected to religious Judaism. Third, American Jewish education clearly affirmed America as Home and rejected the notions of *shlilat ha-golah* or of Israel as a physical homeland for American Jews. Finally, pre-1948 American-Jewish curricula bequeathed a legacy of ideological ambiguity about the meaning and place of Israel—an ambiguity that was to accompany Jewish education for the remainder of the century.

Solidifying Norms: From 1948 to the Six-Day War

In terms of the overall dynamics of Jewish education, the era from the founding of the State until the Six-Day War is characterized by the emergence of the Orthodox Day School and the Conservative and Reform supplementary schools as the dominant forms of Jewish education.

The two major studies that examine this period point to the emergence of Israel as a recognizable part of American Jewish education (Dushkin and Engleman, 1959; Schiff, 1968). By the end of the 1960s, almost half of all Jewish schools taught Israel as a separate subject, and the majority had at least one Israeli born teacher on staff. Maps and books were present in almost all schools. In the mid-1950s the first denominationally sponsored youth trips were initiated, and by the 1960s they were an established part of the Jewish educational scene. The Six-Day War aroused great interest and pride and led to the creation of a national commission on teaching Israel by the American Association for Jewish Education, an educational manifesto on teaching Israel, and a series of new texts. At the same time, Schiff notes the beguiling ideological ambiguity: What ultimately was the meaning of Israel for Jewish education? In this period, Israel found its place in the life of the schools even if the significance of its presence was unclear.

Consensus and Questions: From the Six-Day War Until Lebanon

The third period, which extends from the end of the 1960s until the 1980s, is characterized educationally by the dramatic growth of the non-Orthodox Day School, the decline of the supplementary school, and the increased recognition of the Israel trip (now increasingly known as the "Israel Experience") as a powerful educative force. In terms of a broader Jewish context, this period is characterized by the "New Ethnicity"; the Yom Kippur and Lebanon Wars; the increasing isolation of Israel internationally; the explosion of Palestinian nation-alism; and the emergence of diverse political stances towards Israel in the North American Jewish community.

The story of Israel in Jewish education is chronicled in two studies that were closely coordinated with Schiff's earlier work so as to enable a comparison with previous periods (Chazan, 1979; Pollack, 1984). These studies affirm the pattern of the continuing institutionalization of teaching Israel as a part of Jewish education. By 1984, 97 percent of schools reported that they taught Israel in some form or another. This was the golden era of the publication of textbooks and instructional materials on Israel by denominations, Israeli-based organizations, and commercial publishers. In his period, Israelis (several hundred *shliḥim* as well as many others living abroad) were becoming a quantitatively significant staff presence in American Jewish schools. In the Orthodox world, extended study in Israel during or after high school was becom-ing a norm and other movements and organizations were sending thousands of youngsters to Israel every summer. By the 1980s an in-creasingly large number of young people were experiencing Israel firsthand.

At the same time, the ambiguity that Schiff had noted earlier contin-ued, and outside of the Orthodox and Zionist youth movements, edu-cational goals were fomulated in the most general terms ("creating a positive attitude and pride towards Israel" or "the overall commitment to Jewish survival") and continued to be defined in nonspecific or non-binding ways.

From Consensus to Dissent: Lebanon to the End of the Century

The most recent period in the history of teaching Israel has not yet been definitely documented, but various studies and analyses point to a fairly clear picture. The broad context of this period includes: Oslo and beyond; the economic blossoming and the "Americanization of Israel"; the emergence of the issues of "Who is a Jew?" and religious pluralism; terrorism; increased focus on a North American Jewish agenda; and the growing sense of the need to reappraise the Israel–Diaspora connection.

Educationally, this period is marked by a homeostasis and even decline in teaching about Israel in Jewish education. With a few ex-ceptions, there has been a paucity of new textbooks in the past decade. While there is an abundance of curricula, instructional units, and audio-visual materials, there are indications these resources are underused.

Rabbis, teachers, principals, and Jewish communal leaders have openly shared their increasing ambivalence vis-à-vis teaching about Israel, and they sadly admit that their confusion has sometimes made it difficult for them to be effective gatekeepers of this subject.

While the Israel Experience has received major new atttention in North American Jewish life, the difficulties in significantly increasing the number of young people who go to Israel is sometimes seen as an indicator of a larger cultural crisis (Chazan, 1997).

The turning inward of American Jewry and its increased focus on issues of continuity, intermarriage, day schools, and local Jewish education have sometimes been interpreted as a shift of focus away from Israel-oriented issues. This situation led one educational commentator to sum up the last decade (in an article entitled "J'Accuse") as follows:

> The state of Israel in American Jewish education is moribund. It is time to say it loud and clear: Israel plays an insignificant role in the world of contemporary Jewish education, and contemporary Jewish education plays an insignificant role in shaping the world view of young Jews vis-à-vis Israel (Chazan, 1995)

The Thesis Revisited

The brief journey that we have taken through American Jewish educational history in the twentieth century reveals a diversity of emphases and approaches toward the teaching of Israel. While there is no one exclusive route, the map generally does seem to point to a (mainstream) road taken—and a road not taken.

Overall, the educational system has loyally represented the dominant, decades-long, American Jewish approach to Palestine and Israel that focuses on the unity of the Jewish people (*klal yisrael*); the ingathering of the exiles (*kibbutz galuyot*); Israel and Judaism; Jewish survival; and Israel and the Holocaust. In other words, this approach highlights Israel in the context of the Jewish religious heritage and the Jewish struggle to survive in the twentieth century. In that sense it may well be contended that the Jewish educational system has quite loyally served the dominant consensus position of American Jewish life towards Israel.

The road not taken by most of North American Jewish education (with some powerful and notable exceptions) would have presented Israel as a contemporary Jewish society that confronts individuals with the meaning of their Jewishness and invites them to develop a personal relationship with the Land, the Language, the People, and the Promise. It would focus on Israel as a presence rather than a problem. Such an approach would have highlighted Israel as a contemporary society, the centrality of the Hebrew language to cultural revival, Israelis as peers and colleagues, and Israel as a positive and attractive place to visit.

The twenty-first century is here. The Jewish world has changed, Israel has changed, and the Israel–Diaspora connection will also have to change. As Jewish educators contemplate the teaching of Israel in the twenty-first century, they might well want to acknowledge its past route and at the same time seek out a fresh path, aimed at creating a new relationship with Israel and a new place for it in the hearts and souls of young American Jews.

Bibliography

Berkowitz, H. *The New Education in Religion.* 1913

Chazan, B. "Israel in American Jewish Schools Revisited." *Jewish Education,* 1979

_____. *Does the Teenage Israel Experience Make a Difference?* 1997

_____. "J'accuse." *Jewish Education News* 6, 3 (1995): 15–17.

Chomsky, W. "The Curriculum for the New Jewish Weekday School," *Jewish Education* 5: 26–30.

Cohen, S. *The Progressive School: An Integrated Activity.* 1932

Curriculum. Mizrachi Teachers Institute. 1918–19.

Dushkin, A. "Sanity in the Teaching of Palestine," *Jewish Education* 2 (1930): 65–67.

_____ and Engleman, U. *Jewish Education in the United States.* 1959

Ediden, B. "Teaching Palestine Through Pupil Activity," *Jewish Education* 5 (1933): 103–8.

Franzblau, A. *Curriculum in History for Jewish Religious Schools.* 1935

_____. *An Introduction to Jewish Religious Education.* 1937

Frishberg, Y. *Tokhnit limudim kellalit.* 1946

Gamoran, E. *A Curriculum for the Jewish Religious School.* 1942

Gittelsohn, R. *Modern Jewish Problems.* 1935

Golub, J. and Honor, L. "Some Guiding Principles for the Curriculum of the Jewish Schools of Tomorrow, " *Jewish Education* 5 (1933): 22–26.

Grand, S. *Palestine in the Jewish School.* 1947

Honor, L. "A Zionist Program of Jewish Education in America." *Zionist Quarterly,* 1939

Jung, L. and Kaminetsky, J. *A Model Program for the Talmud Torah.* 1942

Katzoff, L. *Issues in Jewish Education.* 1949

Landsman, A. *A Curriculum for Jewish Religious Schools.* 1922

Lehman, E. *Curriculum for Jewish Religious Schools.* 1910

Pollack, G. "A survey on Israel/Zionism in American Jewish Schools," *The Pedagogic Reporter,* 1984.

"Proceedings of the 11th Annual Conference of NCJE," *Jewish Education* 8 (1936): 147.

Sampter, J. *A Course in Zionism,* 1915

Schiff, A. "Israel in American Jewish Schools," *Jewish Education,* 1968

Special Report: Revised Curriculum, Union of American Hebrew Congregations, Commission of Jewish Education, 1924

Wechman, R. *Emanuel Gamoran: Pioneer in Jewish Religious Education,* 1970

Olga Zambrowsky and Malka Or-Chen

American Jewry as Reflected in the Secondary School Curriculum in Israel

The mutual relations between Jewish society in Israel and American Jewry are multifaceted in character and can be examined and understood in many different ways. The quality of the ties between Israeli Jewish society and the American Jewish Diaspora is intimately bound up with the general question of Jewish identity. The heart of this question lies in the existential nature of Judaism and in the implicit duality between such terms as *The Jewish People* and *The State of Israel* and between *The Jewish Nation* and *The Jewish Religion*. Examination of the ethical, political, historical, and cultural aspects of these dualities has been ongoing for many years in both theoretical and practical frameworks.

This paper examines one of the many aspects that characterize those ties—specifically, the place held by the topic of American Jewry in the socialization process of Israeli Jewish youth, as expressed in the formal study programs in the junior and senior high schools. This examination relies on two basic assumptions. The first is the relative weight of the formal education system in the socialization process that shapes the civic-national image of Israeli youth. Among the many agents of socialization—the family, the mass media, the youth movements, the political parties, etc.—only the formal education system is totally structured and institutionalized. Through the contents of its curricula, the system's established and official frameworks affect almost all the young people, and their influence is continuous over many years. Thus the focus of this study is the system's intentions—and their implementation—as expressed in its courses in all that relates to the topic of American Jewry, and not the degree to which these in fact shape the students' stands on the subject. It is difficult, perhaps even impossible, to isolate one factor from all the many others in this complex process.

The second assumption is that courses of study and their various contents reflect in some degree the positions of those who determine and create them, and who are part of Israel's educational/intellectual/political elite. From this we can surmise that the courses will provide an indication of positions and approaches that are acceptable to this elite in all that pertains to the topic of American Jewry.

Two central questions were raised: What degree of importance is given to the topic of American Jewry, based on the amount of time and space devoted to this subject in the curricula? And what image of American Jewry is presented to the students in these curricula? These questions were examined in different frameworks: types of schools, age levels of students, and specific courses taught. The degree of continuity and consistency that characterized the study of American Jewry over the years was also examined. The topic itself refers to the complex of social and political qualities of the American Jewish community: its history, culture, religion, literature, its influence on the life of the American people, its integration within that society, its contribution to research and to the scientific community, and its ties with the State of Israel.

The project included courses of study in state and state-religious junior high schools, which are intended for 12–15 year olds and which constitute a part of the compulsory education system; and in state and state-religious senior high schools, which are intended for 15–18 year olds, and which include both academic and technical schools. The independent Torah-oriented schools were not included in the study for the following reasons:

1. It was difficult to collect data from them.
2. Because they are independent frameworks, their curricula are varied, so that each of these schools might in fact teach in a different way, and any attempt to draw general conclusions with regard to them would be problematic.
3. The students in those frameworks account for only a small percentage of all the students in Israel.
4. Some of those frameworks, and the yeshiva senior high schools in particular, were already included in the study, since their students take the matriculation exams and their curricula are subject to the Ministry of Education curricula.

A number of methods were chosen for the collection and processing of data:

1. Interviews with those in the Ministry of Education in charge of the preparation of curricula, including those responsible for the relevant subjects.
2. An examination of the compulsory curricula in the junior high schools and in the state and state-religious senior high schools, both academic and technical. These curricula are prepared by professional teams that include, along with Ministry personnel, representatives of the academic world who are appointed by the Ministry of Education.
3. Interviews with teachers of the relevant subjects, based on a random sample, while preserving a representation of all the above-mentioned types of schools, and attempting to include experienced teachers in the interviews along with younger ones, and teachers in big city schools as well as those from smaller towns, kibbutzim, etc. The teachers were asked about the relative place given to the study of American Jewry in their teaching schedules; about the substance of their training in, and the attitude of the students toward the subject.
4. A study of civics and history textbooks, with emphasis on locating the material relevant to the topic of American Jewry and determining its extent.
5. A content analysis of the relevant material as it is presented in the texts
6. A representative examination of the students' choices of reading material for the matriculation examinations, as reported by literature teachers in senior high schools. The investigation was in order to identify the students' preferences in reading fiction and the place of Jewish-American literature within those preferences.
7. A survey of the courses of study in universities and teacher training colleges recognized by the Ministry of Education in Israel, in order to examine what learning opportunities they offer in the field of American Jewry. The assumption was that these are the courses in which the future teachers of the higher grades receive their teacher training—and that the very presence or absence of this subject in the curricula of those institutions can influence the future ability of the teachers to teach this subject, as well as their interest in doing so.

The period of the early 1990s was chosen as the basis for the study of all the above components. Later the results of the study were compared with the data existing for previous years.

Before presenting the findings of the study, it is necessary to present a number of relevant facts about the education system in Israel. The number of persons studying in all the educational institutions (including kindergartens and universities) in the 1993/94 school year was 1,654,210, of which the great majority (1,599,810) were enrolled in the system under Ministry of Education supervision.[1] In the upper grades (junior and senior high school), there were 383,183 students in that year. In the junior high schools, 81.4 percent studied in state schools, 18.2 percent in state-religious schools, and 0.4 percent in the independent schools (mainly Agudat Yisrael). In the senior high schools, 74.2 percent studied in the state schools, 18.2 percent in the state-religious schools, and 7.6 percent in the independent schools.[2]

At the beginning of the 1990s, there were noticeable indications that the education system was organizing for a change in the existing structure at the policy-making level to increase the scope of studies on the topic of American Jewry and prepare new courses and suitable textbooks. This change was a direct result of self examination by the education system following the recommendations of the committee chaired by Professor Aliza Shenhar, appointed by Education Minister Zevulun Hammer to study the status of Jewish Studies in the state education system. In its recommendations, published in 1994, the committee pointed out that it was necessary to reinforce the subject of Diaspora Studies within the general curriculum of Jewish Studies:

> In the teaching of Jewish History it is necessary to emphasize the fate of Jewish communities in the Diaspora, their extensive cultural creation and their efforts to cope with the challenges placed before them by the surrounding society. It is necessary to emphasize the tie and the mutual responsibility that connects Israel and the Jewish Diaspora.[3]

Findings

1. The topic of American Jewry is given a relatively prominent place in terms of extent of studies, which indicates the importance ascribed to it by those responsible for the curricula.
2. The extent of place and time given to this topic is similar in both

state and state-religious schools. The few differences between them
are incidental.

3. American Jewry is taught in the framework of two subjects: history
   and literature. It is given more extensive coverage in the history
   courses than in the literature courses. Most relevant for our discussion is the program of chronological study (particularly found in
   grade 9), which focuses on "The Westward Immigration and the
   Development of the Jewish Community in the United States," as
   well as "The Jewish People in our Time" and "The Jewish Collective in the United States."

4. As for the allocation of study hours to this subject, the findings show
   that the state-religious schools allocate fewer hours to the topic than
   the state schools.[4] In the state schools, approximately 10 percent of
   the history curriculum for grade 9, or 6 study hours, is devoted to
   American Jewry.

5. In the literature curriculum, the literature courses do not include
   any American stories at all. In the state-religious schools, there is
   one required story by Isaac Bashevis-Singer, who can hardly be
   considered an American author.

6. In the grade 9 history textbook, the topic accounts for about 18 percent of the entire content of the text, which is used in both state and
   state-religious schools.[5]

The last two years of high school (grades 11 and 12) are not included
in the framework of compulsory education. Moreover, the senior high
schools are divided into academic, trade, technical, and agricultural
schools, with only a small number of the last-mentioned offering matriculation certificates. Thus it is important to note that only some of
this age group are exposed to a three year study program, and there is
no common study program for them all. In the technological track,
within the framework of the unit entitled "The Contemporary Jewish
Diaspora," the subject is generally defined as "Aspects of Jewish Existence in the Free World," and the total amount of time allocated the
entire subject (including the map of the Diaspora, Soviet and Eastern
European Jewry, and the Jews in the Islamic countries) amounts to two
lessons.

In the academic schools, the program is richer in topics relating to
American Jewry. The subject is taught in the framework of a number
of different study units, which include:

1. "The Creation of the New Jewish Centers on the American Continent" (within the general topic "The Jewish World in the 1880s")

2. "The Jewish Concentration in the United States" (within the general topics "The Jewish World in 1920" and "The Jewish World in 1945")[6]

However, it is difficult to calculate the exact amount of time devoted to American Jewry, since these programs (consisting of three lessons) include a variety of other topics. For example, the history curriculum for the state schools upper level in 1977 presents the general topic "The Principal Jewish Collectives in Recent Generations," with the following sub-topics: Jewish identity and its problems, inter-group national solidarity, assimilation and disappearance in different Jewish groups, traditional Jewish centers, centers in the throes of change since 1900, urbanization, and migration.[7]

In the senior high school literature curriculum, the teaching goals include: giving the students "emotional experiences," inculcating moral, social, and national values,[8] and acquainting them with the main topics of the cultural history of the Jewish people. The curriculum includes the best of Hebrew literature and provides the opportunity to become acquainted with world literature as well. The list is varied. Classical literature is included with popular, and students are introduced to varied styles and genres. The reading lists include hundreds of works, but American Jewish writers are represented by only six authors, some of whom can only marginally be considered as "American": Bernard Malamud, Saul Bellow, Philip Roth, Chaim Potok, Elie Wiesel, and Isaac Bashevis Singer. Interestingly, in the state-religious schools, only the works of Bashevis Singer are compulsory, and those of Potok and Malamud are optional.[9] In a similar study program for the technological track, there are no American Jewish writers on the compulsory reading list, and only Singer is mentioned as an option. The most extensive suggested reading list, from the upper grades of the state schools, contains 167 authors, of which only five are American. The same list includes 10 Russian authors from the period following the October Revolution alone.[10]

The Image of American Jewry Presented

Compared to the quantitative analysis presented above, the description of the image of American Jewry presented to Israeli students in their textbooks is far more complex and its messages ambiguous. Together with descriptions of a dynamic, achievement-oriented, adaptive community, quickly freeing itself of "the miserable European exilic mentality" in order to organize its strengths and flourish, another picture is presented—that of an archaic community, living in the past rather than in present reality. Along with descriptions of success in community organizations, emphasis is placed on the central role of Zionism as the focus of American Jewish identity. Together with stories of prosperity, we find enumeration of difficulties of living among non-Jews.

A basic history textbook for the junior high school gives broad coverage to the development of the American Jewish community from its inception and up to the beginning of the twentieth century, with emphasis on its transition from a suffering community in European Exile to a free and organized community in the New World.[11]

The picture that emerges in the senior high history texts is not much different. The two volumes of David Shahar's *Mi-galut le-kommemiyut: Toledot am yisrael ba-dorot ha-aharonim* (From Exile to Independence: The History of the Jewish People in Recent Generations) are studied in both the state schools and the state-religious schools as a basic compulsory textbook. In the first volume, which focuses on the national movement, the *yishuv* in *eretz yisrael*, and the Zionist movement from the end of the nineteenth century and up to 1939, the American Jewish community is depicted against the background of the introductory discussion on the subject of antisemitism and migration.

Volume Two presents a broad description of the Jewish Diaspora from the 1920s to the 1940s, which constitutes perhaps a quarter of the entire volume. The text also includes chapters dealing with the Holocaust, the Yishuv in *eretz yisrael*, the Zionist movement during World War Two, the struggle for a Jewish state, and the War of Independence. Along with the development of the Jewish concentration in the United states, the section devoted to the Diaspora also surveys the Jews in the Soviet Union, Iraq, Persia, Syria, Egypt, Yemen, North Africa, Algeria, Tunisia, Morocco, and Libya.

American Jewry is protrayed in a 4 paged chapter out of the 76 devoted to the Diaspora. It discusses

1. The rallying of American Jewry to assist Jewish victims of the First World War in Europe and the Middle East (establishment and operation of the Joint Distribution Committee)
2. The special importance of the Zionist Federation in the U.S., its strengthening at the time of the First World War, and its central role in unifying American Jewry.

The significant innovation here, compared with the junior high texts,

is the discussion of the American Jewish dilemma of assimilation versus distinctiveness. Assimilation is presented in the book as the result
of the freedom and egalitarianism that encourages intermingling with
non-Jews. The community's ability to maintain distinctiveness, on the
other hand, is dependent upon its size, its concentration in a limited
number of places, its organization, and its ties to the synagogues.
Along with these factors, there is special emphasis on the attitude to
Zionism:

> One factor that preserved American Jewry from widespread as-
> similation was the strengthening of Zionism in the American Jew-
> ish community. Zionism was supported by almost all levels of
> American Jewry, and through adherence to the Zionist idea the
> American Jews found an answer to their special problems and
> difficulties as immigrants in a strange land. Zionism provided
> them with a group distinctiveness and released them from the
> difficulties of the encounter with strangers.[12]

It is important to note that in all the chapters that describe the different
Diasporas, with the exception of that in the Soviet Union, a special
sub-chapter is devoted to a description of Zionist activity.

Even in Yisrael Guttman and Haim Shatzker's *Ha-Sho'a
u-mashma'uta* (the Holocaust and Its Meaning),[13] the major part of the
discussion relevant to our study deals with the attitude of the U.S. Jewish community to the Holocaust, and to the operational efforts of Jewish organizations in this regard. The discussion does not recoil from
asking: Did the Jews in the United States indeed do "everything within
their power in order to prevent the disaster or lessen it?"[14] The discussion of this topic presents facts and considerations that give the
students plenty of material for studying the issue in all its complexity,
without passing judgment. But it does not discuss the role "Remembering the Holocaust" plays in the maintenance of American Jewish
identity.

From the above survey it seems that despite the fact that in the
courses examined the discussion of American Jewry is said to focus on
its present problems, the history textbooks, for both the junior and senior high schools hardly refer to those problems. In literature, on the
other hand, the few American Jewish books read emphasized the problems. The reports of literature teachers in the high schools in the
1990/91 year lists the names of works chosen by students and teachers
as optional reading for the matriculation exams. Of 211 classes and a

total of 5,587 books, only 251 were by American Jewish writers. Of the latter, 162 were by Bashevis-Singer and 61 by Malamud. Interestingly, the most popular works were Malamud's *The Assistant,* about a Jew in existential distress, and Singer's *The Slave.* If Singer's years in Florida and New York qualify him as an American author, *The Slave,* with its Polish characters and setting, certainly does not. Be that as it may, the point is that the works of American literature chosen by Israeli youth seem to emphasize the suffering and misery of Jews in the Diaspora. And we may conclude that contact of the students with contemporary American Jewish literature is extremely limited. The result is the loss of one more opportunity to learn about the varied, expansive, and rich contemporary life of American Jewry through the avenue of its cultural creations.

Teaching of the Topic in Practice

From interviews with the teachers, we found a significant gap between the stated intentions of the system and their implementation. Although American Jewry appears in the senior high school curriculum, in actual fact it is often not taught. A no less important finding is the existence of a certain sense of discomfort with all that relates to the topic, particularly to its present aspects—so much so that it is defined by the teachers as a "controversial" subject. The impression of most of the teachers is that the attitude of the students toward American Jewry is generally emotional and ambivalent: admiration and interest along with anger and criticism of the very act of living in the Diaspora, especially vis-à-vis the phenomenon of *yeridah* (emigration from Israel) to the United States.

While in the junior high school history courses the teaching is compatible with the curriculum and the subject of American Jewry is indeed taught, this commitment to the curriculum applies only to the historical description of the development of the Jewish comunity in the United States up to approximately 1920. In contrast, interviews with high school teachers in both state and state-religious schools suggested that the subject of American Jewry was in fact not studied in all schools in the proposed form. Teachers commonly claimed they did not have time to cover all the subjects in the programs and since the topic of American Jewry has not been included in the matriculation exams— and the curriculum is overflowing with other subjects more crucial to professional and civic goals—they felt that the meager attention paid to American Jewry was justifiable. Those teachers that did include the subject did not necessarily do so for professional considerations but rather because of their own American backgrounds, family connections to the U.S., or the presence of students with American backgrounds in their classes. Significantly, only a few of the interviewed teachers reported being exposed to the subject in their professional training—which probably also explains their reluctance to delve into it.

Examination of the programs of study in the universities and teachers' colleges showed that in the majority, the subject is included in one form or another. In the teachers' colleges it appears mainly in the framework of general courses, while in the universities specific courses in different departments are offered. The greatest variety is offered by Bar Ilan University, where the subject is studied as a specific topic in General History, Jewish History, Hebrew Literature, Comparative Literature, and Political Science. At Ben-Gurion, University of Haifa, Tel Aviv University, and the Hebrew University of Jerusalem, possibilities are more limited, and sometimes the subject is taught in the framework of a more general course as one issue among many. As a result, the study of the topic depends on the student's personal interest.

The Significance of the Findings

In light of the above findings, we may conclude that the heads of the education systems and the creators of the study programs, particularly in the subject of history, recognize the importance of the the study of American Jewry at the junior and senior high school levels. In theory if not in practice, it seems that the subject is given suitable quantitative coverage in terms of both the time required for teaching it and the required space in the textbooks. This assessments holds true for both the state and the state-religious schools, as no significant differences were found to exist between them.

At the present time, however, a flat and superficial image of the American Jewish community emerges—probably because topics discusssed with the students are restricted to the primary organization of the community, its adaptation to life in the new society, and the development of its new religious trends. In addition, there is sparse reference to the contemporary cultural aspect of American Jewry, as evidenced by the small amount of contemporary American Jewish literature included in the framework of the literature courses and the lack of focus in history texts on the contributions of the American Jewish community to the cultural and scientific life of the United States.

In our estimation, the source of the difficulty lies in the tension created by the conflicting goals the education system has set for itself: the transmission of knowledge versus the inculcation of values. Within this basic contradiction, teaching about American Jewry is fraught with other tensions: the commitment to openness and pluralism versus the commitment to the unique character of Jewishness; the commitment to the Jewish people and its Diasporas versus commitment to the Zionist idea and the State of Israel. It is no simple task for the teacher to transmit these values at one and the same time, and with regard to American Jewry the task is doubly difficult. The size of the American Jewish community, its political power, its cultural and economic achievements, and the very fact of its existence as a flourishing community despite its being a part of the Diaspora, place a very difficult challenge before the educator who is obligated first and foremost to teach commitment to the idea of Jewish uniqueness and the Zionist ideal. This explains the turning to historical descriptions and the absence of engagement with the present situation, thus avoiding conflict or harm to educational goals.

Interestingly, the distress and suffering of Jews in the general Diaspora are the preferred focus of both literature studies and history studies. The life of the Jewish communities of Eastern Europe, the Soviet Union, and the Islamic countries are portrayed from this viewpoint. According to the teachers, when the unit "The Jewish Diasporas" was taught in the framework of the course in civics, both teachers and students preferred the subjects connected with Jews in conditions of distress rather than discussions of the American Jewish community.

This emphasis on the central role of Zionism in Diaspora life and the preference for the "miserable exilic Jew" can almost certainly solve the dilemma that results from the need to teach about Jewish communities living in the Diaspora while still teaching commitment to the State of Israel. It is significant in this regard to note that in the history texts, and later in the civics studies in the 1960s, the coverage of American Jewry is greater than it was at the beginning of the 1990s. In the history texts of Shlomo Horowitz[15] used in the state schools and the state-religious schools, the history of the American Jewish community is spread over a number of extensive, detailed chapters that include a lot of information about the variety of community organizations, even including a biography of Louis Brandeis and other Jewish leaders. In addition, the discussion relates to the contemporary situation of this Jewry at the time. But there is a basic pattern of thinking evident both in the 1960s and in the 1990s, as the following extract indicates:

> The tremendous assimilative power of the American "melting pot" constitutes a serious danger to the existence of American Jewry as a national-cultural unit. There are those who console themselves with the fact that within the cultural pluralism of the United States, the Jews too will be able to preserve their cultural uniqueness. Thus far the reality has not supported these rosy hopes, and in view of the increasing blurring of minority cultures it is very doubtful whether the Jewish minority will be able to preserve its existence. "American Jewish culture," that is so much talked about recently, is really more wishful thinking than reality. Only a large Zionist movement, which will place Hebrew education at the top of its priorities, and a large youth movement, which will relate seriously to its Zionist slogans, is likely to prevent in America that which happened to Western European Jewry in the nineteenth century and which is threatening Soviet Jewry in our time, and that is: the burning of the soul and the living body.[16]

While a normative harshness that was present in the 1960s has become modified in the course of the years, there is no change in the patterns of thinking and in the education system's difficulties in coping with the topic of American Jewry. The approach that views Jewish life in the Diaspora as a source of danger to the very existence of the Jews as a people, and that emphasizes the centrality of Zionism in the life of the Jewish Diaspora, still stands. Here is the place to point out that no evidence was found to indicate that the educational reality described above is the result of conscious or directed activity. It is a complex and problematic process, the main focus of which is the consolidation of Jewish-Israeli identity as a direct result of the existential condition of the Jewish people.

The education system, in its struggle with the above difficulties, in fact mirrors the processes that are taking place within Israeli society, in its position as a reflection of that society. Therefore the expectation that the schools will provide solutions for problems facing the society as a whole is unrealistic. A number of representative examples illustrate the current debate, both in the academy and in the written media.

Eliezer Schweid, in his article "Gilgulei tsurah shel ha-zehut ha-yehudit ha-modernit ke-tahalikh histori" (Changes in the Form of

Modern Jewish Identity as a Historical Process)[17] raises the thesis that Israeli society is presently in the throes of a process of assimilation expressed in the exchange of Israeli identity for Jewish identity. He claims that the continuation of this trend is liable, among other things, "to lead to a total break in the ties between the Israeli culture and its historical sources. The result is liable to be total alienation between the Israelis and the Jews in the Diaspora, and an even more shallow level of the spiritual creation that develops the identity of the individual."[18] In his analysis of the sources of the process, the writer points to the tension that was created with the establishment of the State between its Jewish residents and the Jewish Diaspora, along with the unifying significance of the establishment of the State for the Jewish people as a whole.

> The question whether the Jews of the "prosperous" and "free" countries are to be considered exiles or Diaspora dwellers who are not subject to the law of "shlilat ha-golah"—this question once again became controversial immediately upon the establishment of the State. Moreover, a qualitative and quantitative difference crept in and established itself between the Jews of *eretz yisrael* and the Jews of the Diaspora in such a way that it constituted a new and more serious challenge to the question of a unified identity of the Jewish people.[19]

In a similar spirit, Yair Oron presents his recommendations regarding the educational issues in his article, "Ha-Am ha-yehudi ve-ha-tza'ir ha-yisraeli" (The Jewish People and the Israeli Young Person):

> It is necessary to "step out" of the Israeli reality to the Jews of the Diaspora and, through the questions that are important for Jewish existence in Israel, "reach out" to the Diaspora Jews. In this way the study and discussion of Diaspora Jewry will become relevant for the young person being educated in the State of Israel and will become part of his sphere of knowledge and his framework of relationship, and they might also enable him to examine himself in a different perspective.[20]

Oron's evaluation of the place of the subject of Diaspora Jewry in the curricula is identical with that which our findings have brought to light (although limited to the general education system): "The Jewish people in Israel and in the Diaspora in the period following the Holocaust and the establishment of the State is hardly touched upon. Study and research, clarification and discussion of current, existential and present- day issues of the Jewish people in the proper perspective of time and space (Israel and the Diaspora)—Forget it!"[21]

So a trend in the philosophical sphere does call for more interest in Diaspora Jewry, as an important part of Israeli culture. With this trend, another one, prevalent among part of the intellectual and political elite, is rearing its head. It is more familiar to the general public, as its varied expressions are found in the newspapers at regular intervals. A cursory and uncommitted glance at the written media presents a picture of which the open letter of Shulamit Har-Even to Avraham Burg, Chairman of the Jewish Agency, is a good example:

> Perhaps there really is not much that separates political independence and life in the exile if you do not take into account the oppression (of the Jews) by the kingdoms. But it is we who are creating Hebrew culture here, it is we who are defending what exists, and not Irish policemen or black sergeants. Channels of influence on the government—both in the ballot and outside the ballot—are very short here and very long there, and the responsibility is placed on each and every one of us [...]. It is here and not there that the independent pattern of daily life is being created, here and not there is a flourishing Hebrew language culture that only a few there are familiar with. What is left for them? Gastronomic Judaism?[22]

In a similar vein, Meir Shalev wrote a sarcastic sketch that describes the visit of an American Jewish youngster whose trip to Israel was obviously based on a reconstruction of the voyage of the "Exodus":

> Here there are no "Jews," "Arabs," "illegal immigrants," "war," "blood," "dead," "pioneers," "Zionism," "struggle," "bereavement," "pain," and "hope." Here there are Jews and Arabs and illegal immigrants and war and blood and dead and pioneers and Zionism and struggle and bereavement and pain and hope. Whoever wants to participate is welcome to do so. Whoever wants just to visit, let him come just for a visit. But Israel is not the Disneyland of American Jewry, so leave the quotation marks at home.[23]

The last two quotes express in no uncertain terms an attitude of Israeli monopoly on Jewish identity, on the Jewish cultural and political experience, together with an openly expressed anger against American

Jewry. This sense of anger blends well with the ambivalent feelings of the school students mentioned earlier. This gap essentially parallels the gap between the declared intentions of the education system curricula and their actual implementation. And perhaps more than any other evidence, these philosophical and journalistic expressions clearly demonstrate the existing gap between the context of academic ideals and reality.

Looking to the Future

The gap between intentions and actions is likely to decrease in the near future in view of the change presently emerging in the approach of policy makers of the educational system. The new trend is due to the acknowledgment by a part of the intellectual academic elite of the urgency and indispensability of the subject, and also the result of self examination by the system—especially the establishment of the Shenhar Committee and the pervasive willingness to implement its recommendations.

The first practical attempt to deal with the complexity of this issue is found in the 1994 textbook *Ha-kiyyum ha-yehudi be-tefutzot ba-me'a ha-20* (Jewish Existence in the Diaspora in the Twentieth Century),[24] prepared by a team of writers under the auspices of the Minister of Education, with the guidance and cooperation of academics. Although for the past few years this book has been an optional text for high school history courses. the very writing of a new and updated volume devoted almost entirely to the subject of the Diaspora is an indication of change. In the introduction, teachers and students are presented with a summary of the new approach:

> In general we have not made do with presenting one style of Jewish coping in the Diaspora with its problems. We have presented a number of conflicting solutions that were proposed for each dilemma, and have attempted to avoid evaluating and taking a stand with regard to the quality of the solutions.[25]

These words indicate a new perception of openness and willingness to deal, for the first time, with the complexity and difficulties of the subject. From the methodological aspect also, the book is different from its predecessors in that it presents substantive discussion issues instead of a historical chronological framework. The book consists of the following topics: "Integration of the Jews in the Modern Era," "Between

Socialism and Nationalism," "From Immigrants to an Organized Community," "The Jews as a Minority in a Colonial Regime," and "The Diaspora at the End of the Century."

The volume devotes a relatively larger section to the subject of American Jewry. Even the "classic" chapter, the one dealing with the Jewish community in the United States at the beginning of the twentieth century, is different in character from earlier texts. The history of the community, spread over about sixty pages, presents a complex and fact-filled picture, supported in many instances by American Jewish sources.

The presentation of the role of Zionism is also different. No more does it play "the crucial role in consolidating Jewish-American identity at the beginning of the century," but rather

> Up to the Balfour Declaration, the Zionist Movement did not, as a social and political movement, take hold of American Jewry. [...] True, the Zionist Movement fulfilled an important role in the cultural flourishing of the period. [...] Until the First World War the "spiritual Zionism" of Ahad Ha-Am took hold among the intellectuals who were seeking a secular self-definition for the national-Jewish uniqueness.

Further on, there is a survey of the activity of the "Brandeis Group" and its successes, as opposed to those of the American Zionist Organization during that period. As to the latter: "Unlike the case in Europe, the success of the Zionist Organization in the United States was not sizable until the Second World War."[26]

The other significant innovation in the book is without doubt the attempt to grapple with the current situation in three distinct chapters: "Political and Demographic Changes in the Second Half of the Twentieth Century," "Because of the Holocaust," and "The Establishment of the State of Israel as a Turning Point in the Life of Diaspora Jewry." However, although the discussion raises the issue of the transformation of American Jewry into a very powerful "political community," there is a lack of the called-for interest in its cultural and scientific contributions and achievements. On the other hand, trying to present American Diaspora–State of Israel relations objectively, the authors have presented different positions by means of quotes from original American texts, and this is done without taking any definitive value-oriented stands. The quotes focus on two concepts: one that views immigration to Israel as the supreme commandment of the Zionist idea and rejects the existence of a Diaspora and, opposed to it, the concept of the Diaspora as a permanent factor in Jewish history and the impossibility of a complete ingathering of the exiles.[27] Among the authors whose articles are quoted are Shimon Halkin, Jacob Blaustein, Mordechai Menahem Kaplan, Jacob Neusner, Haim Greenberg, and Nahum Goldmann, all of whom provide fascinating descriptions and illustrations of the perplexities that characterize the American Jewish community's attitude toward Israel.

To what extent is the book a harbinger of significant change in the attitude of the education system to the topic of American Jewry? What are the chances that the subject will be expanded and broadened even more in Israeli courses of study? And most important, will it be taught, if at all, in an up-to-date form and not just as an historical survey? In our view, the answers to these complex questions depend not only on the education system but on the development of the ideological-political debate in Israeli society about national identity, especially in reference to the subject of relations with the American Diaspora. The stronger the element in this discussion that recognizes the dangers of a split with American Jewry and the mutual need for strengthening of ties—a trend gaining strength in the academic world, as well as in part of the political elite and Ministry of Education leadership—the stronger will be the chances for practical changes in the whole education system.

Perhaps these changes will not satisfy the requirements of American Jewry, which sees itself as an equal partner in the dialogue. It is reasonable to surmise that texts like the new book will not fully satisfy the expectations of this Jewry, since the discussion of the present situation of American Jewry in them will almost certainly be based on the centrality of the State of Israel in Diaspora life. But it is unreasonable to assume that the state education system in Israel will adopt an anti-Zionist approach.

At the same time, we can expect little change in the ambivalence of the students and the difficulty the teachers have in discussing controversial subjects. Our examples from the world of journalism also reflect angry and harshly critical stands against American Jewry, stands that reflect a mood that belongs to part of the public and the political elite and can hardly be expected to change quickly. The presentation of the subject in terms of the dilemma and the question, as was done in the new book, could raise the question of whether the education system with its declared value-oriented objectives can allow itself to relate to the subject of American Jewry with the same level of ambivalence and lack of decisiveness that is prevalent in the public debate. While among the public such a discussion is natural, vital, and fruitful, in the education system there is concern that such an approach will only have a negative effect. Teachers and students are both likely to avoid discussion of problematic issues, in which the questions far outweigh the answers.

In summary, then, the education system has two principal options: it can distance itself from the oppressive and confusing ambivalence that we discussed; or it can be wise enough to make use of that ambivalence to encourage a lively and fruitful discussion. Of course, there is also room for the development of different variations of the above options.

Notes

1. *Statistical Yearbook of Israel, 1994*, No. 45 (The Central Bureau of Statistics, 1994), p. 646.

2. Ibid., p. 654. The gap between the number of students in the independent education system at the junior high level and the senior high level is explained by the fact that in this framework there is no division into junior and senior high schools.

3. *Am ve-olam: Tarbut yehudit be-olam mishtaneh* (Nation and World: Jewish Culture in a Changing World) (Jerusalem: Ministry of Education, Culture, and Sports, August 1994).

4. *Tokhnit ha-limudim be-historia le-kitot tet be-veit ha-sefer ha-mamlakhti veha-mamlakhti-dati* (The History Study Curriculum for Grade 9 in the State and State-Religious Schools), (Jerusalem: Ministry of Education and Culture, 1974/75).

5. *Reishit ha-zionut, shi'urim be-historia le-veit ha-sefer ha-mamlakhti* (The Beginnings of Zionism, Lessons in History for the State School), (Jerusalem: The Center for Study Programs, Ministry of Education and Culture, 5736, 1975/76).

6. *Toledot yisrael be-dorot ha-aharonim ve-yedi'at ha-am ve-ha-medinah* (Jewish History in Recent Generations and Studies of the People and the State), A Study Program Proposal for the High Schools (Jerusalem: Ministry of Education and Culture, 5727, 1966/67), pp. 2, 3, 6.

7. *Tokhnit limudim be-historia* (A History Study Program for the Upper Level of the State School (Jerusalem: Ministry of Education and Culture, 5737, 1976/77).

8. *Tokhnit limudim be-sifrut la-hativah ha-elyonah* (A Literature Study Program for the Religious Senior High Schools) (Jerusalem: Ministry of Education and Culture, 5740, 1979/80).

9. *Tokhnit limudim be-sifrut la-hativah ha-elyonah be-veit ha-sefer ha-dati* (A Literature Study Program for the Religious Senior High Schools), (Jerusalem: Ministry of Education and Culture, 5740, 1979/80).

10. Olga Zambrowski, *Sifrut yehudit-amerika'it ve-tzibur ha-kor'im be-yisrael* (American Jewish Literature and the Reading Public in Israel), (Jerusalem: The American Jewish Committee and Bar Ilan University, 1995), p. 8

11. *Reishit ha-zionut, shi'urim be-historia* (The Beginning of Zionism, Lessons in History), (Jerusalem: Ministry of Education and Culture, 5737, 1976/77).

12. Ibid., Vol. 2, p. 13.

13. Yisrael Guttman and Haim Shatzker, *Ha-Shoah u-mashma'utah* (The Holocaust and Its Significance), (Jerusalem: Zalman Shazar Center, 1987).

14. Ibid., p. 190.

15. Shlomo Horowitz, *Kitzur toledot yisrael ba-eit ha-ḥadashah* (A Short Version of Jewish History in the Modern Era), Parts A, B, C (The Hebrew Reali School of Haifa, 1970); Shlomo Horowitz, *Toledot zemaneinu 1918–1950* (The History of Our Time, 1918–1950), (Tel Aviv: Yehoshua Chechik Publishers, 1961.)

16. Shlomo Horowitz, *Kitzur toledot yisrael ba-eit ha-ḥadashah,* Part C, p.110.

17. Eliezer Schweid, "Gilgulei ha-tzurah shel ha-zehut ha-yehudit ha-modernit ke-tahalikh histori" (Changes in Modern Jewish Identity as a Historical Process), *Iyyunim be-tekumat yisrael,* Vol. 4 (Beer Sheva: Ben-Gurion University, 1994), pp. 1–32.

18. Ibid., p. 32.

19. Ibid., p. 17.

20. Yair Oron, "Ha-Am ha-yehudi ve-ha-tza'ir ha-yisraeli" (The Jewish People and the Young Israeli), *Gesher* 1985 (Summer 5745): 27–35. See also Yair Oron, *Zehut yehudit-yisraelit* (Jewish-Israeli Identity), (Tel Aviv, Sifriat Hapoalim, 1993).

21. Ibid., p. 31.

22. Shulamit Har-Even, "Ha-Nosei she-assur lehazkir" (The Unmentionable Topic), *Yedi'ot aḥronot,* February 20, 1995, p. 5.

23. Meir Shalev, "Ha-Olam ke-Merkha'ot" (The World as Quotation Marks), *Yedi'ot aḥronot,* July 9, 1994, p. 3.

24. *Ha-Kiyyum ha-yehudi ba-tefutzot ba-me'ah ha-20* (Jewish Existence in the Diaspora in the Twentieth Century), (Ministry of Education and Culture, 1994).

25. Ibid., p. 4.

26. Ibid., pp. 201–3.

27. Ibid., p. 313.

Harvey Shapiro

Response
Readmitting Tensions in Cultivating a Relationship to Israel

Should we be concerned that the enterprise of cultivating a relationship between American Jews and Israel is replete with mutual ambivalence and seemingly contradictory purposes? How should educators respond to the ambiguity and dissonance that characterize the subjects of Israel and Diaspora?

What Zambrowsky and Or-Chen raise as reasons for concern—ambivalence and contradiction—are also, paradoxically, sources for the relationship's sustenance. Their findings that the Israeli intelligentsia, educational policy makers, textbook writers, journalists, teachers, and students may, as groups and as individuals, frequently hold conflicting attitudes toward American Jewry suggest that the relationship's qualities are deeply stratified. Their findings further reveal that educational efforts to slacken particular ideological resolutions, e.g., *shlilat ha'golah* (negation of the Diaspora), have resulted in Israeli students being engaged with American Jewish life in a less ideologically mediated relationship. What may lie behind these researchers' conclusions are educators' struggles to legitimate a new kind of relationship that allows tensions to coexist with positive interdependencies and affinities.

My assertion that dissonance is inevitable does not deny the veracity of Chazan's findings that there has been a notable failure to teach Israel's modern cultural, ethnic, and linguistic dimensions or even a lack of clear purpose in teaching Israel at all. What Chazan critiques as American Jewish education's avoidance, Americanization, or fabrication of Israel may be more than a symptom of the American Jewish community's need to make Israel consonant with its own values and needs. It may be a symptom of modern education's distaste for contradictions, dissonance, and tensions.

But contradictions do, nonetheless, exist. Zambrowsky and Or-Chen suggest that there is a dissonance between the educational policy

150

makers' declared intentions for teaching contemporary Diaspora culture and society and the actual execution of these intentions—a discrepancy that might reflect the dichotomy between a pluralistic perspective of world Jewry and a particularistic perspective of a uniquely Jewish life in the modern State of Israel. An enduring tension between negation and acceptance of the Diaspora thus informs the reticence of Israel's educational practitioners to implement policies that call for a renewed engagement with an efficacious Jewish life outside of Israel.

Similarly, what Chazan refers to as the linguistic, cultural, and ethnic dimensions of Israel may each evoke particular stresses in the relationship. These stresses include the struggles between affinity with one's native language and with modern Hebrew, between American Jewish culture and that of Israel, and between diverse forms of Jewish ethnic identity as perceived and expressed in America and in Israel. Even directly experiencing Israel may present a challenge to the nature of North American Jewish life, creating a strained relationship between the two societies.

There is thus a perceived dissonance between Israel and the Diaspora that is likely to be evoked by educators' emphasizing the linguistic, cultural, ethnic, and experiential dimensions of Israel. This dissonance leaves educators with a choice—to suppress the tensions in the interest of making the subject matter more "relevant" (perhaps suppressing the subject altogether), or to engage students with these contradictions, encouraging students to struggle with them.

As Zambrowsky, Or-Chen, and Chazan suggest, both Israeli and American Jewish education have opted for palatability and consonance over contradiction and dissonance. Avoiding challenges to the compatibility of the two communities' values, for example, Israeli education has taught the subject of American Jewry only primarily up to the 1940s and has referred to the community as "distressed." Similarly, American Jewish education has tried to make the case for consonance between what are in many ways discordant realities and idealities—Americanism, Judaism, and Israel.

Tensions as Educational Opportunities

But overlooking challenging contradictions and artificially unifying dissonant values deprives us of the edifying power of tensions. I suggest that skillful presentation of, anticipation of, and response to tensions are critical to cultivating a viable relationship.

Certainly, incorporating tensional dimensions of the Israeli–Diaspora relationship is valuable simply in the interests of accuracy and in respect for the other. However, I maintain that there are three further rationales for educators' and students' confronting the tensional qualities of relationships to Israel. The first derives from the nature of culture in general. The second is based on the particular nature of the Jewish relationship to Israel. The third is based on the educational theory supporting the notion that understanding tensions can invite students to explore and deepen their own relationships to Israel.

Culture comprises what Geertz calls "webs of significance"—complex interplays of discordant values, concepts, and practices. As webs, cultures must be tensional; the tautness of each web is a necessary condition for holding its defined, though somewhat stretchable, shape. "Cultural web" defines culture as holding together not only because of interrelated concepts, but also because of tension; the web collapses without the two of them. Thus, tensions are both precarious in that the web could break, and necessary in that there would be no web without them.

Tensions in a culture derive, in part, from the use of metaphors that lend expression to a culture's aspirations and concerns. As Geertz suggests:

> The power of a metaphor derives precisely from the interplay between the discordant meanings it symbolically coerces into a unitary conceptual framework and from the degree to which that coercion is successful in overcoming the psychic resistance such semantic tension inevitably generates in anyone in a position to perceive it.[1]

Thus this interplay between discordant meanings and semantic, conceptual coercion gives the cultural concept its shape and its power. But the "semantic tensions" created by cultural metaphors invite interpretation.

Bruner sees the explication of cultural metaphors as dynamic and necessary. Inviting, displaying, and interpreting cultural tensions contributes to a culture's strength and health:

> Once one takes the view that a culture itself comprises an ambiguous text that is constantly in need of interpretation by those who participate in it, then the constitutive role of language in creating social reality becomes a topic of practical concern ... a culture is

as much a forum for negotiating and renegotiating meaning and for explicating action as it is a set of rules or specification for action.[2]

Israel, as a conceptual framework and cultural metaphor, at once symbolically coerces discordant meanings and provides a semantic unity. Consider the potential discordances between such values as *reshit tz'miḥat ge'ulatenu* (the dawn of our redemption) and secular political autoemancipation, between *goy eḥad ba'aretz* (a unique nation in the Land) and *or la-goyim* (a light unto the nations), and between *kibutz galuyot* (ingathering of the exiles) and *merkaz ruḥani* ("spiritual center"). These juxtaposed values represent seemingly binary qualities of the concept of Israel as well as reconcilable distinctions.

On a personal level, a relationship to Israel often involves a struggle between what are taken to be cultural norms and idiosyncracies of personal circumstances. For example, many consider the concept of aliyah to be normative, and living in Diaspora to be a deviation from the norm. Yet for others, the inverse may be true. These latter may consider aliyah to be situationally untimely or undesirable, and living in Diaspora to be a fulfillment of the Jewish mission in the world that either supplements the building of the State of Israel or supersedes it. Thus even the notion of a relationship to Israel is a case of enduring cultural tension between the normative and the exceptional.

An Example

Among the tensions in the relationship to Israel is the tension between Israel as a time and Israel as a place. In S. Y. Agnon's story, "Tehila," the protagonist, reflecting on the comings and goings at the Western Wall in pre-state Jerusalem, relates his perspective on Israel as a place:

> From Jaffa Gate as far as the Western Wall, men and women from all the communities of Jerusalem moved in a steady stream, together with those newcomers whom The Place has restored to their place, although they had not yet found their place (*shehevi'am ha-makom li-m'komam va-adayin lo matzu et mekomam*)… Those who had come to pray were herded together and driven to seek shelter close up against the stones of the Wall, some weeping and some as if dazed.[3]

A natural restoration to their place brought about by The Place is accompanied by a certain confusion, a sense of unsettled dislocation, as the newcomers struggle to learn how to be in place—a habit lost throughout the years of dispersion and exile from being in place. Their return has left them weeping and dazed. The protagonist, too, shares this instability:

> I found a place for myself at the Wall, standing at times amongst the worshippers, at times amongst the bewildered bystanders.[4]

The narrator thus waffles between worship and bewilderment. This is no simple disorientation brought about by arriving at someplace new. It is a struggle to achieve a comfort in dwelling in the very place that is one's own and which, in the mind of the narrator, has been designated as such by God, the very Place of the world itself.

For the modern Jew attempting to embrace an experience of being in a place, Israel in particular presents a challenge when we consider the Jewish predilection for sanctifying time and suppressing a sense of being in place. This challenge is true for the traditionalist as well as for the modernist, for both traditional Judaism and secular modernism have, in their separate ways, elevated time to a privileged position, suppressing the importance of place. For different reasons, both have engaged in a kind of temporocentrism in which "whenabouts" is of far greater concern than "whereabouts." Is it then any wonder that consideration of the place of Israel in modern Jewish education, as well as in modern Judaism, perplexes us?

This perplexity is compounded when we consider that Israel is not only placial, but temporal as well. Indeed, our contemporary educational struggles are rooted, in part, in the tension between time and place that is embedded in Jewish tradition and Jewish historical experience. Within Judaism, Israel informs two categories, as it were. Temporally, returning to Israel is a renewal, as in the petitionary prayer, *ḥadesh yamenu ki-kedem*, renew our days as of old. Returning to Israel is seen as a kind of temporal restoration. Facing eastward (*kedmah*) during prayer is, metaphorically, an expression of aspiration for temporal renewal and redemption. In the placial sense, however, going to Israel is a movement forward and upward (*aliyah*) in space, and restoring Israel is a rebuilding of the place itself. Israel the place is what is ahead of the Jew as he turns eastward. Thus, going to Israel is a kind of progression forward and upward in space, on the one hand, and a retrogressive turn in time, on the other,[5] encompassing the Jewish sense of being in place and being in time, placing them in dynamic tension with one another.

However, this tension is further enhanced and intensified by moder-

nity's suppression of place. As Edward Casey asserts in his phenome-
nological study of place:

> In the past three centuries in the West—the period of
> "modernity"—place has come to be not only neglected but ac-
> tively suppressed. Owing to the triumph of the natural and social
> sciences in the same period, any serious talk of place has been
> regarded as regressive or trivial. A discourse has emerged whose
> exclusive cosmological foci are Time and Space. When the two
> were combined by twentieth-century physics into the amalgam
> "space-time," the overlooking of place was only continued by
> other means. For an entire epoch, place has been regarded as an
> impoverished second cousin of Time and Space, those two colos-
> sal cosmic partners that tower over modernity.[6]

Modernity's suppression of place and Jewish tradition's predilection
for time—could there be a more formidable alliance against which Jewish educators must struggle to find a place for Israel in contemporary
Jewish education? It is unmodern to be concerned with place. Such a
concern is dissonant with the dominant dogma of post-exilic Jewish
tradition, and Zionism itself has emphasized place primarily for its utilitarian value of progressive (temporal) improvement of the Jewish condition. Is it any wonder, then, that confusion and ambiguity confound
the place of Israel in the curriculum to a degree seemingly incommen-
surate with Jewish education's efforts to be both "modern" and "Jewish?" Perhaps the impediments to finding a meaningful and appropriate place for Israel are found less in a particular Americanization of
Israel in Jewish education[7] or in the sociological and political disaffec-
tion between American Jews and Israeli society,[8] than in this underlying tension between Jewish tradition's accentuation of time, Zionism's
emphasis on place, and modernity's suppression of place.

Both placial and temporal, "Israel" is a place with which Jews have
a relationship and through which they define relationships to places in
which they live. But "Israel" also refers to root experiences of the Jewish people in history and to Jewish aspirations for the future. These two
senses, place and time, have been agonistic at major transitions in Jewish history—for example, during the first centuries after the destruction
of the first Temple in 586 B.C.E. and during the emergence of Zionism
in the last two centuries. In both of these periods, Jews have struggled
between temporal and placial poles and have experienced a transfig-
ured relationship to Israel.

This struggle between time and place shifts when we seek a distinctive relationship to place. To become implaced is to be in concordance with a place, to embrace it as something that is ours and that informs our existence in the world. As Casey writes:

> To be in concordance with something and to embrace it is to relate to it as something possessing more than a merely instrumental significance ... To be in concordant embraces with regions through our bodies is to know regions as familiar parts of our experience.[9]

This concordance with a place may be most intimately and engagingly experienced by one's presence in the place. However, the struggle for concordance with a place may also exist when we are not present, but oriented toward a place. Having a relationship to a place may involve attending to the place, facing it ahead of us, striving to envision it, and (perhaps) moving in its direction as we seek to intensify and deepen this confrontation. These phenomena of attending to, facing, striving, envisioning, and moving toward a place help make the relationship to a place what Casey would call "familiar."

Educators' Expressions of the Time-Place Tension

In previous research[10] that I conducted on the tensions Jewish educators construct in their own narratives of cultivating a relationship with Israel, the tension between time and place (among many others) emerged repeatedly. Each of the educators I interviewed has been deeply committed to the process of cultivating the relationship to Israel and has had substantial experience seeking to do so in a variety of contexts. Despite this profound commitment and experience, these educators suggest that the process of cultivating a relationship is conflicted.

Jim, a 23-year-old camp educator, begins by describing how he spoke to a group of teenagers leaving from camp for Israel. His "charge" to the group exemplifies the tension between time and place:

> You're going to be waking up in Jerusalem. Within 24 hours of my talking to you you're going to be in Jerusalem. Two or three generations back, let alone ten generations back, people would have literally given their lives to step foot in the Land. You get to wake up there every single morning for five weeks.[11]

Jim is conveying a sense of this event as both a momentous episode in their lives and a significant episode in history. The importance of the students' visit is both in the context of their position in time ("Two or three generations back") and their relationship to place ("to step foot in the Land … to wake up there …"). There are thus two commingling narratives—their lives ("Within 24 hours of my talking to you…") and history ("ten generations back")—in which this episode is significant. Jim's exhortation to the group may be considered an acknowledgement of the frictions between these two narratives. One is a story of insurmountable obstacles, seemingly unattainable goals, and exile. The other is a story of ease of movement, a tendency to take distance in time and space for granted.

The tension between time and place is further expressed by the fact that Jim's relationship to Israel is largely a relationship to moments in time. He can temporalize Israel through discrete moments:

> It's in scattered parts in camp. It's when we have *mifkad* at night, when we say *kol od ba-levav*… And there is a certain part of *mifkad* when we do *kol od ba-levav* … the Hatikva, and I look at that flag and I think about Israel and I think about, for example, two of my friends over here who have shared Israel experiences with me… It's something that small. It takes thirty seconds. But it's the internalization of the thought of Israel. That time is set aside…[12]

Thus internalizing Israel in particular moments in camp, Jim seeks to cultivate an affinity with a place that he presently finds in time. For in this excerpt, Israel is "when"—"*when* we have *mifkad* at night," "*when* we do *kol od ba-levav*." This "when" has a short duration—"thirty seconds"; it is in those few seconds that he finds Israel, the State, the Land, the experience of being there. But Jim shares his intention of making aliyah to Israel in the near future. The "when" will become the "where"; these moments in camp will themselves dissolve into memories, now sources of nostalgia as Jim actually travels to Israel. Thus Jim experiences Israel as a duality of time and place.

Rachel, an educator in a Jewish day school, also expresses tension between time and place:

> '77 was the first time that I felt I had done the country and the Land. We were doing scuba diving all the way down … we slept on the beaches and … we went on all this rough terrain and we talked to Arabs and to … nomads in tents. It felt really *mamashi* [real, palpable], something that … I never did before. That was

really exciting to me and I really felt that I had a handle, a real
feel for the Land ...

I'm being very concrete now. I'm talking about the Land, the
physical Land of Israel. It wasn't this entity. Up until that point,
we went to Masada, we went to the things that represented the
symbolic entity of Israel, whether it was historical or modern,
whether it was Knesset or Masada, it didn't really matter. They
were things that represented what Israel is. This time we went
traveling through the desert over mountains. We went through
tough terrain. We were sleeping on the beaches. I went swimming
in the seas. It was a real physical connection to the Land ... The
image—I just have this feeling of this grittiness of the sand and the
heat, and really feeling, I don't know, it was just something — I
could feel comfortable ... It was Israel but it was a different experience of Israel than I've had before. It wasn't historical, it wasn't
political ... It was really tangible. And it was a very different experience ...[13]

In these passages, Rachel expresses a story of transition and concordance. In Casey's terms, it is a story of giving increasingly "explicit attention... to the lived body in relation to its whereabouts," thus making
"the importance of place ... fully evident."[14] Her relationship with Israel now goes beyond particular historical, religious, political, or idea-
tional references. It becomes a relationship to the Land, its dirt, its people, its terrain, and its places. Her relationship is not only an embracing
of a time, but of a place. It is an assertion of the relationship's *mamashut,*
"a real physical connection to the Land," in contrast to the relationship's symbolism or reference, of "things that represented what Israel
is." The historical, political, and hence, more purely temporal and ide-
ational dimensions of the relationship recede into the background. Yet,
in her day school work, she struggles between teaching the significance
of Israel in the context of Jewish history, Jewish time, and teaching a
sense of affinity with Israel as a place that transcends time.

Tension between time and place is also expressed by Rabbi
Silberstein, an ardent religious Zionist educator who made aliyah from
the United States about eleven years ago. Working at a Jewish summer
camp in the United States, he relates an educational struggle between
emphasizing a connection to the living reality of Israel—as a
place—and emphasizing a connection to a religiously transformed
construct of the relationship as expressed in time.

Today in camp if I go over to the *madrikhim* [counselors] and I say, "For *motsa'ei shabbat* [Saturday night] let's have *shirah sh'ketah ve-nashir shirei erets yisra'el sh'ketim* [quiet singing of soft songs of the Land of Israel] you know, '*Erets, erets, erets,*' '*Al ha-d'vash ve-al ha-oketz*,'" they look at me and say, "You're from Mars, man. We're going to sing all of the Mordecai ben David songs... and all of these American Diaspora *ḥasidishe frum* songs—*Mizmor L'david.* We'll do a *melaveh malkah.*" I say. "O.K. Let's do a *shiluv* [combination]" "We don't want a *shiluv.*" Then I say, "What makes this camp different than other religious Jewish camps?" So it's a dilemma...[15]

Here, a "dilemma" concerning emphasis confronts the Jewish educator. It emerges from a tension between expressions of affinity with the modern reality of Israel and religious expression detached from that reality.

This distinction between what Silberstein calls "*shirah sh'ketah al erets yisra'el*" and "*ḥasidishe frum songs*" provides a useful metonymic expression of differing perceptions of traditional observance and piety. These include Rabbi Silberstein's perception of the spiritual and transcendent that he finds in the relationship to the restored living Land and State of Israel—the place—and the *madrikhim*'s perception of finding these transcendences in traditional religious observances and theological expressions, detached from any particular palpable bond to a particular place and expressed in time.

For the *madrikhim*, the palpable Land and State are conceptualized and collapsed into a matrix of religious observance and expression that celebrates time rather than place. Rabbi Silberstein struggles to balance this transfiguration with the vision and the experience of a real living people of Israel, in their Land, building their State.

An Alternative Educational Paradigm

In the dominant or standard paradigm for teaching Israel, the overarching purpose is to teach Jewish values and practices. The student evaluates the efficacy of these values and practices and considers incorporating them into her personal life. This educational process emphasizes Israel as vehicle.

The standard paradigm thus implies that teaching about Israel serves an extrinsic principle or need and that Israel represents or evokes these principles. The paradigm asks: "What does Israel represent, that justifies teaching it?" Israel might represent, for example, developing Jewish character, confronting or adapting to modernity, or unifying Jews. In such an approach, Israel becomes a means toward extrinsic goals that serve the broader agenda of Jewish education. Its purpose is to serve those goals, and the merits of its use may then be evaluated based on its effectiveness.

However, the expressions of tension between time and place, and the notion of tensions as having powerful educational value suggest an alternative paradigm[16] for the place of Israel in Jewish education, more invitational than representational. Rather than as a referent to which one's life must correspond, Israel as challenge characterizes this approach. The alternate paradigm's primary question might be, "How might Jewish education cultivate a viable relationship between American Jews and Israel?" Less concerned with value judgments than with embracing and struggling with a complex and often contradictory inheritance, the invitational paradigm asks, "How could we enable students to view themselves as inheritors of a tradition that is laden with tensions and ambiguities, even imperfections?"

Narratives of personal experience comprise one powerful (though often neglected) form of presenting and exploring discordances. The process of inviting interpretation of a culture's stories and of constructing our own stories in response to those that have preceded us, resists what has been called "the historical sedimentation of the language we use."[17] According to Rorty, storytelling enables a culture to "keep the conversation going rather than to find objective truth."[18] Continuing the conversation prevents the reification of knowledge, what Rorty calls a "freezing-over of culture … the dehumanization of human beings." Cultural continuity, it would seem, requires a kind of tentativeness, a "suspicion of certainty and precision."[19] Thus, presenting tensions and constructing narrative interpretations of those tensions may help educators avoid the stasis of certainty, and perpetuate a relationship to culture.

But how can cultural strains and confusions sustain a relationship? First, these discordant stresses on the relationship create and reveal a disequilibrium that beckons us to intervene; unreconciled discordances and ambiguities invite imaginative interpretation. Thus educators might see fruitful results if they carry out a process with their students of constructing and interpreting contradictions, articulating personal reactions to the tensions that these contradictions suggest, and narrating experiences that react to, or contribute to, understandings of such discordances. These activities of interpreting, reacting, and narrating experiences are critical means of cultivating a relationship and rediscovering the stratified nature of that relationship.

The educators' narratives cited above are examples of stories reflecting struggles for concordance between seemingly irreconcilable values and perspectives. Thus these narratives serve both as expressions of tensions in these values and perspectives, as well as examples of how constructing stories in response to tensions can cultivate ones's sense of being in concordance with dichotomous aspects of a tradition.

Such storytelling also reflects struggles for concordance between what are perceived to be cultural norms and departures from those norms. As Bruner writes:

> The function of a story is to find an intentional state that mitigates or at least makes comprehensible a deviation from a canonical pattern.[20]

When we perceive our experiences, values, or circumstances as exceptions to the norm, we struggle, through our stories, to make this "deviation" comprehensible in our cultural terms. Our telling stories reflects our struggle for concordance between canonicality and exceptionality.

By concordance I mean that the story of Israel finds a place in the student's life story so that it enhances and informs that student's story. By struggling for concordance I suggest that the student makes a sustained effort to respond to tensions between her personal story and her encounters with Israel. These encounters may be with visits, stories, texts, lessons, simulations, dramatic presentations, music, art, or other media. The struggle for concordance assumes that there will be dissonance perceived in these encounters. The question for the educator, then, is how to enable the student to respond to this dissonance and, by that, to struggle to build Israel's place in the narrative of her life.

As we develop educational experiences and policies for cultivating a viable relationship between American Jewry and Israel, we need to confirm the manifold often contradictory qualities of the relationship, and to engage the student with them. In so doing we may deepen a still existent relationship and cultivate its dormant possibilities.

Notes

1. Clifford Geertz, "Ideology as a Cultural System," in Geertz, C., ed., *The Interpretation of Cultures* (New York: Basic Books, 1973) p. 211.

2. Jerome Bruner, *Actual Minds, Possible Worlds* (Cambridge, Massachusetts: Harvard University Press, 1986) pp. 122–23.

3. S. J. Agnon, "Tehila" (1950), trans. Walter Lever, *Firstfruits*, ed. James A. Michener (Greenwich, Conn: Fawcett, 1973) p. 62.

4. Agnon, p. 62.

5. In this regard it is significant that the term *kedem* connotes both the meaning of "days of old" that have preceded the present moment, as well as eastward direction (*kedmah*) and forward movement (*kadimah*).

6. Edward S. Casey, *Getting Back Into Place, Toward a Renewed Understanding of the Place-World* (Indianapolis: Indiana University Press, 1993) p. xiv.

7. For the critique of the Americanization of Israel in Jewish education see, for example, Walter Ackerman, (1986). "The Land of Our Fathers in the Land of the Free," *Jewish Education* 54(4) :4–14; David Breakstone (1988) "The Dynamics of Israel in American Jewish life: An Analysis of Educational Means as Cultural 'Texts'" (Doctoral Dissertation, Hebrew University, 1986), Ann Arbor: University Microfilms International.

8. Steven Cohen. "Are American and Israeli Jews Drifting Apart?" *Imagining the Jewish Future*, D. Teutsch., ed. (Albany: State University of New York Press, 1992), pp. 119–33.

9. Casey, 96.

10. Harvey Shapiro, "Cultivating a Relationship Between North American Jews and Israel," (Ph.D. Dissertation, Hebrew Union College, Los Angeles,1996)

11. Shapiro, p. 225.

12. Shapiro, pp. 228–29.

13. Shapiro, pp. 235–36.

14. Casey, p. 46.

15. Shapiro, p. 215.

16. Shapiro, pp. 286–331.

17. As quoted in Cleo Cherryholmes, *Power and Criticism: Poststructural Investigations in Education* (New York: Teachers College Press, 1988), p. 150.

18. As quoted in Cherryholmes, p. 147.

19. Cherryholmes, p. 147.

20. Jerome Bruner, *Acts of Meaning* (Cambridge, Massachusetts: Harvard University Press, 1990) pp. 49–50.

William Cutter

Response
Myths and Realities in Teaching Israel

Barry Chazan has suggested that Diaspora Jews have sacrificed ethnic, cultural, and linguistic understanding through the way they teach about Israel. The suggestion is that Americans have obviously needed to see Israel in a certain way, and have presented their perceptions in terms that serve extrinsic agendas: the need to function as patron; the need for Jewish mythology; the attachment to behavioral surrogates. But I would add that the inherent social conditions in America and certain general educational realities have played an even stronger role in biasing our epistemologies and in influencing our pedagogues.

One cannot teach much of any subject that is value-laden (as our relationship with Israel is supposed to be) without taking into account the learner's development and social context. So my comments begin with certain social and developmental elements within the American and Israeli pedagogical situation. Client is a commonplace notion, yet client character has been too little addressed in these discussions.[1]

We have tended, I am afraid, to deal paradigmatically, and in terms of the content we want to impart. But the American setting produces a highly-defined learner, and the Israeli setting yields definite character traits. The Jews we try to bring to Israel are often—even usually—the products of successful homes where parents have adapted brilliantly to the American socio-economic climate.

Indeed, Jewish Americans have by now participated in the creation of that climate through their roles in marketing, the service industries, and the media. American children come to Israel with a sense of comfort (I'm speaking sociologically and not necessarily psychologically), and that sense inflects their encounter with a nation whose ethos has been to serve a needy Diaspora. Just as Israel's children define themselves as being part of a nation with military might, so America's Jewish children identify themselves as being part of a nation with social and economic might. Educators in the U.S. cannot foster any commitment

163

that is based on notions about our social frailty, and so they must provide antidotes to compensate for our successes. Any affirmations American children might develop about Israel have to operate within a sensible context (or what some scholars are now calling "plausibility structures").

Parental and communal aspirations in America add yet another impediment to identification with Israel instead of adding a force for identification. It is difficult for American parents, or their agents—the educators—to foster full engagement with Israel, because they have a commitment to American values and America's way of life, corrupt though those values may appear to people with a more continental or Levantine sensibility. American Catholics experience a similar problem when certain of their children decide to enter religious orders. The ethos of America has been embraced by second and third generation immigrant progeny.

Did anyone in the Zionist year of 1897 understand that the people on whom national renewal would be most reliant would turn out to be the very people most resistant to its passions? And it is not only parents and family who reject the Zionist passion. Harvey Shapiro's idea of a "narrative relationship" between the learning communities of the two nations comes about because the ambivalence about teaching Israel often comes from the teachers themselves. The teachers are, in their own way, part of the powerful American mainstream.

In addition to the societal realities and their psychological implications, there are three general areas of concern that I have gleaned in these meetings, and that Steven Cohen has helped place into the discussion: 1) the meaning of place in a learner's life—in this instance, Israel as Holy Land vs. Israel as modern political unit; 2) representation of that place and its people—how to achieve that representation properly and helpfully; and 3) the concept of the ethical way of relating to an "other"—any other, even if she is already a relative. Psychology, epistemology of education, and moral education remain the thickets of the Israel–American dialogue, whose thorns aren't much different in regard to the question of teaching Israel than they are in regard to many educational issues. Each must be addressed by any educator, whether implicitly or explicitly.[2] And, finally, we can add to this list two of the current hot topics in educational theory, which are more general and less personal: 1) canon (What is the material that must be studied?) and 2) the function of mythologization of the heroic past within a modern industrial or post-industrial information culture. The question of Israel and Diaspora education is a virtual laboratory for educational theorists.

These broad theoretical scaffoldings are challenging enough, but they occur within the context of more specific warnings about an erosion in the American–Israeli conversation. Some of our erosions have emerged, as I noted above, from forces that at least one culture in this discussion will view as positive (like a richer domestic Jewish life within America). The so-called attention to spirituality in America has helped de-materialize experience and to create a metaphoric Israel in place of a geographic homeland. (Some descriptions of new spirituality in America have been unfairly burlesqued, but I acknowledge a move "inward" among many of our more committed people.) I see other signs of distancing from the physical Israel throughout the breadth of the American social landscape. I learned recently that a favorite delicatessen in St. Louis changed its name from "The Tel Aviv" to "The Pumpernickel"—a label, I contend, that suggests Eastern European American nostalgia in preference over loyalty to Israel, even though ostensibly the name change was purely coincidental. A major Reform conference recently dropped the reference to "Diaspora" in its title, though Diaspora was definitely part of its work.[3] And few American born writers (Philip Roth and Anne Roiphe excepted, in my opinion) have drawn on Israel as part of narrative explorations of the meaning of being a Jew in contemporary America.

My take on these isolated examples is that Americans do not think of themselves in association with the word "Diaspora," though Israelis who have migrated to America might.[4] I hear almost no serious discourse about Israel within the informal life on university campuses where I work from time to time, except where war and peace issues or an election are at stake. The excellent *Jerusalem Report* is read by only a few people—a cohort that may be a modest exception to my general statement. Israel in the flesh and blood and in present time seems most real to American business people. Business is an emerging area of communication and engagement that might contribute to more generalized Jewish understanding, if the challenge can interest its players. There will be connections, willy/nilly, as mergers occur and as business forums open up. Whether relationships that begin in economic activity can transfer directly to children, or whether such economic connections can take on an educational responsibility remains to be seen. So far, business people do not seem interested in engaging academics or educators in order to enrich their non-economic or non-political insight. The increased attention to the oriental component in Israeli life may enhance an emerging distance from a Eurocentric pumpernickel-oriented Jewish community, and we have to seek antidotes to that distance, perhaps by adding the "oriental" mode to American youth's appreciation of Israeli life. Thus, those who want American youth to feel closer to Israel through a more realistic relationship to its life are faced with the paradox of acquainting youngsters with the aspect of Israeli life that is least familiar to occidentally oriented teenagers.

I am not as pessimistic as some of the presenters at this conference have been, and not as critical of our idealization. Though times are always forcing us to rethink our relationship to ideals, I believe that a good case could be made for holding on to some of the ways in which Americans and Israelis have visualized each other—even some of the ways that we would now call dysfunctional. A perspective that needs correcting is at least a compelling perspective, a place from which to begin. Furthermore, some of the old themes are still with us, and remain quite functional in certain ways. Let's take Barry Chazan's note that American textbooks imagine Israel in a way that serves American needs. I would submit that most curricula that teach about other cultures do so in ways that serve their own needs. In this regard, it may be our task to work mutually to see where the needs of each country's educators can be made to intersect.

The "mobilization" model put forth by Steven Cohen and Charles Liebman may be a little out of date in light of Israel's putative prosperity, but it is not entirely dead either, as Steven Bayme has argued. Do we assume, Bayme notes, that an economic prosperity means the end of social needs that might stimulate mobilization? Is the cynicism and iconoclasm of Israeli life today fundamentally different from some of the efforts at demythologization that we have seen in curricula throughout the world?[5] And, finally, we don't really have the proper data from camp or youth movement. Does not the very existence of this volume, and many others like it, signal an interest in discovering some of the spiritual intersections between American Jews and Israeli Jews? My informal observation of the day school and camping movements in America tells me that Israel is still on the program agendas that affect our young people. (Camp settings actually come closest to suggesting our idealization of Israeli life).

We seem to have agreed here that notions of mutuality and equivalence are hard to come by in the American Israeli dialogue. If we desire more open exchange and less naive, more realistic attachments (as in

Harvey Shapiro's suggestion about the invitation to narrative), then we are going to have to modify some of the larger and even more abstract elements that have come to characterize the relationship. Yet, though I endorse Shapiro's antidote to misperception and disappointed ideals, I insist upon the inevitability of that mythology even if it actually gets in the way of the dialogue. Part of the narrative, after all, is the dialogue between the mythologized ideals (grown from the past) and the experienced reality in the present. And a component of most human relations is the experience of affiliation with others, while one struggles with and sometimes recoils at their otherness. For example, youth in most Western countries can communicate with each other about relationships with their parents, and about clothing, sports, and music styles. The foreignness often emerges when it comes to proclaiming values or patriotism, or defining Jewish life as religious or ethnic expression. Any people possessing a group character will experience some of that abrasion when it meets another group of people.

Many of the old mythologies still function as educational tools. I saw an instance of this in a contest sponsored by the Behrman House Publishers, where I consult as an editor. Several hundred essays were submitted by youngsters ages nine to fourteen. The submissions captured some of the great myths of blooming deserts, saving Jewish souls, and defending frontiers—the very ideals that some say get us in trouble when the Israel Diaspora dialogue tries to include the day to day realities of our mutual lives. Though the subjects were prompted by the contest titles, the essays were clearly heartfelt. For me, this was an encouraging index, not an obstacle to be overcome, and it was re-enforced during the first day of our conference by the group of Reform Jewish youth who were playing Frisbee on the Sde Boker lawn. (Shlonsky first called it *"tzalaḥat me'offefet"* [a flying saucer] in one of his 1950s poems.) I was struck by the irony that we were discussing the decline in the old idealized relationship at one of the key locales in Israel for enhancing that idealization. Sde Boker is, after all, the origin of the blooming metaphors.

Shall the distance between Israeli and American young people (which concerns me and which need not be inevitable), and the mutual difficulties in representing each other (which does not concern me but is partly inevitable) surprise us entirely? Given the complexities of relating to other human beings at all, and given the importance of place in the development of one's day to day identity, what may we honestly expect? The way we look at what we are *not* inevitably distances the viewer (or subject) from the object; and our attachment to where we are and where we perform the projects of our lives requires that some kind of maladjustment—even *disease*—move us to passion about near-far places that distorts vision even as passions clarify the longing.

The religious community, which originally fostered the longing for Zion, has bequeathed a vision that even nonreligious people cannot shake. Haftarot, wedding blessings, invocations involve Jerusalem! It is as if the dreams and visions of the Prophets, whether addressing social justice or promises of national redemption, cannot be reiterated within the prophetic literature without creating myths that distant. The setting for reading the prophetic literature is during the highly ritualized and mythically charged Shabbat service. For those who live the contrast, the distortions are ironic and sometimes tiresome; while for those who come to the contrast for the first time, the distortions can be as attractive as they are treacherous. We must welcome these contrasts as inevitable and as rich occasions for engagement.

Olga Zambrowski and Malka Or-Chen remind us that distortions in perspectives are not simply in one direction. Israeli youngsters, it seems, are taught to view their American relatives from the same perspective of national interest that—as Barry Chazan notes—Americans exhibit. Idealization here sometimes turns to anti-idealization. The historical data—"the real truth"—play only a marginal role in the consciousness of a young person. And, like any analysis of relationships between two nations, there are more data than any one study can draw upon.

In my own academic field of modern literature, interest in the Diaspora is plentiful in Nathan Shaham, Ya'akov Shabtai, A.B. Yehoshua, Ruth Almog, and the mock mythologies of Yona Wolloch, among others. Rissa Domb's *Home Thoughts from Abroad*[6] describes aspects of attachment to foreign soil, and Menucha Gilboa has written[7] about the mythologies that America offers the Israeli reader. It is not entirely surprising that California's coast represents the kind of openness and freedom that one may feel are absent from the small and surrounded physical land called Israel. Of course, mythology about America lacks the theological overlay or the element of national destiny, and attaches more to personal "salvation" than to national redemption. But it is precisely the personal-national dichotomy that seems to interest us here. We ought to explore that dichotomy.

Serious educators must dwell on the contrast between personal and national impulses of their learners when considering the teaching of idealized relationships. As educators ponder the poles of national identity and individual need, the poles assume at various times foreground or background roles in our curriculum considerations. When do the values of the civilization take precedence over the status of the student as learner? When are we indulging in too much concern with the individual and losing sight of the broader communal ideal? To what extent can the child learner be viewed as the repository of the parental (perhaps super-ego/communal) ideal? And, since in the United States individual fulfillment is one of the high ideals, when does the entire goal become obfuscated by an outright rejection of communal goals? Whatever our response to these questions, it appears that children and parents of both nations share these concerns to one degree or another. The discourse may need to be over that "difference in degree."

We cannot and perhaps should not expect to exist together without distortions and without mutual disappointment. The beauty of the dialogue is that we can only be partly of this place. As the late poet T. Carmi said in his erotic, but metaphorically suggestive poem:

You are from around these parts.
I withdraw a lot of money
for tickets
and what not: maps and guides.

I try to dress like the people
Speak their language
And eat their food –

But it is clear right away
that I am not from these parts. [8]

This poem suggests—ever so lightly—that physical place and human otherness are forever related one to the other. It is possible that the less lyrical, the less aesthetic, and more social scientific solution is possible, that a Jew may be able to be educated from life's insistent polarities: the public vs. the private self, and the idealized vs. the lived condition of place.

So we live with many dualities. In Israel, as in America, there is a difference between the public and the private Jew. But the duality that may more significantly affect young learners has to do with the programs we establish for them and the lived experience that addresses the volatile and unstable status of any young learner. For American Jews, Israel travel has been a chance to turn young people loose into a kind of freedom that many are having for the first time. The same is true to some extent with regard to Israeli youngsters who come to the States. I don't have much confidence that we can change some of the basic human reactions to the experience of the Israel–American youth dialogue. Their nearness and farness is a kind of inter-youth abrasion—far more interesting than it is destructive.

Whatever our textbooks reveal, and however dimly we have succeeded in imparting the Hebrew language, a relationship is still in place from which some firmer programs ought to be and probably will be developed. I would not worry about the images within textbooks, and I would certainly cast aside—as a practical matter—the argument that textbooks distort. I would also not be concerned too much about the numbers that are at stake: for the textbooks will always reach the greater numbers, but the leadership among young people will always come from those who have shared the tangible experience, with all of its messy contradictions. Existing textbooks, in my view, do not serve us too badly, considering our limited ambition for them. And while most of us in this business have reservations about the way in which "the Israel Trip" is conducted, few of us would discourage expanding the concept and improving it as it expands. Full scale reconceptualizations strike me as a waste of time. The clients' needs change too swiftly.

While most of the articles in this volume suggest greater discouragement than I feel, they *have* made me reflect on the things I have been seeing around me as an educator for 35 years.

Allow me to take this opportunity to suggest a few changes in the way our educational planning has been carried out. And though I bring to my suggestions a skepticism about the way in which adults stimulate the representational faculty of young people, I will nonetheless hope that I can add something by way of proposals:

1. I would propose a pedagogy of public vs. private valuing throughout our curricula, whereby students are sensitized to this strain regarding issues beyond the Zionist concerns that we in this volume share. In that framework, spirituality vs. national or communal identity would be the abstraction for much of what we have written about here.

2. Michael Rosenak's notion of an ideal in becoming, vs. the lived reality (a point of departure for Harvey Shapiro's paper), may be the link to another kind of sharing between Israelis and Diaspora Jews. That is, we are both struggling between the paradigm and the real.

3. Similarly, Avi Ravitsky's holy–home dichotomy could be folded

into our teaching. Israel *is* "other" (and even "holy" to many), and yet the learner must experience and even revel in the quotidian, the gritty, as it were, which often rubs against the grain. In this regard, our educational work has to find a way to take Israeli religious life seriously, and to describe it in its own terms rather than in American terms. Indeed, the other side is also true, and that is that Israelis must come to understand the nuances within American spiritual life more broadly, and thus reduce its "foreign-ness." This has a better chance of happening if we are a little careful when we place youngsters with families on exchange trips. (I am sure that some would agree that too much reality may not be a good thing if the host family is cynically secular.)

4. This note leads me to an item that I think cuts across all areas. There is a kind of gap in our understanding of which American quirks are easily adaptable to the Israeli environment, and which are the quirks that are simply too distant for an Israeli to grasp. This is a theme that recurs frequently in our discourse: Levis and movies come easy to Israelis, but American religious patterns look strange. The American weekend looks attractive to Israelis, but American manners seem too mannered. An inventory of which items cross barriers and which don't easily cross might be very helpful.

5. We ought to develop teaching processes that reflect Israel's history of engagement with America—as a subject in itself. In that subject, young Israeli and American participants might see themselves as part of a longtime process of engagement with each other.

6. Harvey Shapiro's narrative-invitational model gives us an excellent opportunity to consider the status of the individual's experience in contrast to the expectations the individual has before the experience.

7. The concept of exile within Judaism begins in theology, and perhaps an element of that theology can be preserved (even for non-God-oriented people) by tying it to a Jewish history that is also free of belief systems. Diaspora, from the point of view of the literary mind, is a fundamental Jewish experience—whether in spiritual or in geographical terms. The ebbs and flows in the various weights of the concept might become a self-conscious part of the discourse if it can be historicized into "where it has been" and "where it might be today." The American teaching of Zionism continues to be decontextualized— as if Yehuda HaLevi's passion has a meaning that carries into the twenty-first century. If we cannot speak of Diaspora today, perhaps we can do so as a historical datum. But Jonathan Sarna is right, *shlilat ha-golah* is and was irrelevant to American Zionism.

8. We Americans ought to quit complaining about Israeli teachers. We have hired them, and then demonized them into an "other" to be feared and resented rather than as an "other" to be admired or inquired after. Alterity can be made to work for a relationship rather than against; an occasion for curiosity and not anger.

9. I hope we can continue to seek a common language, *tarti mashma* (in both senses of that expression). Hebrew, however weakly learned, is a living Jewish organism—a tool that takes one beyond pure representation or mimesis and scriptural exegesis. It also is the element within Jewish life that reflects the dichotomy between the Holy and the "Daily," while the bridges language provides can be made more attractive. I disapprove of the American abandonment of modern Hebrew as we try to create a synagogue literacy; and I believe that a meeting of youngsters can include consideration of some of the strain between classic and modern linguistic attachments.

I am convinced that our work must reside in the rub between the daily and the idealized; between the narrative and the paradigmatic, between the strange and the familiar. I am also convinced that the more contact we create between Israel's children and our own, the more we will pave the way for closeness and otherness in whose tension both Homeland and Diaspora find growth. I continue to believe that a lot of learning goes on without benefit of programmer or planner.

Yehuda Amichai's poetic reflection captures this dichotomy:

> A group of tourists was standing around their guide and I became their target marker. "You see that man with the baskets? Just right of his head there's an arch from the Roman period..."
> "But he's moving, he's moving."
> I said to myself: "Redemption will come only if their guide tells them, 'You see that arch from the Roman period? It's not important, but next to it, left and down a bit, there sits a man who's bought fruit and vegetables for his family.'"[9]

This poetic rumination works in two hermeneutic directions. The traveler, the Diaspora reader, the American Jewish child, must be urged to reflect on the arch and the grocery basket, and on the two ways the Messiah comes: on the very poles that create restraint and that constitute our human sense of redemption. A full mutuality would exist if we in America engaged in a parallel fantasy near, let us say, a Civil War site. The American discourse is different: most of our poetry lacks national resonance, and our grocery shopper does not carry history or theology with his vegetables. But we all carry more than we think. Only an "other" can make us realize that. Therefore, we should be grateful even for the unrealistic, the incomplete, and even the misdirected perceptions between us. We need more—before we will get better. As always, in these cases, the tired phrase is true: There are opportunities in our problems.

Notes

1. I mean by this the kind of thing discussed by both Ilan Troen's response and the Zambrowsky / Or Chen paper: "Social realities in America are more powerful than received ideological positions and preferences. Students operate under multitudes of influences. It is difficult, doubtful if even possible, to isolate any one factor among the complex arrangement of factors ..."

2. For a discussion of locus and placement, see, especially, Edward Casey, *Getting Back Into Place, Toward a Renewed Understanding of the Place World* (Bloomington: Indiana University Press, 1993). The literature on alterity and representation is vast, and cuts across many disciplines.

3. The Union of American Hebrew Congregations' annual summer study institute began with the title of *Diaspora*, and wound up with a title having to do with conflict, since that more realistically captured the concerns after the Rabin assassination. My point here is that *Diaspora* would have fit nicely into the title, but that it is a concept alien to activist Jewish citizens in America.

4. See, especially, *The Counterlife* and *Operation Shylock* by Roth; and perhaps Anne Roife's *Lovingkindness*.

5. Note especially the national history curriculum produced by a federally appointed committee of professors and teachers, Gary Nash and Charlotte Crabtree, Directors, *National Standards for United States History*, 1995. (Los Angeles: University of California, the National Center for History in the Schools, 1995). Note that since this paper was written, *The New York Times* (Aug. 14, 1999) featured an article on demythologization within Israel's curriculums.

6. Rissa Domb, *Home Thoughts from Abroad* (London: Valentine Mitchell, 1995.)

7. Menucha Gilboa, "America as Place, Metaphor and Symbol in Three Novels," (Hebrew) in *Migvan,* ed. Stanley Nash (Jerusalem: Makhon Haberman, 1988).

8. The translation is mine. The latest edition of the Hebrew, "Mekomi," is contained in T. Carmi, *Shirim* (Tel Aviv: Devir, 1994), p. 211. The word for place—*makom*—provides a pun: "my place" and "native."

9. Translation by Hannah Bloch and Stephen Mitchell, "Tourists," in *The Selected Poetry of Yehuda Amichai* (Berkeley: University of California Press, 1996). The poem is originally from *Shalvah gedolah: She'elot u-teshuvot,* 1980.

Shaul R. Feinberg

Response
Soul Searching

We advance towards the twenty-first century with great uncertainty, anguishing over the horizon of Jewish community and continuity. Worse yet, there are multitudes of the people who have little or no awareness of heritage.

In this context, of distress and slightly guarded hope, we come together to share studies as well as visions and strategies for teaching and appreciating each other—Diaspora and Israel. The obstacles and challenges ought only to inspire us more towards fulfilling the mandate of "teaching (them) diligently" to our children. The way I see it, "Next Year in Jerusalem" is not a messianic aspiration, but chiefly a continual anthem expressing hope in the face of spiritual threat.[1]

Our classic response to critical paradigmatic shifts in the geo-political-cultural strata has been education: from destruction to rebuilding and the ordinary times between. The compelling, effective response to crisis is found in the uniquely stated essence of education, from *educare*—to lead forth, to draw forth" (the learner) or, better, "to draw *out of*" (the learner). This notion is a worthy complement of the Hebraic value,*leḥanekh* (to educate) or, better, *lehakdish*, to dedicate through sanctified commitment to oneself as teacher and to one's students. At each successive stage of one's lifetime, the tradition has set guidelines effecting this commitment in delineating new levels of learning and perspectives for living.[2]

In this vein, the alert educator ought to realize that one teaches *persons* a subject matter. Human beings are to be the focus. Taking some liberty with sources, the teachers are required to "know before whom they stand." Educators clearly need to recognize the complexities of the learners: their fears, biases, hopes; in other words, who they are. Guarding against their own biases in making such evaluations, the teachers additionally need to recognize who the students are not.

To be sure, in efforts to effect changes that carry the learner and the group beyond mere existence, the nature of the environment plays a predominant role. However, the environment will "educate" only through the skill and imagination of the teacher who engages not only the mind but the spirit, senses, and conscience. This kind of education has been designated as "enculturation."[3]

In other words, the *teacher* mediates the *student's* cultural experiences of the world at large—the *milieu,* and the texts (*subject matter*) that both challenge and help make sense of that world. These four foci of curriculum work have usefully been identified as common-places.[4]

Regrettably, our misconceptions of the learner and the milieu have sorely affected our teaching of Israel. For too long, the emphases have been on the religious, sociological, political, and humanitarian aspects of the Israel we have wanted to impart to our pupils.[5]

While these foci continue to be important, our students, like ourselves, are living in an era when the classic mission has been accomplished. In our era, defined by some as "post-Zionist,"[6] we need to open up new perspectives from which to look, interpret, and act towards Israel. We need to know better our brothers and sisters who dwell in Zion, be they on the extremes of secularism, triumphal Orthodoxy or, more notably, the expanding middle range of the population. Teaching them demands going beyond harsh headlines and propaganda. At the same time, Israelis need to learn about the Diaspora, notably North America, with all its imperfections. Israelis need to be on a kind of educational mission to pluralistic America.[7]

This volume is predicated on the belief that more creative and enduring ways must be cultivated, educationally, that take us "beyond Survival and Philanthropy"—i.e. to go beyond the now *passé* understanding of the other. The multi-faced communities in both locations today are engaged in varieties of ways of self-definition and norm setting. Here, Ahad Ha-Am is inspiring for the contemporary situation: I suggest we recognize the "potential" place of not one but many "spiritual centers" *and* spiritual radii of communities that feel themselves living interdependently with Israel. I would like to suggest that within Israel herself, a similar paradigm exists: a multiplicity of centers, radiating ideas and beliefs to the surrounding milieu. Israelis and Diaspora Jews will still frequently speak of *dati* and *lo dati* or *ḥiloni* as if they are clearly uniform descriptions of religious and cultural life; nevertheless, the desire for observance, learning, and some kind of participation, especially around life-cycle events, go beyond the stereotypes conveyed by these terms.[8] Expanding congregations, schools, centers, life-cycle celebrations, and learning within the Progressive Movement alone are encouraging.[9]

Guided personal encounters with a changing Israeli milieu will expose a vast array of "alternatives" that ought to be taught and that go beyond the "ultra" label that seems to be media-made for excitement. If our Israel–Diaspora educational focus is to know the "other," then we must learn about this societal mosaic, the colors of which are drawn from the widest prism of a hundred ethnic groups. The modern Israeli is invited to make a choice today that engenders new directions of teaching Israel.[10]

Hopefully, a more pluralistic society will continue to emerge—one that will not pigeonhole Judaism into false dichotomies of religious vs. non-religious; this society will become even more open to the educational initiatives of non-Orthodox Jewish groups. And teachers in the Diaspora need to convey the multifaceted expressions of these cultural realities.

I advocate a model of empathetic learning that emerges out of living connectedness, despite the fact that notions of mutuality and equivalence are hard to come by in the America–Israel dialogue.[11]

We have witnessed the opposite, which culminated in Yitzhak Rabin's assassination, inspired by a dastardly distorted vision of Judaism, God, Torah, and Israel. Moreover, despite our abhorrence and disgust of noxious ideas and practices, they will not disappear with the expression of our repugnance. Yet the proliferation of newer religious and cultural communities have provided positive responses. Note the recent yet brief histories of the newest congregations of the Israel Movement for Progressive Judaism—where harsh, violent confrontations have spurred degrees of interpersonal and institutional communication. American Jewish supporters, especially those who visit, learn of these stories first-hand and teach them as part of new Israeli realities to their own communities, including federations and other authorities.

We must do all that is possible to regain the sense of *klal yisrael* as a family, as *our* family, amidst all of the dissonances and bitter antagonisms that have been so painfully prominent on public agenda. What is there of our lives worth knowing and sharing that can enrich and nurture the soul of this living yet chaotic organism? What is there for us to learn about ourselves? We may begin with the spiritual-therapeutic notion of soul as that which is at the heart of the family: "Soul is not a thing but a quality of a dimension of experiencing life and ourselves. It has to do with depth, value, relatedness, heart, and personal substance.

I do not use the word soul as an object of religious belief or as something to do with immortality."[12]

As a lens, this concept and phenomenon of soul allows us to look closely at what we, as family members, see in ourselves and others across the geographical, ideological, and religious divides. As in family, so in a people: the elements that comprise relationships, in their building up and breaking down, cover a broad spectrum; I contend that the degrees of dysfunction emerge from the gradual ignoring of symptoms, often with acts of self-delusion. Care of the soul, claims Thomas Moore, does not require fixing the so-called dysfunctional, becoming free of it, nor interpreting it pathologically. We may need to recover the soul, "by reflecting deeply on the 'soul events' that have taken place in the crucible of the family."[13]

Briefly, in the context of the Diaspora–Israel relationship, "soul events," according to my interpretation, can be seen as the moments that shape the ethos of the group; the daily rigors of trying to make order out of chaos: e.g., the absorption of masses of immigrants, continual needs for vigilance against a heritage of aggression and defense, new visions of reconciliations, memories of terror and genocide, and the revival of old and new learning. Every child and adult, new immigrant or veteran Israeli, wealthy or indigent citizen, and all those in between, have their own basic, thoughtful or visceral responses, by *living through these acts*, that draw us together or wrench us apart. As teachers, we must interpret these acts as more than just happenings in our biography or in theirs; they are "soul events" that affect the family, near and far, in transcendental ways. Whether we embrace the enduring legacy of Ahad Ha-Am's "spiritual centeredness and radiating spokes outward," or a more elliptical model of the two centers,[14] our legacy is one of the struggle into which we are born. It is a struggle that must be born not of passion and self-assured authenticity but *knowledge* of the "other"—nationally, religiously, politically, ethically. We may reach such knowledge of one another in these days by a candid sharing of our written and oral traditions. To be "Yisra-el" is to struggle to be straight and honest with ourselves and others, with all the pain of perhaps not liking what we find.

How to engage in this sharing? We need to be bold in addressing one another, knowing that the lives and ideas of those we meet and teach are not necessarily our own. This will require composites of new Jewish learning, not only of the texts that inform the lives of persons different from ourselves in faith and practice, but the contexts and contours of their lives. Considering the different roles tradition plays in American Jewry and Israel is crucial for mutual understanding.[15]

We can discover the shadows and the lighted byways of the "soul events" that mark the daily lives of different communities. In this era, the nurturing of different narrative traditions, of who and what we are— beyond the headlines and narrow research studies—is of monumental significance.[16] Empathic relationships may grow out of this new discourse—however cacophonous or dissonant that may be. Dissonance, in the service of learning, tells us a great deal about ourselves.

Our joint task is to refine our ideas and plans of action for nurturing "the soul of the people," through the most immediate, knowledgeable discourse possible. To ask the question, as at the Seder table, is the beginning of the pursuit of wisdom. Here, the ritual guides us to acknowledge one another—we who may be idiosyncratic, neurotic, vulnerable, aggressive, or optimistic. Knowledge of the other, however, begins with knowing one another's hopes, fears, failures, and successes. In this spirit, let us invest new meaning and energy in the words of the morning service: "Let us learn in order to teach; let us learn in order to do."

In the spirit of the Four Children who ask (or don't), we would applaud the fundamental notion of "engagement." Recall that even the so-called "wicked" one who seems to count him/herself out is, in fact, *sitting at the Seder Table* when this outrageous statement is made. In a nostalgic moment, I recall vividly reciting the words from the old *Union Prayerbook* each Shabbat—words that sound even more compelling today, "O Lord, open our eyes that we may see and welcome all truth, whether shining from the annals of ancient revelations or reaching us through the seers of our own time."[17] In this prophetic expression, in a siddur not known for reconciling Diaspora–Israeli visions, we are awakened to classic, progressive revelation that resonates today. Seers may be found in those who most passionately and candidly call attention to dysfunction in living and learning. There is much risk in being open to such conversation. I trust, though, we are mature and ready for it.

Notes

1. Donniel Hartman, speaking at a Hebrew Union College Colloquium, January 29, 1998: *What Do We Reform Jews have to Offer a Discussion on Pluralism?*

2. Mishnah Avot 5:20

3. John Westerhoff, *Will Our Children Have Faith?* (New York: Seabury Press, 1976), quoted by Isa Aron in "Instruction and Enculturation in Jewish Education," paper presented at the Conference on Research in Jewish Education, Los Angeles, May 1987.

4. Joseph J. Schwab, "Translating Scholarship into Curriculum," *From the Scholar to the Classroom*, ed. Seymour Fox and Geraldine Rosenfield (Jerusalem: Melton Research Center for Jewish Education, 1976).

5. Barry Chazan, above.

6. "Post-Zionism?" *Avar ve-atid*, 2(1), (1995): 36–44.

7. Paul Liptz, Hebrew Union College Colloquium, January 29, 1998.

8. Shlomit Levy, Hanna Levinsohn, Elihu Katz, *Beliefs, Observances, and Social Interaction among Israeli Jews* (Jerusalem: The Louis Guttman Israel Institute of Applied Social Research, 1993).

9. Meir Azari, "Let's Broaden the Margins," *CCAR Journal* 43, 1 (1996): 17–21.

10. Art Vernon, "Why is Teaching Israel so Difficult Today?" *Jewish Education News* (Summer 1995): 12–14.

11. William Cutter, above.

12. Thomas Moore, *Care of the Soul: A Guide for Cultivating Depth and Sacredness in Everyday Life* (New York: Harper Perennial, 1994), p. 5.

13. Op.cit., pp. 26–27.

14. David Ellenson, Hebrew Union College Colloquium, March 3, 1998: *Zionism and (My) Reform Judaism*.

15. See, e.g., Arnold Eisen, *New Role for Israel in American Jewish Identity* (New York: The American Jewish Committee, 1992), p. 3.

16. Harvey Shapiro, above.

17. *The Union Prayerbook for Jewish Worship* (Cincinnati: CCAR), p.34.

Gidon Elad

Response
The Multi-Rootedness of the Israeli Jew

In responding to the very constructive comments of Dr. Harvey Shapiro, I would like to add a Jewish-Israeli perspective that is not usually discussed among us, and when it is, is presented, without justification, as a part of the post-Zionist outlook.

The Haskalah and historical research brought to light the fact that religion is no longer the only national entity that represents the Jewish people. It seems that this was actually Dubnow's contribution when he said that "as a result of the secularization of the national idea among Jews, our historiography was also released from its subordination to theology, excessive spiritualism and scholastics—the object of scientific historiography must be the nation itself, the national personality, its coming into being, its growth and its struggle for existence."

There is a need for a return to a renewed creative confrontation with this thinking of Dubnow's; a historical thinking that is not Israel-centered, difficult to grasp by the average Jewish Israeli. Dubnow tied this view of his to an additional perspective: "A new perception of our contemporary history is emerging, more suited to its true content and extent. People of our generation are beginning to understand that for thousands of years our people not only 'created ideas and suffered adversities,' but also constructed the framework of its life under all sorts of strange circumstances as a unique community." This ideological-historical perspective was further developed by the historian Salo Baron, and this is not the place to elaborate on it. After the Holocaust, it is difficult for the Jewish person in general and for the Jewish-Israeli in particular to completely reject the nation's "history of tears." Even the political leadership uses it for its purposes.[1]

I believe that the "paradigm of tension" that Dr. Harvey Shapiro presented to us does not exhaust the optimal network of relations between the Jews of Israel and those of the Diaspora. There is a need for a two-fold comprehensive "paradigmatic leap": first, a creative revival

180

of the Dubnowian concept of *am-olam*, a "world-wide people" as a reality based on Jewish political sovereignty, which guides its agenda; and second, a conscious rejection of the "lachrymose theory" as the dominant characteristic of the time axis narrative of the Jewish people.

This "paradigmatic leap" must first and foremost be carried out by the Israeli. The "Zionist Condition" is the continuation of his responsibility for the creative and viable future of the Jewish people. True, some Israelis have been caught up in post-modern deconstructionist tendencies, but I cannot discuss them here. We live in an era when Diasporism, i.e. life as a Diaspora facing a cultural or a political center, is not exclusive to the Jewish people. More than two hundred and fifty million men and women share this "style of being," and both the center and the Diaspora relate to it as a challenge. The Diaspora that most resembles ours is the Armenian one. For example, the leader of its church said in 1987:

> The permanence of the Armenian Diaspora is now an irrefutable reality. In the future, the framework for return to the Homeland may be established. And in fact, it is likely that such programs for repatriation will be organized. As the catholicos of all Armenians, we will be the first to offer prayers and rejoice on the occasion.
>
> However, we do not think it would be possible to resettle the entire Armenian Diaspora, numbering two million people located in the Middle East, Europe, and the Americas, to our Homeland. Therefore, the existence of the Diaspora should not be a source of fear and despair. On the contrary, destiny has thrust upon us the Diaspora—a challenge which we must confront with courage and honor, structuring our life on a firm and enduring foundation for today, tomorrow and far off decades.[2]

Harvey Shapiro says: "I suggest an invitational paradigm that seeks to engage the student with a struggle with tensions that have been embedded in the Jewish relationship to Israel for millennia."

It is the Israeli's paradigmatic leap that will create the change of heart that will allow for the paradigm proposed by Harvey Shapiro and for the necessary internalization of the "constructive tensions" system that exists in the network of relationships between Jews of Israel and the Jews of the Diaspora.

Allow me to present two poetic quotes and one prose statement by two unique educators:

In the 1920s, Uri Zvi Greenberg, the great detester of treacherous Europe, wrote:

We loved the forest, stream, the well and the mill;
We loved the fall of leaves, the fish, the bucket and the *Challah,*
and in deepest secrecy we loved also the ringing of their bells ---
And even the little Gentile urchins with their blonde hair.
We loved the harmonica, flute and Ukrainian melody;
Village maidens in their dances and colored ribbons;
We loved the white cotes with roofs of straw and with roofs of red tiles,
We loved the winter's end that dripped from these ...[3]

"And even that which we loved," he said, "we were forced to hate." Is this the bi-focal emotional structure of an emigrant–oleh or might there be more lurking behind this confession?

At the end of the 1970s, the poet Erez Biton, who immigrated from Morocco, asks/tells us:

What does it mean to be authentic?
To run in the middle of Dizengoff shrieking in Judeo-Moroccan
"Ana Min Elmagrab, Ana Min Elmagrab" (I'm from the Atlas Mountains, I'm from the Atlas Mountains).
What does it mean to be authentic
To sit in Cafe Royal in gaudy clothes (*agal* and *Zarbiya*),
or to announce loudly: My name is not Zohar, I'm Zaish, I'm Zaish (a Moroccan name).
And not this, and not that,
and in any case another tongue swells in your mouth until the gums explode,
And in any case, beloved discontinued odors are condemned
and I fall between the lingos
at a loss in the babble of voices.[4]

Is this also a bi-focal emotional structure of an emigrant–oleh?

And what of the following joint statement by Dr. Michael Rosenak, an Israeli immigrant from the United states, and of Dr. Arnie Eisen, who lives in the "land of limitless possibilities."

The heart of the matter, we suggest, is that this nation, living in Israel, will never be as normal as others. It will always have a people beyond its borders. It will be a national homeland for

Jews, but even Israeli Jews will never be defined only by territory, while those who live elsewhere will hopefully be well aquainted with the land which is, in some undefinable sense, also theirs.[5]

There must be a transformation in the fundamental experience of the Jewish Israeli in order for the conversation to take place as a true dialogue. I am referring to the dual- or multi-rootedness presented above not as an anomalous situation that must be overcome, as it is presented in the poems of U.Z. Greenberg and Erez Biton, but rather as a normal form of being, as expressed—in what seems a radical statement—in the words of Michael Rosenak and Arnie Eisen. There exists a national Jewish form of thought that political Zionism ignored, and today, in the era of de-facto rapprochement between political sovereignty and Diasporism, we have the right, and indeed the obligation to reopen the creative dialogue with that mode of thinking.

It is a case of the Israelis changing skin and spots. They are certainly capable of it. Do they want to?

Notes

1. See Simon Dubnow, *Divrei yemei am olam* (Tel Aviv, 1958), vol. 1, pp. 2–3; Mark Cohen, "Neo-Lachrymose Conception of Jewish-Arab History," *Tikkun* (May–June, 1991): 55–60; Robert Liberles, *Salo Wittmayer Baron: Architect of Jewish History* (New York and London, 1995), 338–57.

2. His Holiness Vasken the First Diocese of Armenian Church of America, Presentation (New York, 1987), typescript in author's archive, p. 36.

3."Compulsion," by Charles A. Cowen, in *Yerushalayim shel mata*, trans. from the Hebrew (New York, 1939), pp. 33–34.

4. "*Taktzir sihah*," in *Tzippor bein yabashot* (Tel Aviv, 1990), p. 61.

5. Arnold Eisen and Michael Rosenak, *Teaching Israel: Basic Issues and Philosophical Guidelines* (Tel Aviv, 1997), p. 38.

AMERICAN JEWISH INSTITUTIONS AND THE JEWISH STATE

Samuel Norich

Can the Center Hold?

For the past two years, the top echelon of United Jewish Appeal (UJA) and community federation leadership have been developing a plan for the reorganization of their institutional complex that, in its latest formulation, called for the merger of UJA and the Council of Jewish Federations (CJF). That plan has now stalled. There has been much speculation as to why it stalled, ranging from unkind references to overweening individual ambition to criticisms of the failure of the federation and UJA leadership to prepare their constituencies to support the measures being proposed. Such ad hominem references and observations about faulty "process" may carry some truth, but they can only hinder adequate understanding of the far more significant truths about the structure and functioning of this sector of American Jewish communal life, which would have to account for the considerable impetus toward a merger, on the one hand, and for its derailment, perhaps even its eventual failure, on the other. The institutional patterns to which I refer have, after all, the weight of several decades of experience behind them. Americans used to reinventing or re-engineering their corporations every fifteen minutes may think they can ignore such ingrained patterns of behavior, but the patterns are woven from habits and cultural constructs that change much more slowly. It may even be helpful to think of these institutional patterns as a kind of unwritten constitution of our communal life. Only by reminding ourselves of this unwritten constitution can the institutional complex that has dominated American Jewish communal life for the last three or four decades devise a strategy that can keep its role central, that can free it from the impasse it has now boxed itself into, and that can point the direction of the changes that must be made if this institutional complex is to evolve in harmony with its constitutional patterns.

The proposed merger of UJA and CJF has been promoted as an efficiency measure. Two large bureaucracies were to be combined, a few executive positions and their six-figure salaries would be eliminated, and at the end of the day, American Jewry would at last have one central organization whose name would emphasize the UJA, although its internal political structure would resemble that of CJF. By imposing the governance structures of CJF, with their vaunted accountability to the hundreds of federated communities, on the cowboy culture of UJA, the federations would at last gain "ownership" of UJA, which they had come to regard during recent years as a loose cannon. With federation annual campaigns failing, during the early 1990s, to keep up with the rate of inflation, the imposition of CJF's political structures and fiscal controls on the $30 million annual budget of UJA would bring a measure of accountability and perhaps even some parsimony to UJA operations.

In point of fact, the compelling rationale for this merger had much to do with control and little to do with efficiency or cost-savings. UJA and CJF perform different tasks for American Jewry, and the merged entity would have to carry those tasks on whether under one hierarchy or two. The saved expense of several executive positions would be largely offset by the administrative cost of a merged entity whose top echelon would have to have a larger span of control. Any real saving that could have been hoped for would have come from relocating the two organizations, as well as the United Israel Appeal (UIA) and American Jewish Joint Distribution Committee (JDC) headquarters, into one building, where administrative support functions could be combined. Such relocation was urged by at least one of the four organizations from the outset. It could have been accomplished without a merger, and it may now become the "consolation prize," for which the national system will settle if it fails to combine UJA and CJF into a single organization.

The Jewish Telegraphic Agency's report, when it first analyzed the prospects of the joint committee established by UJA and CJF two years ago to study the national structure, spoke of a "pac-man" situation, as if CJF were seeking to swallow everything in sight.[1] But a combination of CJF and UJA cannot be understood as a power grab, neither on the part of the individuals who stood the best chance of acceding to the senior lay and professional positions in the joint entity, nor by the larger group of leaders of the large metropolitan federations who were its prime advocates. A merger would certainly have increased the power of these same individuals, but the logic of their advocacy had more to do with the rationalization of the federation system, with its continuation on the trajectory on which the federation system had already embarked one or two decades earlier. What they sought was not loftier titles and larger spans of control. They sought to vest control over the federations' income stream in the federations themselves, rather than leaving it largely in the hands of what they had come to regard, during the past decade and more, as a not very well-managed ancillary organization, an organization whose first obligation was to its overseas beneficiaries rather than to the federations and their local member agencies. In the eyes of the federations, that arrangement immobilized their strategic options. Only by wresting control over the nation-wide fundraising operations from the UJA and from the overseas agencies that are its present "owners" could the federation system introduce the kinds of flexibility into both its fundraising and its allocating mechanisms that would enable it to respond to the challenges and the opportunities that changes in the Israeli political economy and the American social welfare system are sure to pitch their way.

Federation leaders may have been slow to acknowledge the good news, and whether it was Yossi Beilin or Yitzhak Rabin or Beige Shochat who finally hammered the point home,[2] they have understood for at least two years that Israel is now a wealthy country, with a per capita income just behind that of Great Britain (and gaining fast), with a higher rate of scientific innovation (i.e., the number of scientific articles published per capita) than any other country, with a burgeoning export market in the Far East and in Eastern Europe, with a new-found appeal for Western capital investment that is drawn by Israel's human capital and by the prospects for peace and stability in the region. Just the increment in Israel's government budget from 1990 to 1995—the budget grew by 80 percent—is 20 times larger than the entire budget of the Jewish Agency.[3] They have seen these recent developments with their own eyes, and, much as they resent being told that Israel no longer needs their charity, they and their major donors have come to the conclusion that if they were to judge on purely economic grounds, the costs of immigrant absorption that their donations to the Jewish Agency have helped to cover could now be covered entirely, and no longer just largely, from Israel's own tax revenues.

Having had their contributions to Israel's immigrant absorption relegated to secondary importance by the country's meteoric economic growth, the federation leadership see far more urgent fires burning closer to home. American Jewry's generations-long struggle to overcome Christian and nativist barriers to full acceptance seems to have been victorious during recent decades, and the notorious intermarriage rates demonstrate this victory as vividly as any statistics can. To counteract the now regretted by-products of that acceptance, the federation system has issued a clarion call to "continuity" (a call to learning or prayer or acts of loving-kindness would probably have been too divisive) which is beginning to mobilize energy and to draw funds to Jewish educational programs, mostly to informal Jewish educational programs, that had previously been the almost exclusive preserve of the synagogues and, less so, the community centers.

The continuity agenda is beginning to take shape, at an uneven pace and with uncertain impact. Meanwhile, all federations are feeling the devastating effects of the sharp cut in social welfare expenditures by all levels of American government. Whether the Contract with America is ever enacted or not, the federations already see parts of the billion dollars they receive annually from government agencies for their affiliated agencies' social welfare programs disappearing, and they fear that unless they can find new donors or shift more of the contributions of present donors to those urgent domestic needs, there may well be a free-for-all as every agency goes after new sources of income. The centrifugal pull of desperate local agencies, each deciding it has to fend for itself, could well tear the entire federation system to shreds.

Faced with a set of pressures that raise the marginal utility of federation allocations to local and domestic programs and lower their utility to overseas programs, the expected tendency would be that federations, on average, would shift funds from the latter to the former. That is in fact what they have done historically, and it is what they have continued to do during the last ten years. The so-called "partnership share," the proportion of their annual campaign totals allocated by federations to UJA and its overseas beneficiaries (mainly the Jewish Agency and JDC), has declined from 52.3% in 1985 to 41.8% in 1994.[4]

Such a slide could have remained no more than a worrisome statistical detail were it not for the concomitant leveling off of the annual campaign totals. Particularly after the special supplementary campaign for Operation Exodus crested in 1992, and the UJA's overseas beneficiaries had to absorb very real dollar cuts, not just drops in their percentages, the federations' failure to "convert" the additional donations they were able to raise during the emergency of the early 1990s into higher regular contributions to their annual funds during the following years created a fiscal crisis for the federations' main overseas beneficiary, the Jewish Agency. By last November, the crisis had loomed to such proportions (the Agency's leaders were projecting an accumulated deficit of a half billion dollars within a few years) that the Agency was forced to cut $120 million, one-fifth of its total expenditures, from its 1996 budget, by turning the affected programs over to the future exclusive responsibility of the Israeli government.[5]

This fiscal crisis of the federations during recent years was only the most obvious manifestation of a profound transformation in their internal political structure, a transformation that had been proceeding slowly for some time and had accelerated with a generational succession during the last ten years. The federation system's historic success during the post-war period had been built on a partnership between two very different and often contentious constituencies, distinguished from one another in their organizational cultures, their federation roles, and often in their social origins. A small group of wealthy and generous donors, many of them self-made entrepreneurs, often the children of immigrants or men who had immigrated during their own childhood, whose principal commitment was to the rescue of endangered Jewish communities or to the upbuilding of the fledgling Jewish state, a group with strong *espirit de corps*, was given the leadership of the local fundraising campaign organizations and of their national coordinating structure, the UJA. A much larger group of people of more modest means, often lawyers and other professionals, men and women devoted to the various agencies of the local community and practiced in the articulation and negotiation of competing agendas, generally considered more cerebral and less muscular types than the first group, were expected to volunteer for one of the committees charged with oversight of the federations' allocation and communal planning activities. The fact that the overseas causes to whom UJA was committed were linked in a single, unified campaign in most communities (in 1973 New York became the last to conform to the otherwise universal pattern) with the domestic and local needs coordinated by the federation, gave the system an overarching unity of purpose. Whatever differences of style and priority divided the two constituencies, the federation system regarded the tensions between them as productive for the needs of both American and Israeli Jewry. UJA leaders, who took it upon themselves to donate and to solicit the ever larger sums that Israelis at the helm of the Jewish Agency asked of them, particularly during times of war or other emergency, were able to provide a rising tide to raise all ships. As large segments of American Jewry were opening their checkbooks out of concern for Israel's or other Jewish communities' needs, they were providing the funds that would also build an increasingly elaborate and professional organizational infrastructure in their local communities, as well as on the country-wide level.

Two changes transformed this internal structure of federation leadership. First and most important was UJA's inability to attract the energy and time of members of the wealthiest Jewish families, or to hold on to the energy and time of those it had managed to attract. Though they continued to donate their six or seven figure annual gifts to their federations, these leaders were lost to the top positions of the national and Jewish Agency structures, preferring instead to devote their time to their private foundations. This had much to do with the excruciatingly slow and hard-fought struggle that leaders of the federation system were waging at the time to wrest the parity with Israelis in governing the Jewish Agency that the Agency's reconstitution had promised them over a decade earlier. The glacial progress made in this struggle by the federation leaders "cooled out" some of their most powerful and dynamic champions. It was not until Brian Lurie formed them and others like them into the "mega-givers group" when he took the helm of UJA in 1992 that the system found a place—albeit a tenuous one—for that echelon of leaders.

The other change was that the erstwhile differences between UJA people and federation people had by and large disappeared by the 1980s. As the founding generation of UJA leaders retired or passed from the scene, the lay leaders who took their places were increasingly people who had held leadership positions in the campaign as well as in the federations' planning and allocations activities. Many of the larger federations set up their own campaign operations, even their own Israeli missions, organized by their appointed staff representatives in Jerusalem, and largely dispensed with the services of the National UJA staff and lay leadership. What UJA leaders now lacked in elan they gained in the breadth of their experience. The two hierarchies increasingly shared common social and professional backgrounds. They both acknowledged their responsibilities to the local community as well as to the larger agenda of the Jewish people. While a few UJA leaders, both veterans and "young leadership" types, could still give impassioned appeals on behalf of our obligations to the Jews of Israel and other lands, most had ceased to be distinguishable from the ranks of federation and CJF leadership, of whom some were personally just as identified with Israel.

UJA leaders still pushed the priorities of their overseas beneficiaries, but often their energies were noted more in the pressure they applied to the federation board or allocations committee to avoid another cut in their "partnership share," than in their efforts to solicit larger gifts from their largest donors. They ceased to be the undisputed leaders of the federation system and were increasingly regarded as the same as everyone else—another pressure group in the federation constituency. And the fact that their pressure was being exerted on behalf of the Jewish Agency, a distant and increasingly disrespected beneficiary, may help to account for the consistent drop in the partnership share during recent years.

The federation and CJF leaders, for their part, recognized the emotional saliency that the rescue of endangered communities and their absorption in Israel continued to hold for the majority of their donors. If they wished their institutions to maintain the centrality, both symbolic and political, that they had acquired in the communal life of American Jewry, they—certainly the wisest of them—knew that federations would have to remain actively engaged with Israeli Jewry and indeed with the Israeli political elite. They knew they could not afford to shift their focus entirely to domestic or local agendas, whether the new agendas of culture and education or the old agendas of social welfare. But they could no longer accept what must have appeared to them as an increasingly obsolete, anachronistic and indeed anomalous structure, in which the institution that ran their fundraising campaigns and mediated their relationship with Israel was the UJA, an organization of American Jews just like them, but an organization putatively owned by its primary beneficiary, the allegedly inefficient, immobile, politically compromised, and even embarrassing Jewish Agency. If American Jewry were to devise a new relationship with Israel, that structure would have to change, and it would have to begin with the UJA.

Such were the constraints and the divergent strategic vectors pulling on the federation and UJA leadership when they convened their joint "study of the national structure" in the spring of 1994. Almost from the start, the effort was hampered both in its conception and composition. Rather than treat American Jewry's ties to Israel as the flame at the heart of the communal governance structure, they sought to treat it conceptually as a matter, as it were, external to the system, as if it could be considered, even theoretically, as epiphenomenal. Their concern was with the relationships among the four "national agencies": CJF, UJA, the United Israel Appeal (UIA), and the Joint Distribution Committee (JDC). These relationships were to receive the closest and most intense scrutiny of a committee of 26 people over two years, and while "the public" would be encouraged to air their views, whatever debates and disagreements arose among committee members would be kept behind closed doors.

Inexplicably, representatives of UIA and JDC were not included in the committee's original ranks, only to be added a year into the process. The consultant appointed to staff the committee had had only limited experience with the relevant institutions, having produced major strategic planning studies for several large federations during the prior few years. Only a year into its deliberations did they add to the committee's consultants a scholar with a profound understanding of and vast experience with the institutions involved, including the Israel-based institutions. But having defined the problem as a matter of reconfiguring the relations among a group of American Jewish organizations, the results were broadly predictable from the outset. At least, the committee's recommendations were broadly predictable. What was surprising was that its first set of recommendations would be rejected, and that the second, more transparent and more blatant set would be roundly criticized and effectively tabled when they came up for discussion at the quarterly meeting of federation and UJA leadership five weeks ago.

The two sets of proposals were variations on a theme. The first set, floated for leaders' comments in May 1995, would have given the federations and CJF the prerogative of naming half the members of the board and the executive committee of UJA, and it would have eliminated UIA from the scene, dividing its functions between UJA and CJF. Even if UIA's functions consisted of nothing more than that of conduit for funds allocated by federations to UJA for the Jewish Agency and recipient for refugee resettlement grants for Israel made by the U. S. Congress, it could not have been dispensed with so easily. In fact, UIA's most sensitive function is to assure American tax authorities that tax-deductible contributions by U. S. donors are in fact being administered abroad in accordance with our laws. Another function presumes well-established relations with a list of American banks that regularly extend large amounts of credit to UIA on behalf of the Jewish Agency. When UIA leaders flatly refused to accept the proposals calling for the organization's demise without adequate prior consultation, without adequate assurance that all its roles could be smoothly transferred to other players, the committee studying the national structure withdrew its proposals.

Within two months they had come up with a new set of proposals.

A new national organization would be created to replace UJA, CJF and UIA. According to a confidential memo dated December 6, 1995 and circulated to the communal leadership, JDC would "continue as an independent organization with a number of prescribed relationships and mutual obligations to the new entity."[6] "This new entity will probably have the initials UJA somewhere in its name," according to the memo, but its governance would resemble the elaborate representative structure of CJF. The linchpin of this arrangement was a proposal that during a three-to-five-year transitional period, the federations would guarantee allocations to UJA and its overseas beneficiaries of no less than the 1994 amount, $310 million.

It has now been clear for several months that the federations were reluctant, indeed, unwilling, to provide such a guarantee. One of the reasons for the merger was to increase their flexibility, not to tie them to a guaranteed floor. "Guarantee" was softened to "assurance," but everyone was left to guess what that meant. UIA let it be known that it would refrain from taking part in the proposed merger for the first few years, so as to see whether it was otherwise in fact proceeding in accordance with the plan. How the leaders of UJA and CJF could let their now tattered proposal come before their May 1996 meeting, without adequate preparation, without even a written draft with commentary having been circulated, is therefore virtually incomprehensible. But they did. And as soon as they did, the criticisms began to fly, the issue spun out of control, and the chair of the Committee on the National Structure suggested that the proposal be withdrawn for further study.

That of course happened an age ago, before the Israeli elections, before the meeting of the General Council of the World Zionist Organization, before the Jewish Agency Assembly. It is too early to say what lessons the leaders of the federation system will draw from these events, or what direction they will now chart for their institutions. Let me therefore conclude by recalling suggestions that have been put before them earlier.

In March 1995, Herbert Freedman, the long-time professional head of UJA, met with the UJA executive committee and urged them to declare a national emergency over the state of Jewish identification and learning.[7] He asked them to establish an emergency fund of $500 million over the next several years to endow ongoing grants for a majority of American Jewish young people to spend a semester or a year of study in Israel. Almost a year earlier, in June, 1994, the new leader of the Likud opposition, Binyamin Netanyahu, addressed the Jewish

Agency Assembly and asked them, in terms eerily reminiscent of the call—and the reasoning—of Yossi Beilin, with whom he shares not only the same approximate age, that they make a massive shift in priorities towards Jewish education, particularly Jewish education for Diaspora youth in the colleges, seminaries, yeshivot, universities, and ulpanim of Israel.

The federation leaders know that they will have to turn their big ships in mid-stream, that they will have to put the spiritual and intellectual concerns of a younger generation of donors and their children at the center of their new mission. They also know that if their institutions are to reclaim their historic vitality, they will have to find a new agenda to tie them to Israel. Hopefully, a new generation of Israeli leaders will show them the way.

Notes

1. Jewish Telegraphic Agency *Daily News Bulletin,* April 19, 1994.

2. Steven M. Cohen and Charles Liebman, "Rethinking Israel/Diaspora Relations: A Search for New Relationships," *Journal of Jewish Communal Service* 74 No. 2/3 (Winter/Spring 1997/98): 94–95.

3. Personal communication, Haim Ben-Shahar, January 26, 1996.

4. Data provided by UJA National Office, August 25, 1995.

5. UJA National Office, *Leadership Briefing Number 1,* November 1995.

6. Memorandum from Council of Jewish Federations and United Jewish Appeal, Study of the National Structure, "Status Update," December 6, 1995.

7. Personal communication, June 15, 1995.

Shoshana S. Cardin

American Jewish Institutions and Israel

I feel privileged in that I am the only one on this distinguished panel who sits on the board of any, let alone all four, organizations engaged in this re-engineering or restructuring. The four are: CJF–Council of Federations, UJA–United Jewish Appeal, JDC–American Jewish Joint Distribution Committee, and UIA–United Israel Appeal. As chair of the latter, the one slated for oblivion two and a half years ago, I recognized that other leaders were not fully aware that the United Israel Appeal had major responsibilities to the United States Department of State, to the IRS, and to the United States Congress, as well as to individual donors. Therefore, I shall try to be as unbiased as I can in presenting my case in response to Sam Norich's provocative paper.

I would venture to say that the average participant at this conference is about as knowledgeable about the alphabet soup of the federation system as the average donor in the United States.

As a rule, donors to the UJA/Federation campaigns do not seek detailed information as to how their contributions are allocated or specifically to whom. They rely on federation leaders and national leaders to distribute the necessary resources to the appropriate agencies, local or overseas. Perhaps I should explain the genesis of the federation system. It was created in 1895 in Boston to take care of the local Jewish community and its domestic needs. Large numbers of immigrants from Eastern Europe and Russia were coming to United States cities: they needed language and job skills; their children needed Jewish education; their elderly needed assistance and the entire gamut of social services, of which you are aware. Previously, independent agencies competed for funding within their own communities. It was deemed necessary to develop an organized approach to meeting these competing yet vital and diverse local, domestic needs, and this gave rise to an annual campaign whose goal was to raise one set of monies for domestic social service needs through one central entity—the local federation.

During this same period, while these federations functioned independently, some supported separate campaigns for overseas needs—again competing with other agencies concerned with the Yishuv and Jews in distress in Europe and the USSR. The Zionist movements had their campaigns, the JDC had its campaign, and the United Palestine Appeal (which is now the United Israel Appeal) had its campaign. We had the *"berakhah"* of having multiple campaigns for overseas needs.

In the late 1930s, as the situation in Europe deteriorated and Jews needed to be assisted in numbers greater than before, the leadership of the United Israel Appeal and the Joint Distribution Committee met and decided to combine their fund-raising efforts. They created the United Jewish Appeal to raise monies for all of our overseas needs, for Jews in need anywhere in the world, including the Yishuv. The UJA campaign became the coordinated response of the American Jewish community.

In fact, the United Jewish Appeal became a very effective instrument, partly because of the terrible, terrible trauma, the Shoah, and the extreme difficulties encountered by the Yishuv. Monies were raised and sent concurrently to both the Yishuv and Jews in distress in Europe from this newly organized American Jewish communal response mechanism.

The success of these amalgamations was such that from the period of 1950 to 1973, federations questioned the need for two individual campaigns. Could they not combine the local and overseas campaigns into one integrated campaign and create one annual central campaign for all Jewish needs? By 1973, New York City being the last of the major federations to combine its two separate campaigns, every federation had one campaign, one line, and each federation determined how much of that campaign stayed locally and how much went for overseas needs. Overseas needs were dominated by the programs of the American Jewish Joint Distribution Committee and the Jewish Agency of Israel.

This move by federations created a very effective *klal yisrael* campaign because, until that time, those who were interested only in domestic needs did not necessarily give for *medinat yisrael*, and those who were interested in Israel did not necessarily give for local needs. So here was a creative approach to community building, to developing the *am eḥad* concept. Federations were bringing together concerned

Jews who had different interests and different agendas. Moreover, this integrated campaign put Israel at the center of our campaign for everybody, Zionist, non-Zionist, local or domestically oriented. Everybody was contributing to Israel, whether they specifically wanted to or not. There was a central campaign, and few, if any, donors in the country designated their gifts to only domestic or overseas programs.

But this mechanism, so effective in addressing the issues of the 50s, 60s, and 70s did not satisfy the needs of the 80s and 90s. As Israel became a dynamic, viable entity—economically more independent, accepted diplomatically in the international world, recognized as not only a haven for refuge, but an exciting and vibrant country for those who were choosing to make their lives there, there was a realization that the ground had shifted. The coming of age of our North American Jewish community added a new set of responsibilities that demanded collective federation action. Federations became increasingly aware that their raison d'être was not only philanthropy, not only rescue and service. Individual constituents and communities began demanding that they assume ever greater responsibility for ensuring their Jewish futures—our Jewish continuity.

The federation movement had, by its character and nature, already made an enormous contribution to American Jewish life. Federations helped design a way of being Jewish in a manner that was consonant with the best of American values and proffered the best of Jewish values. Federations encouraged American Jews to be full participants in American life, embracing the universality that is embodied in that participation, while simultaneously being committed to an affirmation of the particularity of Jewish interests as expressed through our Jewish communal process. It was this approach that had made it possible for us to withstand the forces of an open society which, by their very nature, tend to contribute to the disintegration of our particularity—our Jewishness.

It was no accident, therefore, that the federation movement consciously adopted a commitment to Jewish creative continuity as the core—the very essence–and central theme of our movement during the past five years.

In addition to the ability to mobilize quickly and to serve in a manner that ensures the here and now, the immediate and the obvious, federations must also have the ability to look ahead—to ensure our continuity—our tomorrow. The question is how to address the new challenges, how to address these shifts. To move this huge, huge enterprise to a different course is a very difficult issue, despite the fact that the concept of merger of the UJA and the Council of Jewish Federations began about twenty years ago.

What we are seeing today is the devolution of a paradigm that was extremely effective. It raised almost a billion dollars for Exodus, a billion dollars in three years for the greatest miracle we have witnessed in this century, and fortuitously the Exodus continues.

What happened was that after that billion dollars, raised *in addition* to the annual campaign, the additional monies that had gone into the Exodus campaign did not translate into the annual campaign. Let us understand that the sum of a billion dollars was *in addition* to the annual campaign. We have had previous experiences where we built up to a peak, for a special campaign, and then funds dropped down or remained flat for the next few years, because there had been a major effort for people to give specific maximum sums, which they did, after which campaigns declined.

Unfortunately, UJA and the federations decided that if the number of *olim hadashim* dropped from 190,000 to 65,000, no special attention was warranted. The leadership thus changed the focus of what had been the main goal of world Jewry, to bring in as many *olim* as possible, and certainly from countries of distress, through the Jewish Agency. At the same time, in the last three years, the absence of a special focus was accompanied by Messrs. Beilin, Yehoshua, President Weizman, and others not of such stature, saying, "Thank you very much, American Jews. This is a new era. Your money is not making a major difference in our economy, so keep it at home. Take care of your own problems, because either you are going to disappear because your Judaism is disappearing, or you are irrelevant to the future of the State of Israel. We don't really need your assistance and interference."

Donors heard this message not once or twice but four, five, and six times, after which those who had struggled to make a maximum gift just two years before, responded, "Wait a minute! If they don't need us, our money, why should we bother to send it to them?"

So it was not that the campaigns dipped precipitously. It was that the allocations from the campaigns—which were flat, and were anticipated to be flat—to the Israeli component went down. American Jewry felt that they were not appreciated and since Israel (via the Jewish Agency) did not need the money, they would look at other foci, other ways to do *tikun olam* for Israelis and for Soviet Jewry. So instead of giving to UJA and subsequently to JAFI (the Jewish Agency for Israel), individuals

and foundations began to give what is called designated, targeted giving. In fact, there probably is a larger aggregate sum being given annually to Israeli institutions from American Jewry than that which is
allocated by the federation system. This threatened the federation system.

We, American Jews and Israelis alike, have to understand and acknowledge that the federation system is central to the vitality of our
organized American Jewish community. The federation system created a cohesive Jewish communal response and community-building
mechanism. While the local federated community is not a *kehilah*,
there is a *klal yisrael* concept that the federations encourage and that
has kept the continental community together. And indeed, federations
continue to address the needs of the over five million Jews who live in
the United States. So to threaten the fabric of the federation system, I
think, would be a serious mistake.

The current federation system is not perfect. Its most serious flaw to
date has been that until very recently the relationship between the leadership of CJF and UJA and the synagogue movements was strained.
That must be corrected if continuity, the newly identified challenge, is
to be appropriately addressed.

Let me get to the basics of this merger, non merger. I don't think
there is going to be a merger in the near future. However, I do believe
that there will be greater coordination, and a greater working relationship between the entities involved. I believe there will be a major effort
to avoid the duplicative efforts that take place, even though, as Dr.
Norich said, there is a healthy tension between the UJA-niks, who are
"farbrente Zionists" in their own right, and the local federation people,
who are more interested either in their local day schools or the geriatric
center. It has been a helpful tension and while lately it has been removed, I hope it can be recreated.

What we will see is a re-engineering for the twenty-first century with
the federations at the center. The issue is more one of ownership than
of possible merger. Federations want more say, more control over the
decision-making process, even though the majority of decision makers
are and have been federation appointees. I recognize the validity of
that construct, although I remain concerned about inclusiveness in the
new entity. I personally believe that anyone who suggests that the centrality of the federation and the annual campaign is not sacred in the
sense that we all have to commit to work for it, is making a serious
mistake. The campaign is the enterprise, the glue that keeps all the

components of the community together. Diminution of the effectiveness of federations will bring about the unraveling of the continental American Jewish community. That, I think, would have a very serious negative impact on all of us.

What are my expectations? There is a recognition that Israel has changed. Israel is not needy. Israel is not helpless. That rhetoric has to change. UJA has changed its slogan in response to federation pressure. At this time, with all of these events occurring concurrently, UJA has changed its slogan from "We are one, from strength to strength, *am ehad*," to "For ourselves, for our children, for Israel, forever." That change was required by the federations, because now that Israel has matured to the level that it has, and is engaging in a peace process, the American Jewish community has to determine how it will interact, as a mature community, with a mature State of Israel and individual Israelis.

The federations and UJA recognize that the challenges of assimilation, alienation, and non-affiliation are serious enough to affect the totality of *klal yisrael* and, in fact, are now focusing on what can be done at home to strengthen the American Jewish community, not at a cost to Israel, but in recognition of the challenges in the United States. These challenges should be and will be addressed by the same people who addressed the challenges in Israel and other Jewish communities who have served as Israel's partners.

The day has long gone when Israel or Israelis were the beneficiaries and American Jews were the benefactors. Just as the focus or the motivation for caring was based on tradition and history, whether it was the Shoah or the birth of Israel, we now have to focus on partnership. Indeed, we are beginning to look for a real, pragmatic, and effective alliance, such as Partnership 2000, where Americans and Israelis come together to determine what is good for specific communities, kibbutzim, moshavim, or regions.

What we are trying to do, and what I hope we will do as we approach the twenty-first century, is recognize that we are still *am ehad,* a partnership with full diversity—diversity of those who want to live in Israel and will come there from the free world; diversity and recognition that we can be, and should be, partners and *mishpahah,* not necessarily living on the same continent, or in the same country, but partners and family nevertheless. We must publicly acknowledge a mutuality of respect and a sense of interdependence between American Jewry and Israelis, no longer *golah* and *galut.*

The world sees us as one people and it is time that we begin to recognize that that one people has a spectrum of colors and intensities. We in the United States must address our concerns and Israeli concerns as equally important: whichever one needing the most attention must be given that attention when it becomes the priority. Our vision and our goal should be to strengthen *klal yisrael*. May our endeavors be met with success.

Bibliography

Bernstein, Philip. *To Dwell in Unity*. Philadelphia: Jewish Publication Society, 1983.

Elazar, Daniel J. "The Federation Movement at 100," *Jewish Political Studies Review* 7, 3–4 (Fall 1995): 13–31.

Feldstein, Donald. "The Jewish Federations: The First Hundred Years," *Journal of Jewish Communal Service* 72, 1–2 (Fall/Winter 1995–96): 5–11.

Toward a New National Structure, a New Working Partnership Between the United Jewish Appeal and the Council of Jewish Federations. New York: Council of Jewish Federations, April, 1997.

United Jewish Appeal: Seventy Years of Partnership. Annual Report 1994–95. United Israel Appeal, New York, 1995.

Howard M. Weisband

Response

I would like to present a number of Israeli perceptions relating to the issues that Sam Norich has presented in his paper and the overview that Shoshana Cardin has provided. These perceptions reflect the perspective of many of the Israelis with whom I have had the opportunity to work and converse in the framework of the Jewish Agency. In addition, I will add a few of my own views of these issues and offer a conclusion.

Perception One: The Israeli addresses his Diaspora counterpart: "You think we are driven by politics, and you don't operate within a political system? UJA, CJF, UIA, JDC, HIAS, NYANA, Big 19, etc., etc. That is not politics?"

What we are dealing with is the difference between party politics in Israel and institutional politics in the Diaspora—politics of a different sort, but still politics. Together, they contribute to the creation of a unique Israel–Diaspora political system, which represents the framework within which we work.

Perception Two: "You are stealing our money. You fund-raise on the back of Israel but we get only 80 cents on the dollar at the Jewish Agency. Maybe we have to run our own campaign."

Perception Three: Shoshana Cardin pointed to the current slogan of UJA ("For Our Children. For Ourselves. For Israel. Forever"), already two years in use. The Israeli perception? "So you have a new slogan. But Israel is last. Israel is no longer first within the UJA, which carries the mandate and used to be the advocate for overseas and Israeli needs only. That is a serious problem." Again, Israeli perception.

Perception Four: "Your fundraising is down. Allocations have dropped off the table. Yet, philanthropic funds coming to Israel are way up. Learn something from that. Americans still respond to Israel."

The fact is, in aggregate, the American friends of all other Israeli institutions have surpassed significantly the amount coming to Israel from the UJA. In the past decade, according to the report of the Bank of Israel, the total figure sent annually to Israel philanthropically, apart from UJA and not including Israel Bonds, has increased from the range of $140 million to $650 million. During the same period, the UJA has maintained a level in its regular annual allocation of approximately $200 million, with Keren Hayesod income from countries outside the United States totaling some $100 million.

"Yes, there has been Operation Exodus," says the Israeli, "but that income has dropped drastically to $15 million or $20 million a year or less. Therefore, you have created a new baseline, which is much lower, given the drop in allocations alongside the decrease in special fundraising."

Perception Five: "You have $3 billion in assets in endowments and foundations. Israel overall receives only 10 percent of the allocated annual grants from these assets."

Never mind that Israelis do not understand restricted vs. unrestricted funds or bequests vs. philanthropic funds. A perception is a perception.

"Your executives are paid $200,000 and $300,000 a year. What are they producing? Campaigns are down. Moreover, you cannot seem to reorganize or restructure. So why do you expect us in Israel to restructure the Jewish Agency and the World Zionist Organization? Get your own house in order."

Finally, "Is this really partnership?" That question is also being asked.

At this point we could articulate the corollary American Diaspora perceptions toward Israel and the operations of the Jewish Agency and the WZO. The conclusion, however would be about the same, focusing on the last question, namely, "Is this really partnership?"

While these perceptions may not be grounded in fact, they represent real feelings and perspectives of key players on the field of Israel–Diaspora relations and unfortunately do not reflect an affirmation of trust and confidence in the relationship and partnership within the Jewish Agency.

Indeed, the major change in the conceptual underpinning of the institutional infrastructure of the Israel–Diaspora partnership is described by Norich. "Rather than treat American Jewry's ties to Israel as the flame at the heart of the American communal structure, they (the American leadership) sought to treat it conceptually as a matter, as it were, external to the system." Precisely the case I myself have observed on a number of occasions: unfortunately, generally speaking,

Israel has become no more than a theme in American Jewish life, competing with a multitude of others, on both the individual and the institutional level. In other words, Israel is no longer central to Jewish life nor the center itself in the Israel–Diaspora relationship.

In my opinion, this change represents more than a chance superficial shift in attitude. American Jewish leaders have moved Israel from the center of consciousness. In fact, this radical change in how Jewish leaders view Israel may already be the cause for what may be termed the distancing or decoupling that has occurred in the Israel–Diaspora relationship.

Norich is correct when he speaks of a common culture. Our efforts as a Jewish people must be redirected around the teachings of Ahad Ha-Am and Mordecai Kaplan, projecting and experiencing Israel as the spiritual and national center within Jewish peoplehood.

Four fundamental principles should be incorporated in redirecting the Israeli–Diaspora relationship. The first relates to the destiny of the polity. The polity of the Jewish people must be independent and not competitive with the government of Israel, the sovereignty of the Jewish State. The Jewish people should be able to make its own decisions as a polity where appropriate regarding issues of peoplehood as opposed to issues of the State, but always in coordination and cooperation with the sovereignty. Therefore, the Jewish Agency, for example, must have the ability to determine its own structure and take determined action, albeit in coordination with the government of Israel.

The reality is that as that government changes, so do its attitudes, priorities, and mechanisms relating to the Diaspora. Such a situation represents anything but consistency, which is an essential dimension within any systemic relationship. Jewish leadership worldwide must control the destiny of the polity of the Jewish people—in this case, of the Jewish Agency—in the face of fluctuating Prime Ministers' advisers, Ministerial committees, and Foreign Ministry desks.

Secondly, the Jewish Agency should formulate an Israel–Diaspora partnership and not an institutional one. The system to date is an institutional partnership—i.e., a UIA–Keren Hayesod–WZO partnership—not one of Israel and Diaspora. It is not a partnership of the Jewish people attempting to realize its best and broadest potential. In order to assure and maximize its own future, the Jewish Agency must broaden and increase the involvement of additional significant Jewish leaders and organizations, both in Israel and in the Diaspora. Some of our best brain power, our business leaders, our professionals, our rabbis, our academics, our literary figures, in Israel and abroad, are mostly excluded from the current structure. When they are included, they are inserted into the constrictions of the system as pseudo politicians or pseudo fund-raisers. A true Israel–Diaspora partnership would construct its governing bodies in a fashion that would capitalize upon the individual potential and contribution of each of its members, all the while seeking to regenerate new involvement and ideas. Israeli political parties must be represented, and similarly, the Diaspora fund-raising institutions must be a part of the basic structure. However, there must be a broadening of the system to include additional Jewish leaders talented in their own right. This should be done with one organizational framework uniting the Jewish Agency and WZO. Such a framework should be redrawn to reflect what is best for the Jewish people, not what is politically desired by officials either for themselves or for their parties or organizations.

The third principle concerns elections. In reality, each of the constituents, including the WZO (which sells itself as a democratic entity), has utilized selection rather than election as the chosen method for putting leadership into place. Representative polities in both western and eastern societies seek more and more to incorporate two key values, democracy and accountability, into their systems through the use of direct elections. It is time that the Jewish polity, the Jewish Agency, provide greater opportunity for its individual constituent members to choose its own leaders. Both interest and confidence in the system will increase, as will ultimately the ability of the organization to define its mission and carry out its responsibilities.

Soon the new technology will allow for an efficient method of international elections. The Jewish Agency Assembly, with 518 delegates, should be utilized to elect directly at least half of the 120 members of the Board of Governors as well as the Chairman of the Executive and the Chairman of the Board. In other words, all of the Assembly, Israel and Diaspora together, should elect both chairmen.

Lastly, philanthropy plays an important role in building a great society. It does what governments cannot or will not do, enhancing the humanitarian, educational, and cultural aspects of the society and its total environment.

In order to significantly increase philanthropic potential, donors must be drawn into the cause. They must be personally acquainted with the ultimate goals and objectives of the fund-raising effort. To succeed, all campaign personnel must be fully aware of how they are helping to build society. Too often the fund-raisers, lay or professional, are more concerned with forging ties between the donors and their institutions. For instance, in creating campaign literature or film, the primary consideration should be the impact of the story being presented rather than the number of times the institution itself is mentioned.

Israeli and Diaspora leaders, together, must put more creative energy into raising funds rather than fighting internecine battles over allocations. Once accomplished, more substantive monies will be forthcoming into the system as a whole, and discussions and debates over allocations percentages will take place in an atmosphere of success and accomplishment, not despair over depletion of resources.

Two additional fund-raising policies should be considered. First, I propose the establishment of a United Israel Campaign in which the United Jewish Appeal and the Keren Hayesod would be combined with the Jewish National Fund. The national agendas and political and governance structures of these organizations are presently so similar that a joint effort would result in a meaningful savings in administrative costs. For the time being, other political, cultural, and territorial factors would keep the various "Friends" organizations outside a United Israel Campaign framework, but the proposed unification would ultimately provide benefit to both the donors and the Jewish polity.

My second proposal will prove even more controversial, but it may be necessary for the integrity and well-being of the system. Ideally, as indicated above, more funds will be raised, allowing allocations to be split more harmoniously and fairly, based upon a mutual understanding of needs. If that does not happen, and if a federated campaign chooses to unilaterally and consistently underfund overseas interests at an unacceptable rate, then an independent Israeli overseas campaign should be considered within that community. The red line, or the unacceptable rate, must be determined thoughtfully, not arbitrarily, and it may be different for different communities. Every understanding and solution must be tried before such a radical practice is employed, but cases may exist where such an effort may in fact be necessary.

Norich utilizes a metaphor at the end of his paper, writing that federation leaders "must turn their big ships in mid-stream." I agree. However, I fear that current discussions in the Jewish Agency and WZO are not serving to turn a big ship around; they seem more possibly, proverbially, to be rearranging the deck chairs on the Titanic. As an eternal optimist, I believe that radical change is both possible and essential in order to put the big ship back on course before waiting so long that the Jewish world has to send down submarines and cameras to observe the wreckage of the glorious institution that is no more. We must not reach that point. The power is in our hands if we are truly ready to work on behalf of the Jewish people.

Eric H. Yoffie

Response

I would like to thank Sam Norich for his paper. I found it to be insightful and essentially accurate, to the extent that I would profess to understand such things. But the real questions are: What difference does it make? Who really cares? How does all this relate to the real problems of world Jewry? I would give this discussion a somewhat different focus, and ask: What are the real problems that we face today? The real problems are: How do we create serious Jews? How do we connect them to Torah and direct them to Sinai? How do we involve them in the drama of Jewish living? *These* are the real problems.

I would agree that part of the answer involves giving Jews a sense of peoplehood and making them understand the centrality of Israel. But I would want to stress very clearly that these feelings flow from a commitment to the religious destiny of the Jewish people. If these feelings are rooted in history or culture, they will fade, as they have already begun to fade. *Jewish peoplehood and the centrality of Israel are primarily religious values.* Therefore, if we wish to revive Jewish peoplehood and the centrality of Israel, we need to revive Jewish religious tradition.

Is reviving religious tradition a problem for Israel or America? I would suggest that the problem is exactly and precisely the same in both places, and throughout the Diaspora, for that matter. Obviously, how we approach these matters in Israel will be different from how we approach them in America. But the problem is still the same.

I would also suggest that resolving this problem is primarily the task of synagogues and religious movements. Having said that, how do federations and CJF and UJA and the Jewish Agency relate to this problem that I have defined? It is not clear. Shoshana Cardin has said, and I agree, that these organizations do very important things for us: they give us a central communal address; they create a measure of communal unity; they provide social services to Jews in need; they fight antisemitism; they work to assure Israel's survival and economic well-being. All of these matters are important and remain on our agenda. But I suggest that they are not the most important problems that we face at this moment in the Jewish world.

Can these agencies direct some of their energy and talents to the new tasks, the Jewish tasks, the religious tasks that I have defined? I do not know. Generally speaking, referring in particular to the American situation, they have chosen to maintain community unity by avoiding entanglement with religious issues and religious institutions. But I would argue that it is precisely the passionate particularism of religious institutions and religious traditions that is needed now to assure the future and survival of the Jewish people.

At the same time, there has been some progress. While national federation and UJA structures have defined the religious area as outside of their realm of concern, some local federations have tried to grapple with religious questions and work with religious institutions in order to promote Jewish life. Boston provides some encouraging examples, as does New York.

Of course, in many cases what we hear is that communal institutions do not work with synagogues because they are difficult and contentious. They have a point of view, we are told; they are stubborn, they advocate their own particular religious ideologies. As a result, communal institutions often try to work around the synagogue, preferring a partnership instead with their own agencies, even if these agencies are not qualified to provide religious programming and direction. Still, I would emphasize again that local federations can point to some significant accomplishments, and to some groundbreaking initiatives. If I were to generalize, therefore, I would say that what we have seen up to now is very modest success. The amount of resources allocated by communal institutions to religious institutions constitutes an encouraging start, but is still very, very limited.

Where do we go from here? I believe that if we are to have healthy relations between Israel and Diaspora Jews, we need religious Jews from America who will be immersed in the work of promoting the religious institutions of their movements in Israel. This will be our vehicle to influence Israeli society and to provide a bridge to the citizens of Israel. Steven Cohen has written about this subject at some length, and I agree with him completely. This is how we will promote the religious values that we consider so essential. This is how we will provide a home for our own movement members when they go to study and work in Israel. This is how we will build a stake for ourselves there.

As currently structured, the Jewish Agency is not able to deal with these issues or to help us implement these goals. Much of what has been done, in fact, has created frustration and anger among the religious bodies. For example, we have the resolution on pluralism that was brought to the recent meeting of the Jewish Agency Assembly. I appreciate the goodwill of those who brought it forward. In its original form, it was an excellent resolution. But then the goal became not to advance the cause of pluralism, but to satisfy all major factions at the Assembly. As a result, the word "pluralism" was removed from the resolution. It is now mostly considered a success because it is sufficiently ambiguous as to be essentially meaningless. What is the point of a resolution on pluralism that does not mention the word "pluralism"? It was hardly a surprise when Israel's Orthodox press considered the resolution that was passed to be a great victory for its side.

And what about allocations? Ten years ago, after strenuous effort and protests from the Conservative and Reform movements, the Agency allocated $1.5 million to the programs of each movement, as well as some funds to Orthodox programs. Ten years later, that money has been cut by a third to $1 million for each movement. Furthermore, if truth be told, the money that we are allocated is virtually useless because we cannot count on its delivery. It comes six months, eight months, even twelve months late; we are obligated to spend our own funds first, and then hope for reimbursement later on.

If the Jewish Agency is going to be involved in religious issues and in support of religious institutions, then it must do so in a serious way. Otherwise, it needs to decide that these matters are not part of its agenda, and that it will not engage in this activity. It cannot play both sides against the middle.

I attended a meeting last week between the leadership of the Jewish Agency and the leadership of the Reform and Conservative movements in order to resolve some of these problems. Without mentioning any names, I will say that many of the Agency leaders did not even know who was in the room. At this moment, the Reform and Conservative movements—which constitute the grassroots of American Jewry, with about 2.5 million members—find it very difficult to relate to the Agency at all.

Similarly, during the last year talks were going on among UJA, UIA, and CJF to consider a "grand realignment" of their organizations and a fundamental restructuring of the national fund-raising institutions in America. The Reform and Conservative movements suggested that this would be a good time to think in terms of a new partnership between the synagogue world and the fund-raising world, and urged that a way be found for the synagogue movements to join these talks. But all of these requests were rejected.

In summary, we have little reason at this moment to be encouraged about our relations with the Agency. We hope that this will change, but for now it is cooperation with local federations in America that is most encouraging when we talk about new relationships and new paradigms.

Let me conclude with a statement that is not an institutional statement. We are a covenantal people, constituted by the terms of the revelation at Sinai, and bound thereby to a way of life, a land, and a religious destiny. This is what gives Jewish identity coherence and compelling power. The most important institutions in Jewish life will be those that advance faith, Torah, and covenant.

If the Jewish Agency for Israel and the other national communal and fund-raising bodies will see themselves as part of this religious mission, I will welcome that and bless that, and they will flourish. If they do not see themselves in those terms, they will play a still important but far more limited role in Jewish life.

Richard Hirsch

Response

I speak as one who has been serving as the chairman of an international commission appointed by the World Zionist Organization to reorganize the WZO and the Jewish Agency. I was appointed based on a paper I wrote some four or five years ago (Sam Norich devoted a section to my views in his recent book), which advocates the reorganization of world Jewry, in order to respond to the needs of the twenty-first century. This highly politicized process has now been going on for three years and we have proposed a plan, which will hopefully lead to a reorganization of the WZO and the Jewish Agency.

The fundamental premise of that reorganization is that the terminology "Zionist" and "non-Zionist," upon which the entire Jewish Agency is predicated, namely fifty percent Zionist and fifty percent community leaders, is no longer valid.

I believe the committee has accepted my fundamental premise: in today's world, there is no longer any justifiable distinction between Zionist and non-Zionist. The very fact that Shoshana Cardin is sitting around the table of the Jewish Agency, in her capacity as a non-Zionist, and the President of Hadassah is sitting there as a representative of the Zionists, is in itself corroboration that there really is no relevance anymore to these artificial distinctions.

I contend that either all the Diaspora Zionists active in the Jewish world are non-Zionists or all the active Diaspora so-called "non-Zionists" are Zionists. There is no substantive difference between them.

Therefore, the fundamental partnership has to be predicated on the reality of Jewish life. Institutions have to reflect the reality in which they function. What is that reality today? The true partnership is between Israel and the Diaspora, and not between Zionists and non-Zionists. Hopefully the new organization to be created will be predicated on that new partnership basis.

Having said that, I also want to caution us that just reorganizing does not necessarily make for more effective institutions. You have to reor-

214

ganize and restructure around redefined goals. Our fundamental problem is that as a Jewish people we have not been able to respond to the needs of the twenty-first century by redefining our goals. I will refer to that in a minute.

A further caveat: we are in danger of formulating divergent definitions of Jewish identity, which will potentially lead to a schism between Israel and the Diaspora. What do I mean by that? The American experience has been conducive to the "religionizing" of Jewish identity. In the American context, the distinction between Jews and others is no longer based on ethnicity, but on religion, on which synagogue or church you go to. Jewish identity is no longer comparable to Italian, Irish, and French identity, but to Protestant and Catholic identity. Therefore, the Jew is more and more identified by others, and therefore by himself, as a member of a religion, despite the fact that in many instances he does not observe Judaism.

In that regard, the distinction between "secular" and "religious" is artificial. There are many Israelis who in the Israeli context define themselves as secular, but who are just as "religious" as American Reform and Conservative Jews who define themselves as religious. Just because you define yourself as religious and *say* you believe in God, does not mean that you believe in God, and just because you define yourself as secular and *say* you don't believe in God, does not mean you don't perpetuate Jewish values. From my perspective, artificial delineations can lead to obfuscation of fundamental issues and challenges.

Conversely, if you take a look at what is happening in Israel, the Israeli environment is conducive to a "nationalization" of Jewish identity and experience. I am concerned that we will indeed become what some Zionists aspired to, a people like all other peoples.

What distinguishes American Jews from all other peoples? It is our contact with the land and the state and the people of Israel. What distinguishes Israel from all other states? Only the contact with the Diaspora. Israel was created, to paraphrase Lincoln, "Of the people, by the people, for the people," including Jews who live outside the state. It is the only country ever created in the history of humankind by people who did not live there. Every other nationalism came about as a result of people who rebelled against conquerors and established independence on their own ancestral land, on which they had been living with their own cultures.

I want to comment on the problems of the federation system and the so-called restructuring to which Sam Norich referred in the federated system. Here, I agree with what Shoshana Cardin said, and differ with my good friend and respected colleague, Eric Yoffie. I think the federated system is essential. I do agree that in this new revised plan, the federation leaders have not involved or given sufficient attention to the synagogues and the schools. Where are they going to do the Jewish continuity? Who is going to "Jewish-continuity-it" in America, if you don't have the synagogues and schools? To that extent, I am in complete agreement. But, I think the way to achieve that objective is not for the synagogues to declare that we are going our own way.

The federations, in the final analysis, will learn that they cannot achieve their objectives without the synagogue movements. So, synagogue movements, don't give up. Get in there and fight and demand your rights and your rightful place. Who are the federations? They are composed primarily of Jewish leaders who identify as Conservative and Reform Jews. Some synagogue leaders express concern that in many instances those who are most active in Israeli causes feel closer to the State of Israel ten thousand miles away than they do to the synagogue around the corner. But, don't blame only the federations; also blame some of our rabbis and colleagues for defaulting and failing to make synagogue experiences sufficiently rewarding and attractive.

Another issue is the growing tendency to say Israel has to go its own way. There are a lot of people (Howard Weisband referred to this) who are now saying that we ought to have our own separate campaigns for the United Jewish Appeal and make it exclusively Israel targeted.

Maybe a lot of people are beginning to talk that way. I think that would be a disaster, because despite everything that has happened, despite the growing disinterest in Israel, despite the *hitrahakut*—the distancing—from Israel, I still maintain that Israel is the main, cohesive, unifying force of Jewish life in America today. You take Israel away from the federations and you permit them to raise money for their own institutions and they are not committed to Israel, what is going to happen? You are going to destroy the unified American Jewish community.

I served in Washington when we went through the trauma of trying to unite the UJA and the federation in Washington. No one who has gone through that process can think blithely about having a separate campaign. I believe it would be a great tragedy. Israel would suffer and the Jewish people in America would suffer, so I am opposed to that.

To summarize, I think we are in a March of Dimes syndrome at the present time. What do I mean by that? The March of Dimes discovered Salk, or Salk discovered the March of Dimes. They cured polio. Did the March of Dimes go out of business? No. The March of Dimes went in search of other diseases.

We have a problem. The Jewish people is the problem of the Jewish Agency. It is the problem of our federations and it is the problem of the synagogues. What is the Jewish disease? The erosion of Jewish identity, the dissipation of Jewish values, and the failure to live a Jewish life. We are so used to being worried about being extinguished by our enemies. We don't have so many external enemies anymore, who endanger the very existence of the Jewish people. Now our major enemy is internal, a spiritual malaise.

So, instead of going out of business, we have a primary task: to resolve the Jewish problems of the twenty-first century. As with the March of Dimes, let us get on the march. Let us begin to look for the shared Jewish experiences, the shared sense of destiny of the Jewish people, the commitment to Jewish education, the inculcation of Hebrew, and the intensification of the Israel–Diaspora relationship.

If we look from a historical perspective at the twentieth century, during the first half the energies of world Jewry were devoted to creating the Jewish State. During the second half, those energies were concentrated on our efforts to strengthen the Jewish State and to bring in aliyah. In the next fifty years, it seems to me, we are all going to have to pull together, both Israel and the Diaspora, as true partners. I predict that in time Israel will prove to become the major partner. It will not only be the Jews of the world strengthening Israel, it is going to be the Jews of Israel strengthening world Jewry.

A NEW AGENDA

Avraham Burg

A New Agenda

I want to dedicate some time to analyzing the title of this volume: "American Jewry and Israel: Beyond Survival and Philanthropy."

What is beyond what? Who is doing what? But first, I will share some ideas with you that are not organizational policy, *hashkafah*, or Orthodox Zionist observations or ideology, but rather some thoughts from an individual who moves quite frequently on a very short bridge between Israel and America—which means something like once a week or twice a month.

It looks to me like the next decades or century are going to be very quiet or, relatively speaking, boring years. This means no real events, no disasters, and the majority of the Jewish people are going to live without any immediate physical threat. Moreover, most of the Jewish people, for the first time in our history, are going to live under democratic systems, whether Middle Eastern, Balkan, Russian, American, European, or Latin American, in some form or another. Nobody has promised me, of course, that I am correct. Who knows what will happen? And to develop a discussion based only on one possible assumption is a bit risky, to be sure. But when you compare our times to our very recent four thousand years of experience, we are having a couple of boring generations.

That is one thing. Secondly, we have based our American–Israel dialogue on the assumption that the United States of America will, for the next century or so, be the same nation that we knew it to be in the previous century. I am not sure this is the case for many reasons, but I will state only one. The relationship between our beloved Israel and the United States of America some fifty years ago was based on a kind of partially religious, partially spiritual sisterhood or brotherhood, and a fraternity between the two countries.

If, like I read in the papers, in fifty or sixty or twenty or thirty years' time, the hegemony of white Protestant Christians in the United States no longer exists, we will witness a different America. I don't know what will be different about Israel at that time, but there will be a different America.

Having said these two things, I would like to discuss the topic at hand. People speak a lot about "Post-Zionism." There are even people who speak about "Post-Judaism." Every organization and every religion has its own Fukuyama: the end of Zionism, the end of Judaism, the end of something. I have no idea what these terms mean. As long as there is one Jew who believes in God, belongs to the people, and sees his faith as part of all this, there will be a Jewish people. It goes on. It is part of *netzah yisrael.*

I will say the same thing about the Zionist movement. The Zionist movement, or the World Zionist Organization, for me is an instrument. It is not the *kedushah;* it is not the sanctity; it does not have a holiness of its own. Nor is it a goal. It is an instrument by which to achieve goals. If these goals are being redefined by each new generation, that is fine with me. I do not have a fundamentalist mentality, which says whatever was *kadosh* two thousand years ago, or a century ago, should remain *kadosh* forever. Zionism must be an instrument of something.

Something unbelievable has happened. In our lifetime, we are witnessing a new reality: a mission that was accomplished by a people within a century. One hundred years ago, the two existing demographic centers of the Jewish people were the Tsarist empire and America, both of which together contained eighty percent of the Jews in the world. During the Second World War, one-third of our people were killed in circumstances we all know and cry over, and the rest of the Jews were rescued by their own people. Then witness the unbelievable story of the collapse of Soviet Russia and the now relatively free former Soviet Union; and we are witnessing now perhaps the last chapter of Jewish history over there. It is a beautiful thing, and we are all committed to accomplishing this grand final rescue mission.

Then, all of a sudden, we ask ourselves, "Okay, we rescue all the people, and then what?" Do we—Israelis and American Jews—have something in common? We did have in common the colossal "help mission" for the Jews in Kiev and the other cities of the former Soviet Union. Now, the two sides, Israel and Western World Jewry, look at each other and say, "What the hell are we going to talk about? What will it be? What is the present agenda? What is the future agenda?"

It is very difficult because there are individuals within American Jewry and within Israeli Jewry who are isolationists and say they don't care or won't pay attention. We even have heard Israeli leaders make remarks like, "If you don't send your kids to Israel, you are irrelevant." But there are other isolationist forces within Israel and in North America as well. When we debate the budget of the Jewish Agency, for example, the battle cry is "local needs." I know that there are local needs. I would be the last one to argue against humanitarian services for everyone, for Jewish education, or for Meals on Wheels. I am the last one to object to these causes. But when you make local needs an ideology, what are you actually saying? That there is an individual Jew or a community where I live and I am responsible for them only. I am not further involved, beyond the immediate pressure of the poor of my city.

But there are common denominators. I just want to talk about two. One very simple and the other more complicated. Then I will move into Israel and finish my short remarks.

For many years we have spoken about the concept of giving. Giving because there are needy people. We even have budget lines that we call "the Needy," because the concept was a recipient-oriented one. In our lifetime, this has changed in front of our eyes. All of a sudden, the concept of giving is not just for the recipient but for the donor as well. All of a sudden, in many places, you hear of families, communities, schools, saying "Why give? Because it is tzedakah." *Tzedakah* is a word that is not very well known in Israel. It is a very complicated concept. It means justice, as well as many other things. *Tzedakah* is something that is good for me, the giver. Why? Because, technically, this is the way I buy my membership ticket into a club. If I educate my children to be givers, and if I educate myself to be a giver, then I am unique and different from the rest of my neighbors. I believe that *tzedakah* is going to become the common denominator among Jews. Did you give? Are you a giver? Are you a part of this process? I won't ask you what you give, how much money, resources, experience, motivation, commitment, or involvement. But, whatever you give, giving is a concept for the donor as well as for the recipient. This is a simple concept.

Now I would like to go back to "Post-Zionism." It is true that the last century was dedicated "to Herzl." Herzl fought against the physical distress of the Jewish people. Herzl was not privileged to read the wonderful book written by Dr. Alfred Gottschalk about Ahad Ha-Am, but I can tell you that the next century is going to be the century of Ahad Ha-Am. Ahad Ha-Am thought that Israel should be a spiritual center, a *merkaz ruhani*. It should be a kind of spiritual generator for the rest of the Jewish world. Why? Because Israel is something bigger than just a place. When the founding parents of Zionism first launched their ideas, it was a kind of rebellion against the "mother-shtetl" mentality of Judaism. By their rebellion and revolution, people thought, "We disconnect ourselves from something. We will never go back there."

Now, a century later, the concept of Zionism is still such a revolution, but with its back turned to the future and its face facing the past. It is a revolution that means going back to the land, the language, the Bible, archaeology, and independence in a region of the world that was neglected, that we had left behind. It is a revolution of "going back," of returning. If people ask me, "Avrum, what is Post-Zionism?" I would say that Post-Zionism is Judaism. In the same way that Zionism rebelled against Judaism, we can close the circle by saying that "Post-Zionism" is now Judaism.

Having said that, what is Judaism? What does this new era mean, both here and abroad? We have two sects within our people who do not know each other. One side I will call the Orthodox one, although it does not encompass all the Orthodox. But conceptually speaking, more and more of them are saying, "I want to isolate myself. I care only about my people. I care only about those who keep the Sabbath. I care only about those who eat kosher food. I am not interested in the rest of *klal yisrael.*" Such people have disconnected themselves from the present. But then there are many people on the secular side of the Jewish people who do not have any real access to what Eliezer Schweid calls "the Jewish bookshelf" or our history, our roots, our origins. So one side of our identity, our psychological hemisphere, is not well connected to our roots.

We have to open both sides. The Orthodox have to be open to other forms of Jewish expression. This requires a reform, not just in a political/organizational sense, but also in traditional Jewish thinking. We also need a secular openness and a willingness to reform secular thinking—and traditional Zionist thinking—to enable real communication with Judaism. This task cannot be accomplished exclusively in Israel or in America or wherever. This is the first time, after so many years, that we have the same agenda: Jewish identity, with local variations and with alternatives. The problem is the same problem. Sometimes, it requires cooperation among all parties.

So if I am asked, "Avrum, what is your Zionism and what is your Judaism?" I will define my bottom line, if there is one. For me, Zionism as history was a powerful expression of my people, and of myself, a response to being a persecuted element of history. For me, Judaism is the balance, and the control of power makes me a complete Jew.

Michael A. Meyer

Response
To Stand Within the Covenant

Avraham Burg called his "Proposed Policy Guidelines for the National Institutions of the Jewish People," published a year ago: *Brit am* (A covenant of the people). My response to him today, speaking as a Diaspora Reform Jew, will likewise be formulated in terms of *brit*.

The text that seems most relevant to our present situation, I believe, comes from Amos (1:9): *Ve-lo zakhru brit aḥim* (They ignored the covenant of brotherhood). Although Avraham Burg has forcefully written: "We must present all Jewish viewpoints and life-styles to the Israeli public, and to its young people in particular" (p. 43), the opportunities to do so, it appears, will be diminished. If we progressive Jews are not to be included within Israel in a *brit aḥim*, then we can either withdraw or increase our efforts. I believe we must increase our efforts.

Exclusion is not a new situation for Jews who regard religious innovation to be Jewishly legitimate. Back in the beginning of the nineteenth century, when the Reform movement began, one of its most fervent advocates wrote a pamphlet on its behalf which, employing a verse from Leviticus (26:25), he entitled *Ḥerev nokemet nekam brit* (The avenging sword avenging the covenant). The agenda of non-Orthodox Jews in Israel will require such avenging. Given the centrality of Israel for Diaspora Jews, no less for Reform Jews than for Orthodox, we cannot but take sword in hand.

Yet I believe that like the Jews in Nehemiah's time, who carried swords as they rebuilt the walls of Jerusalem, it is not the use of the sword that is of the essence, but the work of building. As important as the recognition as *aḥim* (brothers) is for Liberal Judaism in Israel, it is the propagation of the *brit* that is of the essence. Highest on the particularist agenda of Progressive Jews around the world, I believe, must therefore be reaching out more effectively to Israelis with an alternative to secularism and Orthodoxy, an alternative to neutralize the *Kulturkampf* that marks religion as necessarily authoritarian on the one hand, and secularism as devoid of religious potential on the other. I am persuaded that this Liberal particularist agenda within the larger agenda of the Jewish people requires the highest priority. It is because we Liberal Diaspora Jews are committed as much as we are to Israel that we cannot think only in terms of *am yisrael* but also in terms of *emunat yisrael*, and for us that means a flexible and broadly meaningful form of Judaism for modern Jews. Within the framework of the *brit am*, Progressive Jews must think of strengthening the *brit emunah* (covenant of faith). In Israel that means, for example, helping to shape and implement religious curricula in the secular schools.

It is, I think, completely legitimate that various groups within the Jewish people should press their own particular agenda. Pluralism may not be a Jewish value *per se*, but Jewish history attests to pluralities of expression competing with each other from ancient times onward. It is indeed heartening that Avraham Burg believes in Jewish pluralism. Only upon recognition of diversity can we build our sense of unity.

But beyond the particular agenda must lie common ones. In the Diaspora we are coming to the realization that host cultures, especially that of America, represent a more serious threat to our collective Jewish existence than ever before. As Jews we enjoy unprecedented acceptance. Not only are Jews more socially acceptable than ever in the past, but so is Judaism. The problem is that Jewish tradition is seen as narrow and prejudiced the moment it makes any claim to exclusivity, the moment it claims any superiority. The common agenda for Jews in the Diaspora must be to stress that Judaism is indeed different and demanding, not merely a cultural ornament in a multicultural society. Israel can help those of us who live in the Diaspora to hold up to ourselves and to the world our irreducible particularity as Jews. If we fail to do that, we will be swept away by the powerful social currents that have already divested most Protestant denominations of any credible claims to uniqueness.

Avraham Burg has written eloquently of the Israeli agenda in terms of relationship to the Jewish people. That this relationship grows ever weaker is a sad fact for Jews everywhere. Israelis not only have to have an understanding of their educational obligation to Jews elsewhere, but also of what they stand to learn themselves in terms of those liberal traditions that are especially at home in Diaspora Jewry.

The most broadly based agenda is, of course, that of the Jewish people as a whole. What can we do together—Diaspora and Israel—drawing upon the various religious and secular expressions of our tradition? Part of the title of this volume is "beyond survival." Yet survival of the people and religion of Israel must be the first point of our agenda for the future. That survival is threatened as never before in the Diaspora, as American Jews, for example, substitute a vague "spirituality" for regular and specifically Jewish expressions of Judaism. At the same time the relationship to a state that seems no longer to require their efforts, politically or philanthropically, becomes less significant. The relationship is just as threatened in an Israel where the landed state rather than the spiritual people increasingly becomes the focus of personal identity in different ways for both Orthodox and secular Israelis.

If the people of Israel is going to survive—and not just with a vague form of Diaspora Judaism set against an Israel that can unite only on political allegiance—we are going to have to pull together despite the differences. We are going to have to *make* Jewish history, not just participate in American history as Diaspora Jews and Israeli history as Israelis.

But if survival is essential for all else, all else is also essential for survival. In other words, there must be a rationale for the Jewish people to exist as a people, and not only for Jews as adherents of the Jewish religion and as Israeli citizens.

What then can we stand for and implement together as a people? The answer is: values. Moral values, religious values, values drawn from our tradition that in their essence, if not always in their application, can unite the various factions into which we are divided. We need to explore these values together, Orthodox and Progressive and secular Jews, Diaspora and Israeli Jews, out of mutual respect and, beyond that, out of *ahavat yisrael* (the love of fellow Jews).

Here too there is a covenant text from the Tanakh that is appropriate for the goal of our collective agenda. It comes from Second Kings 23:3: *Va-ya'amod kol ha-am ba-brit* (and the entire people stood within the covenant).

We need common objectives, based on common respect and the common quest for explicating and applying Jewish values, that will enable all of us to stand together within the covenant.

Daniel J. Elazar

Response
A Reinvented Jewish Polity in a Globalized World

As the twentieth century draws to a close, organized Jewry is in the process of concluding the great mobilizing tasks that have confronted the Jewish people for the past century and for which Jews organized themselves into their present structure. Those great tasks are being completed with extraordinary success. They have revolved around: a popular *rebellion* against the Jewish situation of homelessness, persecution, and impoverishment in the Diaspora; *relief* from the conditions of poverty and oppression that were the lot of most of world Jewry then and throughout much of this century; *rescue* of Jews from countries of distress and danger to Israel and New World Diasporas where the Jewish people could survive and flourish; and *reconstruction* of Jewish life under new conditions of freedom and equality.

Those have been great tasks, greatly undertaken and well done. With all of our mistakes, we have much to be proud of as we draw up a balance sheet at the century's end. Indeed, this century should stand out, even in the long history of the Jewish people.

However, the completion of those tasks leaves a vacuum for organized Jewish life. Jews will continue to pursue their individual goals as they will, but to function as a collectivity they must be moved by important collective tasks. Hence we are at the moment in a hiatus as we turn to identify the tasks of the next century.

World Jewry is at a turning point. This is an unmistakable aspect of the 1990s, regardless of whether one appreciates the opportunities to come or regrets the loss of past arrangements. In some respects, Jews are pulled in both directions, but the fact itself is unmistakable.

After a century in which the civil tasks of the Jewish people dominated the Jewish agenda, we have been witnessing a shift among many Jews, a return to the spiritual tasks of Judaism, sometimes in familiar ways and sometimes in new and even strange ways, but all directed toward matters of the spirit. The result is that the civil institutions that the Jewish people have built are almost all in difficulties at this moment. While those civil institutions may not be able to generate the vision that will motivate Jewish activity in the immediate future, they must share that vision if they are to remain strong and vital institutions, as we need them to be.

There is an irony in all this. While the civil institutions of the Jewish polity are, at least in principle, least able to take the lead in matters of the spirit, at the same time the deep fragmentation in Jewish religious life and the different visions in the presumably more spiritual domains make it even more necessary for the same civil institutions to serve as the bridging and unifying elements amidst great spiritual diversity. Hence, they must take the lead in articulating a common vision for the Jewish people.

Look at the situation in this decade so far. The last great Jewish community in distress has opened up, both for the freedom of Jews to live Jewishly in their countries of origin and the freedom to emigrate elsewhere. Israel has entered into a peace process with the Palestinians, Jordan, and Syria which, in turn, has opened the doors to the state's full acceptance by the rest of the world. Israel's economy entered a period of very rapid growth.

On the other hand, assimilation and intermarriage in the Diaspora reached new highs. The struggle between those who want Israel to abandon its Jewish character and become a "normal" state and those who want it to remain a Jewish state connected to the Jewish people worldwide, took on new intensity. In the last analysis, the Jewish world is dividing into two camps: those who seek normalization "like all the nations" and those who seek the way to perpetuate and cultivate Jewish civilization.

All of this has had pronounced effects on organized Jewish life, whether in Israel, in the organized Jewish communities of the Diaspora, or in the world Jewish organizations that link the two. The response of the leadership in all three spheres has been to pursue tried and true paths of constitutional change, restructuring, and reorganization.

Let us look at the record to date:

- In 1992, Israel's Knesset changed its Basic Law to provide for the direct election of the prime minister and added Basic Laws establishing clear human rights protections under the constitution and expanding the powers of judicial review of other branches of government.

- Two years later the victory of a new slate in the Histadrut elections led to a major reorganization of that venerable institution, and Israel's health care system was reorganized.
- The Jewish Agency for Israel was restructured internally to expand its Board of Governors to include non-party Israelis, inter alia, to change the organization and governance of the departments, and even to transfer traditional tasks to the Israeli government.
- In the United States, American Jewry entered into a process of restructuring that sought a consolidation of the Council of Jewish Federations, the United Jewish Appeal, and the United Israel Appeal into a new broad-based organization that could speak in the name of American Jewry in new ways.
- In the former Soviet Union, organized Jewish communities sprang up throughout the country as soon as it became permissible for Jews to organize freely.
- European Jewry as a whole has begun to explore new continent-wide intercommunity contacts and to provide organizational frameworks for them.

In the wake of all of these and similar developments in other countries, world Jewry as a whole has begun to face the prospect of reinventing itself as old tasks and functions have become obsolete and new ones now demand attention.

What is disconcerting is that the reinventing schemes are being pursued without serious consideration of what the reinventing is *for* other than self-perpetuation. Hence many of the efforts have run into deep trouble, as is often the case with reinvention for its own sake.

What are the basic foundations needed for a renewed Jewish vision? We can identify three eternal ones: *maintaining and strengthening the solidarity of the Jewish people, maintaining and developing Jewish civilization in all of its dimensions, and the maintenance and strengthening of Jewish religious norms.*

The unspoken premise accompanying all of these is the continuing need for appropriate Jewish organization (local, countrywide, regional, and global) to provide the framework through which to mobilize the resources and to focus collective Jewish efforts on those tasks. Without such organization there is no Jewish people. With proper organization the Jews have a community and a whole that is greater than the sum of its parts. In our time, this is especially important since we will continue to see a crumbling along the edges of the Jewish people through assimilation into the new global world society and we will need to maintain a core and a "whole" that can counterbalance that assimilation. For a Jewish renaissance we need not only seriously Jewish individuals and families but strong Jewish communities and a Jewish polity.

Any vision for the Jewish people must rest upon four basic principles: *Torah,* a shared commitment to Jewish learning and the commanding obligations that being Jewish entails; *am yisrael* (Jewish peoplehood), identification with the Jewish people as a whole, not just Judaism as a religion, and the great chain of Jewish tradition that stretches across the generations, binding Jews across time and space; *klal yisrael* (the community of Israel), Jewish unity despite our differences and with mutual respect regarding those differences; *brit* (covenant), the idea that Jews see themselves as bound to one another and to God through a covenant that distinguishes us from members of other peoples or faiths, a covenant that serves to differentiate Jews from non-Jews and to assure in certain critical ways that the Jews remain a people apart, even as we have our *covenants* with those nations who share many of our *covenantal* principles and are bound to all of humanity through the Noahide covenant.

In the new globalized world, we must add another principle, that of *kiruv* (outreach), the commitment of those who affirm these principles to reach out as appropriate to other Jews, to non-Jews who seek to share the fate of the Jewish people, and to humanity in general, each in the appropriate measure, to touch them while strengthening Jewish life at its core.

The advancement of these principles must be based on what seem like two contradictory thrusts: one, provision for more pluralism in Jewish life than ever before, simultaneously with a rejection of those forms of pluralism that are counter to the advancement of Jewish norms, especially those that accept (even reflect) the neopaganism of our times. Moreover, in the recognition and acceptance of greater pluralism, Jews will have to be careful to recognize that different Jewish communities have different understandings of pluralism and not try to impose their community's understanding on others, although they certainly may wish to try to convince others of the validity of their particular approach to Jewish life.

Jew will have to carefully guard against allowing neopaganism to be recognized as Jewishly valid in the name of pluralism. This requires walking a very narrow line. Undoubtedly, those institutions offering alternative versions of Jewish religious and spiritual life will be advocates of one version or another and may have a hard time playing that role. Hence it is a role that the civil institutions of Jewry will have to assume for themselves as they have done, albeit not necessarily in a deliberate fashion, for the past half century at least. To do so they will have to play a critical role in the renaissance of a norm-based Jewish vision.

These norms rest upon value concepts as old as the Jewish people itself, given form in the Bible and the Talmud, in some cases reinterpreted at the time of the Zionist revolution, and now requiring new postmodern applications. These include:

1. Jewishly directed norms such as recognizing that Jews constitute an *edah*, an assembly of all of the people of Israel for joint decision-making and action; that the Jewish people constitutes an *am segulah*, a people with a special destiny, and that we are bound together in a *brit arevut* or a covenant of mutual obligation.

2. For Jews it also includes Zionist norms such as the building of the *bayit le'umi*, Israel as our national home, as a *medinah yehudit*, embodied in a state that will be both Jewish and democratic in *eretz yisrael*, which will be committed to *hithadshut*, that is to say, Jewish renewal, and *tehiyah yehudit*, Jewish revival.

In order to build our new vision on these foundations, contemporary Jews need to strengthen their religious commitments, the Jewish character of their homes and families, and develop a renewed emphasis on Jewish learning (all proper steps necessary to bring about a Jewish renaissance. We also must find Jewish ways to fulfill humanistic norms. These can be stated in traditional Jewish value language as *yishuv ha-aretz*, the proper use of the world and its resources for human benefit in ecologically sound ways; *bnei Noah*, recognizing that ultimately all humans are bound together in the same covenant; *tikkun olam*, or the repair and restoration of the world; and *darkhei shalom*, developing and implanting the ways of peace.

* * *

In light of this renewed vision, we must address the great practical questions of governance, which are:

1. What should be done?
2. Who should do it?

3. How should it be done?
4. In many cases, where should it be done?
5. For or to whom?
6. Who should pay for it?
7. How should those involved in the foregoing work together to achieve common tasks?

Increasingly, the last is one of the most important questions. There is evidence that at least since the beginning of the modern epoch, with the growing interdependence of peoples and their institutions and societies, it has become even more complex.

We begin with some fundamentals:

1. There is a world Jewish polity that is identifiable as such. It serves a Jewish population that has organized itself into a series of concentric circles willy-nilly, consisting of all those in the world who subjectively define themselves as Jews or who are recognized as Jews by their respective communities. It is activated by those who are in some way affiliated with organized Jewry through some organization or institution and is led by those who are active in Jewish life in some way.

2. Those who are so connected, active in, or follow the activities of the organizations or institutions of the world Jewish polity do so on three planes. The first is through Jewishness or identification with the Jewish people. The second is local organizational affiliation with organizations that themselves are parts of the world Jewish network at one or more steps removed. The third consists of those who participate or follow the world Jewish arena.

3. Because of today's crisis of Jewish identity and survival, whereby the old religious and communal models are no longer compelling for so many people born Jews, a more or at least different associational model may be able to contribute something to the resolution of this problem. At least in part this model can be found through the fostering of a sense of Jewish citizenship, locally, countrywide, and worldwide. There are several organized means of connecting with the world Jewish polity. The most common are the world associations of local and countrywide organizations. At the heart of the polity, however, are five entities: the government of the State of Israel, the Jewish Agency for Israel, the World Zionist Organization, the Joint Distribution Committee, and the World Jewish Congress.. We can identify the following as the tasks and functions that are performed by the institutions that collectively provide the governance of the world Jewish polity. They are:

nation building; the development of Israel; relief and rescue of Jewish communities in need; fighting anti-Semitism; representing collective Jewish interests in world affairs; mobilization of leadership and activists to undertake these and other functions; governance functions in the world Jewish polity; assuring that there are appropriate bodies for the carrying on of the functions; raising funds to cover the costs of these functions; oversight of the organizations and institutions handling the functions; and developing appropriate inter-organizational relations both among the authorities that comprise the world Jewish polity and the local, countrywide, regional, and worldwide arenas.

4. Many of the connections that hold the world Jewish polity together are non-organizational, including networks that involve international travel and telephoning by individual Jews to friends and family around the world, reading or watching Jewish printed or visual materials about different communities, global Jewish computer communications through Internet and fax machines, and the like. All of these are important. Most are independent and few are subject to any kind of hierarchical structuring but remain networks whose use and entry is dependent upon voluntary choice by individuals. All are important but none take the place of organized Jewish life.

5. The past century has seen a growing compression of the world into an ever smaller compass. Not only have travel and communications become easier and more widespread, but interdependence has grown by quantum leaps. This has implications for the Jewish people by increasing the ease of communication among Jews worldwide. The need for that communication is also greater since Jews are located in more places and farther apart geographically than ever before. At the same time, they are able to communicate with each other more easily than ever before and to be in touch with every part of the Jewish world almost instantaneously. More and more have connections throughout the Jewish world, or at least across long distances within in it. Increasingly individual Jews, Jewish families, and Jewish communities are dependent upon resources in other communities whether it is religious direction from Israel or whether it is just for inspiration from the American Jewish experience, or whether it is an "Israel experience" as a means of strengthening Jewish identity.

6. Despite the plethora of organizations and organizational activities, a majority of world Jewry seem to be unaware of them. For most Jews, knowledge of their local involvements is all they know about organized Jewish life, if that. In some cases, they also know about the countrywide

confederations of organizations to which their local bodies, or the equivalent, belong. Relatively few even know of the existence of most of the institutions and organizations that guide the world Jewish polity and have even less knowledge of what they do, who their leaders are, and how they spend the funds available to them. It is a constant effort to acquaint them with even the bare minimum of knowledge required for anything that might be described as citizenship. A deliberate and assertive effort must be made to develop that sense of citizenship and provide the knowledge based upon which it must rest. The emotional bases of world Jewish identification will have to be strengthened because of the problems of assimilation abroad in the Jewish world today.

7. Nevertheless, an institutional structure has developed and has generated a network of linkage more or less involving most of the existing organizations and institutions. World Jewry functions even if its functioning is not widely understood by the Jews of the world. While a continuing effort must be made to acquaint more Jews with it, it will continue to function. Those involved in it must help it to function with the maximum possible democracy, efficiency, and effectiveness in the pursuit of Jewish goals.

8. Not only is this necessary for the health of the Jewish people and its body politic but it has become increasingly reasonable in a world that has become far more interconnected than ever before, where dispersed groups survive primarily by formal association and identification and all the informal elements that are part of both. Moreover, the world is more accepting of such phenomena as ethnicity that crosses state borders, national sentiment that is not limited to particular territories, and the existence and maintenance of state–Diaspora relationships. All are critical components of Jewish peoplehood or nationhood that are better recognized and more commonly accepted. The Jewish people now has a better opportunity to maintain worldwide unity than it has had since the destruction of the First Temple in 586 BCE. It is up to the leaders and activists in the Jewish world, those who are connected or can be brought to consciousness of this new reality to make the most of it.

CONCLUDING THOUGHTS

Paula E. Hyman

Bridging Our Differences
An American Perspective

There is widespread recognition that the symbols and myths that linked American Jews to Israel in the past half century have lost their potency, particularly among the younger generation. The myth of "Holocaust and rebirth" that connected the mass murder of European Jewry to the miraculous emergence of the State of Israel no longer speaks to many American Jews. The collective survival guilt of American Jewry after the Holocaust, that was displaced onto concern for the struggling new country, has waned. Moreover, despite Emil Fackenheim's 614th commandment, to deny Hitler a posthumous victory, the Holocaust does not provide a rationale for young Jews in either Israel or America to remain Jewish as we approach the twenty-first century. The fact that the Holocaust was not a major subject of discussion in the conference from which this volume derives attests to its inability to provide a blueprint for the future. As we continue to mourn its victims, we recognize that the Holocaust has become increasingly an historic event.

Most importantly, contemporary Israel is no longer dependent on the largesse of American Jews. Israel is a prosperous industrialized society, and the stereotype of the pioneer ethos of the early generations of settlers hardly accords with the materialism displayed on Sheinkin St. or in the ubiquitous shopping malls. The patron–client relationship of American Jewry and Israeli society is bankrupt and increasingly offensive to the client. The slogan "We are one" is not only untrue; it is no longer effective for fund-raisers or those seeking to strengthen the Jewish consciousness of American and Israeli Jews. It also fails, incidentally, to acknowledge the deep fractures in Israeli society, and in the American Jewish community as well. In Israel those fractures have been powerfully demonstrated by Rabin's assassination, the subsequent elections, and the conflicting visions of the "peace process" and of the role of halakhah in the state. In America those divisions have revolved around approaches to intermarriage, attitudes toward Israel, and concerns about the attempts of Orthodox Jewish leaders to define the public religious posture of Jewish communal functions. From my perspective, acknowledging what divides us internally is an important step in determining where we may cooperate. In a similar vein, paying attention to the divisions between Israeli and American Jews is essential to building bridges between the two communities. Academics might usefully investigate why the symbols that united Jews in the past have lost their power, but the two major Jewish communities of the world cannot wait for scholarly studies to point the way to the refashioning of the grounds of their relationship.

Those of us who are committed to the concept of a Jewish people need to find a way to sustain the concept "All Israel is responsible one for the other" even if we are patently not one. Whether the UJA's new slogan, "For ourselves. For our children. For Israel. Forever" will prove effective in strengthening Jewish solidarity is difficult to predict. As the premise of this volume suggests, the relationship between Israeli and American Jews is in a state of transition and demands thoughtful consideration of the grounds on which a new one will be built. Virtually all participants have pointed to the need for "mutuality" and "partnership" between the Jews of Israel and North America, but have been disturbingly vague about the nature and content of both terms.

There are a number of issues that strike me as essential for discussion if Israeli and Diaspora Jews are to understand each other. First, we need to "invent" and mobilize a common legacy and a common vocabulary, on the basis of an exploration of the symbols that continue to shape our various identities as Jews. I refer here to what has become a virtual cottage industry among modern historians—the investigation of the invention of traditions of nationalism in the past two centuries. Most influential have been Benedict Andersons's *Imagined Communities* and Eric Hobsbawm's *The Invention of Tradition*.[1] These books suggest that the ties that bind and create our sense of identity are not simply naturally acquired; they are constructed by political and cultural leaders. How we construct them through our educational institutions, media, and political discourse will affect our self-identity as Jews in different societies as well as the relationships between us.

Like my colleague Sam Norich, I am calling upon Israeli and American Jews to create a common culture, to construct new symbols and refresh old ones that will bind us together, despite the differences that Steven M. Cohen and Charles Liebman found in the meanings that

Israelis and American Jews ascribe to their Jewishness.[2] Those differences are strong, rooted in the specificities of living as a minority in a voluntary Diaspora community in a country that emphasizes individualism or as the majority in a sovereign Jewish state that emphasizes the collectivity. Yet, if we are to continue the variegated enterprise of the Jewish people, there must be an element that we hold in common. What we share is a collection of texts, but texts in the broadest definition of the word. Our most obvious shared text is Torah, the classical writings that embrace the Hebrew Bible and rabbinic commentaries from the period of the Talmud until our own time. I am referring to an expanded definition of Torah that includes literary, philosophical, and mystical texts throughout the generations. Culture, though, does not reside only in written texts. It comprises the meanings that groups find in the world around them on the basis of their understanding of their experience.[3] Shared memory of past events, then, is crucial to the creation of a sense of solidarity.

The liturgy and rituals of Judaism provide shared symbols and memory to Jews who may have little else in common, but we need symbols that resonate as well with Jews who do not practice Judaism. Fortunately, Jews have also traditionally acknowledged historical events that shaped group consciousness, even when they were not personally affected by those specific events. Thus, in the memorial books that they kept, Jewish communities recorded not only what had occurred in their own domain, but also elsewhere in the Jewish world. The last few pages of the *Memorbukh* of Haguenau in Alsace, for example, written in the nineteenth century, recall incidents from the region but also include references to such events as the Damascus Affair of 1840 and the Russian pogroms of 1881.[4] In the tapestry of Jewish history, there are many threads to weave a usable past. To be effective, such a usable past must be woven from a wide range of historical events.

The historical events that we select to include in our educational and cultural endeavors, particularly when they are chosen to reflect on the Diaspora, cannot simply be incidents of persecution. The Shenhar Report on Jewish Education in the Non-Orthodox Public School System in Israel took an important first step in stressing the need for infusing greater knowledge of Diaspora history into the secular Israeli public school curriculum. As the report is implemented, it is crucial that the full range of Diaspora experience be represented to provide a basis for mutual understanding. In the long history of the Jewish people in the Diaspora there are countless examples of political, cultural, and religious creativity that can serve as models for contemporary Jews. In the modern period alone, for example, one might highlight the political activism of Jewish workers, the social welfare visions of Jewish philanthropists, women as well as men, and the intense spirituality of early Hasidism. Similarly, Jewish schools in the Diaspora should teach the history of Zionism and Israel in its complexity and provide opportunities for exploring differences as well as commonalities.

In our search for common symbols, we must not forget the centrality of language. The establishment of the State of Israel has not halted the decline in Hebrew as the lingua franca of educated Jews that began with the emancipation of Jews in Western societies. Perhaps because of the dominance of America in international commerce, politics, and culture, English has become a necessity for Israeli as well as other non-English speaking elites, and American Jews, like other native English speakers, rarely feel any pragmatic need to master a foreign language. I can only fantasize a time when representatives of American Jewry, European Jewries, and Israeli Jewry meet at a conference in Israel where the common language is not English, but Hebrew.[5] To make that fantasy a reality, we must begin with the elite, so that knowledge of Hebrew becomes a requirement for any self-respecting Jewish communal leader. Jewish elites can now communicate with each other across international borders in English, but strengthening Hebrew among American Jews is essential to forging new links with the Jews of Israel. Like no other tongue, Hebrew provides Jews with a shared Jewish language that connects us across time and space, and that draws together Jews divided along other axes.

Even if American Jewish educators succeed in creating a Hebrew-speaking Jewish communal leadership, American and Israeli Jews cannot strike a partnership with each other without confronting two important sources of friction. The first is the subject of religion and religious pluralism, addressed so passionately by Rabbi Uri Regev, Director of the Israel Religious Action Center. The second is the question of gender equality.

Religious pluralism in Israel, which might appear to be an internal matter for Israeli society, has emerged as an important issue in the relations of Israeli and American Jews. It is widely known that Jews who live in the United States, whatever components of ethnic culture persist among them, define themselves in terms of their religion, a definition that is acceptable in American society, where ethnic particularity is increasingly conflated with racial identity. Whether they are observant or not, most American Jews perceive the source of their identity to be their religion. Most identify with one or another of the Jewish denominations that have been institutionalized in America, even when they are not themselves institutionally affiliated. There is no strict division between "secular" and "religious" in American Jewish consciousness.

All of the denominations of American Judaism—Conservative, Orthodox, Reconstructionist, and Reform—perceive themselves, and are treated by Jewish communal bodies, as legitimate expressions of Judaism. They are free to contend equally in the public arena.

In its commitment to the protection of religious diversity, American societies represent an extreme version of the marketplace of religious ideas found in much of the modern Western world. This phenomenon of the marketplace of religious ideas is, in fact, one aspect of the element of choice that the sociologist Peter Berger has posited as the defining characteristic of modernity.[6] Modernity has offered individuals the possibility to make choices about the nature of their religious affiliation and self-expression as they do with regard to their marital status and their family size. American Jews may take religious pluralism for granted in their own lives, but it is, nonetheless, one of their fundamental values. Those raised in a society where religion and the state are considered separate realms, as in the United States, or where state interference with religion is minimal, as in Canada, find many of the consequences of state-sponsored religion unpalatable. Until recently, most American Jews have not recognized how pervasive state control of Judaism is in Israel; even those who appear in *shul* regularly and are concerned with Israel have scarcely been aware of the extent of the difference between their practice of Judaism in America and its practice in Israel. They have been ignorant of the impact of state-authorized Orthodoxy on the lives of Israelis or on the status of non-Orthodox rabbis in Israel or abroad.

That situation has begun to change. Until 1996 the extent of the constraints on Jewish religious expression in Israel, not to mention the curtailment of secular freedoms, was known only to the minority of American Jews who are regular visitors to Israel, but the attempts by the government-approved, Orthodox religious establishment to delegitimate non-Orthodox rabbis and their conversions has received considerable attention in the American press. In the wake of the 1996 elections, for example, the *New York Times* mentioned the plans of ultra-Orthodox parties to demand the overturning of the Supreme Court decision requiring the registering of non-Orthodox conversions that took place in Israel as well as the closing of the non-kosher MacDonald's restaurant in Jerusalem. The "Law of Conversion" introduced in the Knesset in 1997 has aroused consternation among many American Jews. It is no longer necessary to have personal contacts with Israel to be aware of the issue of the lack of religious pluralism; reading the *New York Times* suffices. Between January 1, 1996 and June 30, 1997 there were no fewer than thirty-six articles on religious conflict in Israel, including stories about attacks on Conservative Jews praying in the vicinity of the Western Wall, about demonstrations over the closing of Bar-Ilan street on Shabbat, and most prominently about the Law of Conversion and its repercussions among American Jews. Insofar as "official Israel" reminds the more than ninety percent of American Jews who describe themselves as non-Orthodox that they are deficient as Jews, it will weaken identification with the Jewish State. The issue of religion in Israel therefore is not merely an internal matter. As the Conservative and Reform movements in North America increasingly mobilize their constituents to become involved on this issue, it will become central to Israel–Diaspora relations. It has serious implications not only for UJA fund-raising campaigns but also for the emotional identification of American Jews with Israel.

Moreover, religious pluralism is not merely an abstract value; it has invigorated the practice of Judaism in North America. The American experience can become a resource for those Israelis who indicate that their own "spiritual hunger" has not been fed by Judaism as it is practiced in Israel. State-sponsored Judaism, it can be argued, has weakened the attraction of Judaism for a substantial segment of Israeli Jews. As many American Christians as well as Jews have noted, the linkage of state and religion corrupts religion. Although the American model of separation of church and state cannot serve as a paradigm for Israelis, to whom it is utterly foreign, the creation of a civil space in which the state is not operative will offer Judaism, in a variety of forms, the possibility to flourish.

Such has been the experience in the past generation in North America. The "return to Orthodoxy" in America has attracted a great deal of attention, largely because it was unanticipated a generation ago, but expressions of what is called "Jewish renewal" flourish in all Jewish denominations, not just Orthodoxy. These manifestations of Jewish renewal are nourished by the willingness of American Jewish leaders and laypeople to assimilate practices, such as meditation, from other religious traditions and Judaize them. This is a historical process, incidentally, to which my teacher Gerson Cohen, in his essay "The Blessing of Assimilation in Jewish History" attributed the long-term survival of Jewish culture.[7] Religion, therefore, is a source of meaning for Jews in America who would fall, or be pushed, into the anti-religious secular camp in Israel.

How Conservative and Reform Jews can best make their case in Israel is a matter for debate. Members of these movements in America can use the power of the purse in Jewish communal affairs in addition to formulating their claims in terms of American values of individual rights and religious pluralism. These strategies do not exist for Reform and Conservative Jews in Israel, who comprise a tiny fragment of Israeli Jewry and live in a society where religious pluralism within Judaism is considered a radical innovation and where individual rights may be subordinated to halakhic norms or national needs. There has been much criticism of the forceful public expression of a civil rights strategy by the spokesmen for religious pluralism in Israel; a quieter, behind-the-scenes approach, it is suggested, would be more effective. Perhaps. But I share the perspective of those who argue that sometimes it is necessary to speak out for what is right, even if it is not currently feasible. Our political and social vision need not be limited by current conditions. Presenting an issue in terms of its moral rightness can prepare the way for its being considered adoptable in the future.

This was certainly the strategy of Jewish feminism in America some twenty-five years ago. Feminist successes in North America have, in fact, created a gap between Israeli and American Jews on the issue of gender equality. A generation ago Jewish feminists who published a list of demands for gender equality, particularly within the Conservative synagogue, recognized that they were not going to achieve their goals immediately. But they were committed to a long term struggle. That the issues were raised publicly and discussed widely in the course of a decade determined that it would become possible to accomplish many feminist goals in the Jewish community within slightly more than ten years. As I mentioned to friends when we went out to celebrate the night that the faculty of the Jewish Theological Seminary voted to accept women as candidates for rabbinic ordination, the twelve years that elapsed between the call for change proposed to the Conservative Rabbinical Assembly in 1972 and the faculty's 1984 decision were a blink of an eye in the context of Jewish history. The radical demand had become institutional policy in a movement that had initially been resistant to such a change.[8]

In the past generation, American institutions have accepted the fundamental premises of the equality of the sexes. Many social critics, including those who oppose its ideology, have acknowledged that feminism has been the most significant social movement of the post-war period in American society. Not only are women more visible than ever before in positions of authority in virtually every sector of society—from the university to the business corporation to the religious ministry—but ordinary people as well as public opinion makers have become sensitive to prejudice and discrimination against women. The absence of women from high-level meetings or from tenured positions in the university, for example, is noted and discussed, not passed over in silence.

Feminism has transformed North American Jewry as well. In Israel, despite the Zionist myth of gender equality, the status of women remains inferior to that of their American counterparts. Women are largely absent from positions of power in government and business and in tenured positions in the university. Women's history, which has traditionally been ignored, is only now beginning to attract scholarly attention. Women suffer particularly within the religious constraints of state-recognized Orthodoxy, where the power to terminate marriages remains a male prerogative. Moreover, many segments of Israeli society, seeing female subordination as natural, summarily reject gender equality as a value.[9] The ultra-Orthodox assault women whom they consider immodestly dressed and many Israelis blame those who are physically attacked for praying publically in mixed groups for "provoking" the violence to which they fall victim. Even those who might profess egalitarianism fail to see evidence of gender discrimination around them.

Israelis might comment that I look at Israeli society, and at the small number of Israeli women participants in this conference, with American eyes. This comment, however, is very much to the point. Dialogue can begin only when we acknowledge that our perceptions are different. If the struggle for equality of women with men continues to be seen as "an American fad," and if fundamentalist elements gain strength in Israeli society, then the "gender sensibility gap" between American and Israeli Jews will grow. That will be, I think, another obstacle to the strong identification of many American Jews, and particularly women, with Israel.

However, the gender issue has provided an opportunity, and will continue to do so, for building bridges between particular groups of

Jews from America and from Israel. We have talked about the personal element in the encounters (*mifgashim*) between American and Israeli Jews, and we have mentioned that the Jewish population is segmented. It follows then that our encounters will be segmented as well. Israeli Jews will not speak as a totality to American Jews in their totality. Those who find common ground to stand on, and shared concerns to discuss, often forge intense ties in their meetings. The issue of the status of women within Israel in contrast to their status within the American Jewish community has thus enabled American and Israeli Jewish women to build a sturdy bridge to each other. Shared interests and goals are the best instruments for bringing together Jews from different societies.

The acknowledgment of our differences is merely the first step in exploring how our various experiences and perspectives can serve as resources for each other. A relationship of mutuality suggests that we must learn from each other: Israeli Jews from the pluralism and relative tolerance and gender equality that characterize American Jews, and American Jewry from the profound sense of peoplehood that Zionism and national sovereignty have brought to Israeli Jews. Discussions as to how to increase the contacts of Israeli and American Jews—both directly and in cyberspace—are essential for the creation of the new relationship between the two communities that so many leaders perceive as necessary.

The "invention" of a common legacy is not simple. It is far easier to debunk myths than to identify symbols that will unite disparate people. Yet, if American and Israeli leaders are serious about strengthening the connections between their respective Jewish communities, it is essential to think and act creatively, to invent as well as to preserve.

Notes

1. Benedict Anderson, *Imagined Communities: Reflections on the Origin and Spread of Nationalism* (London: Verso, 1983); Eric Hobsbawm, "Introduction" and "Mass-Producing Traditions: Europe, 1870–1914" in Eric Hobsbawm and Terence Ranger, eds., *The Invention of Tradition* (Cambridge: Cambridge University Press, 1983), pp. 1–14, 263–307.

2. Steven M. Cohen and Charles Liebman, *Two Worlds of Judaism: The Israeli and American Experiences* (New Haven: Yale University Press, 1990).

3. See Clifford Geertz, *The Interpretation of Cultures* (New York: Basic Books, 1973).

4. A microfilm of the *memorbukh* of the Jewish community of Haguenau of the eighteenth and nineteenth centuries may be found in the Central Archives of the History of the Jewish People, Jerusalem, HM 2/5010.

5. For a discussion of the situation of Hebrew among U.S. Jews, see Alan Mintz, ed., *Hebrew in America: Perspectives and Prospects* (Detroit: Wayne State University Press, 1993).

6. Peter L. Berger, *The Heretical Imperative: Contemporary Possibilities of Religious Affirmation* (Garden City, N.Y.: Anchor Press/Doubleday, 1980), especially pp. 1–29.

7. Gerson D. Cohen, "The Blessing of Assimilation in Jewish History," Commencement Address, Hebrew Teachers College, Brookline, Mass., June 1966.

8. See Paula E. Hyman, "Ezrat Nashim and the Emergence of a New Jewish Feminism," in Robert M. Seltzer and Norman J. Cohen, eds., *The Americanization of the Jews* (New York: New York University Press, 1995), pp. 284–95.

9. On the status of women in the *Yishuv*, see Deborah S. Bernstein, ed., *Pioneers and Homemakers: Jewish Women in Pre-State Israel* (Albany: State University of New York Press, 1992). On the contemporary condition of Israeli women from a feminist perspective, see Barbara Swirski and Marilyn P. Safir, eds., *Calling the Equality Bluff: Women in Israel* (New York: MacMillan, 1991).

Allon Gal

Bridging Our Differences
An Israeli Perspective

Shaping a common culture for Israel and world Jewry, American Jewry in particular, should be very high on the contemporary Jewish agenda. I agree with Professor Paula Hyman that this goal is a most constructive response to the challenge of enhancing our relations, when the traditional "survival and philanthropy" binding-factors are consistently declining.

Undoubtedly, there are meaningful differences between our communities; and, surely, understanding what divides us is the first step toward bridging these differences.

Hyman appropriately has mentioned the recent book of Liebman and Cohen, *Two Worlds of Judaism.* In this work the authors perceptively touch upon differences between the Judaism of the two communities, and they rightly conclude: "American Jews are overwhelmingly liberal, and their liberalism is central to their conception of Judaism. In many important respects, most Israeli Jews are not liberal. More significantly, the core elements of liberalism are rather marginal to their conception of Judaism." When it comes to religious life, the authors convincingly observe that American Jews, when molding their Judaism, intensively employ personalism, voluntarism, universalism and moralism. In Israeli religious life, on the other hand, there is much more emphasis on ritualism, collectivism and particularism.[1]

On the basis of this work and other studies, I would further generalize that American Judaism ever strives to fall in line with American liberalism, emphasizing universalistic and democratic values; while at the core of Israeli Judaism—persistently oriented to sustain sovereignty and security—are ethnic and historic-particularistic factors.[2]

Before elaborating further, it is important to note that when the State of Israel was established, no serious effort was made by the two communities to interact culturally and spiritually. Sometimes it seems that even the opposite was the case, as the leaders of those years—certainly

the Israeli ones—were, in a sense, perhaps more concerned with defining the distance between them in order to clarify to themselves and to
the world the sovereignty of the young Jewish state. Thus, perhaps the
Ben-Gurion/Blaustein accord (1950) reflected, among other things, the
deep urge for the symbols of independence of those years. And it may
well be that until the Six Day War, matters of survival and philanthropy had to be indeed highest on our relationship agenda. In any
case, decades passed without meaningful efforts to develop a shared
spiritual Israel/Diaspora domain. As the years passed, this failure was
also associated, I'm afraid, with emotional estrangement. Perhaps
Canaanism in Israel, as an *ideology,* has failed; but, alas, it too often
seems that a Canaanite *mentality* of sorts has become quite typical of
the native Israeli. Thus, beyond all other difficulties, bringing Israelis
and American Jews together has come to be an emotionally very
complicated task, especially when we are talking about the younger
generations.[3]

Now, to bridge differences and neglect of this serious a nature is not
an easy task. Still, it is attainable, as we are discussing branches of the
same people, *am yisrael,* whose Jewish cultural frames of reference are
basically identical. Furthermore, the real picture on each side of the
ocean is variegated, as in each community there are all the elements of
the other one; the differences are by no means of two rigidly or dog-
matically different Judaisms or Zionisms.

It is still not too late, I think, to effectively work on the molding of
our common culture. This volume is perhaps a modest step in this direction. As for the contributors, I think that their very diversity—
communal leaders, heads of organizations, intellectuals, academicians,
public media personalities, religious leaders, social activists, writers
and artists—may be instructive for further efforts in this vein. I would
suggest, though, that more focused themes should be considered for
similar efforts in the future.

The case of feminism, that Hyman has so thoughtfully discussed,
exemplifies, indeed, the great potential for bringing the two communities much closer. Until about three decades ago, it looked as if the differences between the two communities regarding women's rights were
too sharp to be bridgeable. The Israeli system seemed heavily discriminatory against women, while the American scene was characterized at
the time by liberal women, mostly religious, who gradually and consistently moved toward full equality.[4]

Historically, women's equality had been a basic value in the early *halutzic* period of the Yishuv. However, daily work was too physical, and so were most of the crucial defense roles. The entrenched conflict with the Arabs also worked to confine the roles of women to birth-givers and educators of the children. Thus Israeli women (Golda Meir's example notwithstanding) were cornered for a long period in traditional roles in the kitchen and the family. Still, the ideology of women's equality remained valid and was naturally included in our Declaration of Independence.

Gradually, especially since the late 1960s, Israel's economy has become more sophisticated, and extensively computerized. The sheer physical strength needed for many jobs has sharply declined and women can effectively perform more and more of them, even in the defense sector. Now, the old egalitarian-feminist ideology, coupled with the technological changes, has enhanced women's position in Israel.

It was against this background that, after the Six Day War, the presence of some prominent American immigrant feminists began to be noticed in Israel. They spoke out on the gap between the formally expressed egalitarian ideology in Israel and the actual, disadvantaged situation of the Israeli woman. And they courageously pursued many reforms aimed to improve the situation. A genuine dialogue between American Jewish feminists—some religiously liberal, some modern Orthodox, and some secularist—and their Israeli counterparts developed. From the late 1970s and into the 1990s, the efforts of immigrant pioneer feminists, together with the rise of "home-made" Israeli feminists, has resulted in significant laws and new institutions. Their interaction embraces not just the political and social arenas, but also the educational one. Thus, their efforts have uncovered "feminine elements" in Jewish history and culture. Significantly, "gender studies" have been introduced in universities and in teachers' colleges in Israel. And these studies have been often sustained by American Jewish moral and financial support.

Now, what components of this joint effort can be applied to other areas of interaction? Women's equality has been cherished by both communities, and is considered a challenge for both (though one of them, Israel, has especially failed in this regard). The value is of great relevance to modern life and at the same time is reflected in traditional Jewish literature; the value, which has both Jewish and universalistic implications, can be further advanced as time goes on.

Let me suggest some other cultural themes of shared concern for both Diaspora and Israeli Jewry.

I find the theme of social justice relevant, signficant, and appropriate. Israel in recent decades has achieved a swift modern technological development and low inflation. But these have been accomplished at a cost of high unemployment, social-economic polarization, and the exposure of a great segment of workers to harsh free-market rules. Now, justice and its realization in social-economic life has been the moral value that singularly characterizes Judaism, both conceptually and historically. Both Jewries can address themselves to the implication of this value in our times.

American Jews can instructively contribute to this complex: they live and work in a free economic system while professing, at the same time, responsiveness to social justice requisites. They can also contribute to this bi-communal discussion from their historical legacy—drawing upon American Jews' pioneering role in the development of social work, workers' rights, and the philosophy of "social Zionism" associated with such personalities as Horace Kallen, Louis Brandeis, Julian Mack, and Henrietta Szold.[5]

This is also a promising theme from the Israeli side, as Israel today emerges from its historically rigid division between the socialist and the free-market schools. Hence a shared discussion of social justice in contemporary Jewish culture—focusing on the Israeli case—can be really seminal.

The role of a constitution in democratic society is another cardinal topic that can bring us together. Israel is constructing its constitution in a gradual manner, by the accumulation of "basic laws" individually passed by the Knesset. It is instructive that historically, when emerging Israel discussed a certain "Draft Constitution," American Jewry enthusiastically embraced the idea. Although Israeli politics and polity did not allow the establishment, at the time, of any comprehensive document, a constitution for Israel is still a very hot issue in this country, as is the place of the "basic laws" in the Israeli polity, and the position of its supreme court—which heroically works to back those "basic laws" in the light of Israel's Declaration of Independence. All this may be a subject for a serious and productive discussion to which American Jews, living in a democracy with the oldest constitution in the world, can immensely contribute.[6]

The idea of peace, *shalom*—which derives from sublime traditions—can also offer us a joint opportunity to mold our modern Jewish culture. While in the Bible *shalom* is generally used just to describe a state of affairs, Isaiah's and Micah's vision of an age where there would be no war between nations, is unparalleled. In the rabbinic texts, *shalom* commonly signifies an ethical category, depicted as a blessing, an expression of divine grace. The sages went to great lengths in their praise of peace. On the other hand, they were aware that peace, at times, opposed other values such as justice and the pursuit of truth. In our Middle Ages tradition, peace is a cosmic and divine ontological principle; against this, war is viewed as an undesirable historical phenomenon. At the same time, though, war is considered tolerable within certain limits; our tradition is not pacificistic.

Now, though modern Jewish thought is almost unanimous on the great value of peace, the above-mentioned questions are not only theoretically very complex but also sharply debatable in their implications for the arenas of Israel among the nations and of the State of Israel in the Middle East. All of this, then, presents another set of questions suitable for our shared endeavor.[7]

Another suggested theme is the Holocaust, the impact of which is especially pervasive in molding our identity in Israel. A self-reliant, militarily strong Israel—eternally open to Jewish immigrants—is generally considered here to be the optimal answer to the Jewish tragedy. The emphasis in the American community, on the other hand, often tends to be on the universalistic aspect of the Holocaust, namely, on the merit of democratic and liberal values for avoiding similar catastrophies. This bent is notably shared, for example, by Simon Wiesenthal and Elie Wiesel and is also well demonstrated in the Holocaust Museum in Washington D. C.[8]

In Boston (where I just spent a sabbatical), there is a most remarkable Holocaust memorial monument, built mainly of six tall chimneys visible day and night, and inter-connected by railway tracks reminiscent of course of the trains that carried the victims. These tracks intersect with the American Revolution's famous Freedom Trail; and at this junction there is a plaque that declares that the prevalence of the Freedom Trail's values in the world would prevent another Holocaust from happening.

It seems to me that both perspectives are vital elements in our common Jewish culture. Together we can more effectively forge the desired balance.

Finally, I wholeheartedly agree with Professor Hyman that appreciating Jewish religious pluralism should be a major factor in bringing our communities closer. As a matter of fact, the lack of this understanding from the Israeli side undermines the very solidarity of our communities and threatens the unity of the Jewish people. However, bringing about an Israeli change in this regard is extremely difficult.

At the root of the afore-mentioned successful cooperation in feminist awareness is a shared ideology: indeed, there have been valid links between our communities in all above-noted themes. However, when we discuss pluralism, the scene is dramatically different.

Neither in Eastern Europe nor in the Muslim countries—from which the founders of Israel and the first mass immigrations to the State came—did emancipation, religious freedom, and religious pluralism prevail. Israel reflects this historic reality in its lack of religious pluralism as well as in its rigid division into secularist and religious camps, both of which consider Orthodoxy as the genuine expression of religion. This is a historical burden all of us have to face.

Some scholars emphasize that several social-economic patterns have developed in the Yishuv and Israel; but this background, heterogeneous as it was, hardly produced any pluralistic ideology that asserted the phenomenon. (Little wonder that the very term "pluralism" is quite new in the Israeli vocabulary; and there is still no widely-accepted Hebrew word for it).

This ideological resignation should not puzzle us once we remember the concentrated, heroic effort required for the survival and development of the Jewish *eretz yisrael* community. The relative poverty of the land, the deadly external menace—and other complicated factors—demanded a strenuous and coordinated nationalist effort for many decades. It is only in recent years that Israel has felt secure enough to gradually develop its ethos—as in the prominent case of the Shenhar Commission Report on education—away from centralism and uniformity.

The question then is how to pursue pluralism, particularly in the spiritual and religious realms, when we lack ready-made historical and ideological contexts.

A confined target effort, of a political nature, be it of a loudly-public or a quiet behind-the-scenes nature, is of course necessary; but as the obstacles on this course are formidable, let us also check other avenues. A crucially helpful aid to the establishment of religious pluralism in Israel can be found in the very nature of the Jewish civilization. Historical Judaism has always been distinguished by diversity and at least by a great potential for pluralism. This phenomenon is evident from the time of the First and Second Commonwealths, through most of our medieval history, and up to the modern period.[9]

Coupled with heterogeneity we historically developed a special "debating culture," namely, a culture that allowed for competing ideas at its core. This quality is traceable in the composition of the Bible, in the Talmud, and in most of our ensuing cultural and intellectual history.

The teaching of Jewish history and Judaism from a pluralistic perspective can be, hence, a crucially productive way to sensitize the Israeli ethos. The more the religious pluralism in the West is recognized in Israel as a natural and legitimate phenomenon in the history of the Jewish people and of Judaism, there is more chance for it to be cultivated as part of Israeli identity.

Yet another avenue toward the advancement of religious pluralism in Israel is the illumination of its relevance for upholding the civil and ethical values historically cherished here.

Since the Six Day War there has been a rise in Israel of fundamentalist-nationalist trends that threaten democratic and humanistic values long held dear in this country. The culmination of this tendency was the assassination of Israel's prime minister, Yitzhak Rabin, by a native Israeli and a university law student, a religious-nationalistic fanatic. The religious background and education of the murderer has caused concern about the marginality of such values as tolerance, democracy, and civility in our religious life here. The ideology of religious pluralism is now seen as a way to advance these values tremendously: the emerging consensus is that the more religious pluralism in Israel is associated with deeply rooted democratic and humanistic tenets—the more inroads we have for its integration into the Israeli make-up. Thus, pursuing pluralism in the light of those well-rooted values may be a most effective method for its advancement.

This is not to say, of course, that the only way to bring religious pluralism to Israel is via humanistic-democratic values. The assassination of Rabin by an Israeli Orthodox youth has stimulated in some Israelis a deep interest in more ethically-oriented liberal religious attitudes. This spiritual hunger, which may well develop into subtle appreciation of American liberal Judaism, would naturally bring our communities meaningfully closer together.[10]

The above-mentioned themes are, of course, just suggestions for a possible agenda for working on a common culture and enhancing solidarity between our communities. In any case, the challenge is highly demanding, and that is why we should, I think, attentively consider also the structure of our future work together. The elaborations offered in this conference by Professors Liebman and Cohen—on less "mobilizing" and less centralized frameworks—may be most productive for future projects.

Consistent gatherings along these models, the publication of their results, and particularly their dissemination in the communal and educational systems of both Jewish communities seem to me to be effective ways to mold our common culture.

These gatherings should be conducted, I suggest, in both countries, perhaps on an alternating basis. Also, perhaps an appropriate date for the gatherings would be very close to Israel Independence Day. Perhaps some of these gatherings can be conducted in university campuses; and then a couple of days for a teach-in on a certain topic can be formally set up.

I fully sympathize with the yearning for symbols that would unite our communities. But, especially after the assassination of Rabin, and against the background of fundamentalist-nationalistic currents here, we should cautiously look for those Jewish symbols that express humanistic values that unite us.

Also, most Israelis (clearly more than American Jews) define themselves as "non-religious." It is true, as the Guttman Report has proved, that many of them actually practice some elements of religious customs and traditions. However, I think we should adopt symbols that would fall well in line with the Jewishness of non-religious Israelis, an identity the bulk of them hold to in a modern and democratic context. Although most American Jews see their Jewishness in religious terms, most see their Jewish commitments in a modern, liberal, and democratic context. Hence, let us together look for symbols that reject irrationalism, superstition, and dark chapters in our history. By this I do not mean that we should compromise on colorless and anemic symbols. They should be conspicuously Jewish and derived from our shared history, religious history included. But they should reflect also openness to modernity and especially some orientation to humanistic and universalistic values.[11]

The Hebrew language is vital indeed for the shared building-up of our common cullture. Thus I embrace Hyman's idea for Jewish leaders in the world to seriously study Hebrew and to maximize its use in world-wide Jewish exchanges. Yet, from the Israeli perspective, I also advocate pursuing English as our second language. I would resent an Israel that is mono-linguistic. We need to be connected with the Western world, the Anglo-American world in particular. Despite the fact that the successful history of Zionism, Israel's birth included, is intimately connected with the English-speaking world; and despite the impression some visitors may have as to the Israelis' versatility in the English language—there is much to be desired in achieving the appropriate status of this language in our country. Strangely enough, but for historical reasons, English is rather foreign to the Israeli psyche. For some, it is the language of the "rulers" of Palestine who brutally enacted anti-Zionist policy; for others, it is the language of a world imperialist power that seeks to assimilate, to Americanize, all genuine nationalist phenomena, tiny Hebrew-speaking Israel in particular.

Now, all this is a matter of controversy in Israel, because still other people here, such as the former Minister of Education, Prof. Amnon Rubinstein, are concerned about the shaky position of English, especially in disadvantaged populations. During his tenure as minister (in the early nineties), Professor Rubinstein proposed a special English-spoken curriculum in the Israeli school system. The Israeli Academy for the Hebrew Language, however, concerned more with the purity and strength of the national language, rejected Rubinstein's proposal.[12] To my way of thinking, it is a pity that English is not promoted enough in Israel. English is the practical communicative medium with Jews the world over, and also the medium that would help prevent Israel from becoming too narrow-minded, tribal, and boastful. All in all, from the Israeli perspective, I would like to see our shared culture flourish as a bilingual endeavor.

Notes

1. Charles S. Liebman and Steven M. Cohen, *Two Worlds of Judaism: The Israeli and American Experiences* (New Haven, 1990), p. 96 and chap. 6, respectively.

2. Allon Gal, "Independence and Universal Mission in Modern Jewish Nationalism," *Studies in Contemporary Jewry* V (1989): 242–74; idem, "'Jewish Return to History' in American Zionist Thought," in Shmuel N. Eisenstadt & Moshe Lissak, eds., *Zionism and Return to History: A Reappraisal* (Jerusalem, forthcoming) [Hebrew]

3. For background, *Market Facts, Inc., 1998 Annual Survey of American Jewish Opinion* (New York, 1998), pp.9–11 ff.

4. Rochelle Furstenberg, *The Women's Movement in Israel* (Ramat-Gan/New York, 1995), is the source of this and the ensuing discussion; see also notes 8, 9, in P. Hyman's article in this volume.

5. For "Social Zionism" see e.g., Sarah Schmidt, *Horace M. Kallen: Prophet of American Zionism* (Brooklyn, NY, 1995), chaps. 5–11; Allon Gal, "Brandeis' View on the Upbuilding of Palestine, 1914–1923," *Studies in Zionism* 6 (Autumn 1982): 211–40.

6. Amnon Rubinstein and Barak Medinah, *The Constitutional Law of the State of Israel* (Jerusalem 1996), Preface and chaps. 4, 6, 28 [Hebrew]

7. Aviezer Ravitzky, "Peace," in Arthur A. Cohen and Paul Mendes-Flohr, eds., *Contermporary Jewish Religious Thought* (New York, 1987), pp. 685–702.

8. Michael Berenbaum, *After Tragedy and Truimph* (Cambridge 1990), chaps. 1, 2; Yosef Gorny, "The Shoa and the State's Ethos and Its Impact on Contemporary Jewish People," in Yisrael Gutman, ed., *Major Changes Within the Jewish People in the Wake of the Holocaust* (Jerusalem, 1996) esp. pp. 671–78 [Hebrew]

9. S. N. Eisenstadt, *Jewish Civilization: The Jewish Historical Experience in a Comparative Perspective* (Albany, 1992); idem, "Sectarianism and Heterodoxy in Jewish History," *Jewish Studies* 37 (1997): 7–59.

10. Avrum Burg, review articles in *HaAretz/Books*, Feb. 25, 1998, and July 29, 1998, pp. 1, 14 & p. 7, respectively.; Yossi K. Halevi, "Zionism, Phase II," *Jerusalem Report*, Dec. 26, 1996: 12–18.

11. Cf., Eric Hobsbawm, "Introduction: Inventing Traditions," in idem and Terence Ranger, *The Invention of Tradition* (Cambridge, 1995), pp. 8–9.

12. Tom Sawicki, "We Don't Need No English Education," *Jerusalem Report*, Oct. 20, 1994: 20–21.

Richard J. Scheuer

Postscript
Liberal Judaism's Interaction with Israel

I write immediately after the World Zionist Congress of December, 1997, and I see possible changes in the relationship between American Jewry and Israel that will give more scope to the non-Orthodox streams and to their educational institutions.

First, the pre-Congress voting for the delegates in America demonstrated the gradual disappearance from the Zionist scene of old Zionist parties, of the Jewish Defense organizations, of partisan bodies reflecting parties in the Knesset, and "lodge-based" organizations like Hadassah and B'nai B'rith. The Reform ARZA (Association of Reform Zionists of America) took 47 percent of the vote, the Conservative Mercaz took 27 percent, and the Orthodox parties 10 percent.

The turnout dramatized two important developments. First, the kind of concern and identification with Israel that Cohen and Liebman refer to in their essay is vibrantly alive in the religiously liberal movements. The vote helped communicate to Israeli and worldwide leaders the commitment of non-Orthodox Jews to Israel and the strength of their idealism. And it showed that the way to mobilize the American Jewish community is through the synagogue—largely, the Reform and Conservative synagogues, where the bulk of the votes for delegates to the Zionist Congress was generated.

Indeed, as American Jewry has developed at the end of the century, one identifies as a Jew by joining a neighborhood synagogue. Therefore, the State of Israel will find itself addressing the synagogue movements when it needs to engage with the American Jewish community. The Hebrew Union College and the Jewish Theological Seminary are going to have a greater chance to be heard.

Second, the Congress voted (in Chairman Avraham Burg's words) to recognize that "in a democratic society, expressions of Judaism will be diverse; observant and secular Jews of all streams have the equal democratic right to maintain their beliefs and lifestyles in their own ways; and attempts by anybody to impose religion or prevent its observance by the other side is anti-democratic and liable to undermine respect for Judaism."

Regarding Burg's adopted formulation, the Congress also

> ...out of deep concern for the unity of the Jewish people, calls on the leadership of the religious streams in Israel and the Diaspora to cooperate with the Israeli government to guarantee the success of the Neeman Committee in its efforts to solve the painful questions on the Jewish people's agenda, including those regarding personal status and the ability to act in Israel.

While these resolutions have no force in law, there is every reason to believe they may reverberate in the Knesset, in the Israel Supreme Court, and among thinking Israelis in academic and government circles. The Congress showed that American Jewry is seriously concerned about pluralism and openness in Israeli society. The voting of the delegates demonstrated a change in the make-up of American Zionism—reflecting a younger, family-oriented synagogue membership compared to the previous delegations, which were comprised of older Zionists.

The new American Zionists are, hence, concerned with Israel in a much more intensive way. Their synagogue membership often begins with an interest in Jewish education, in teaching their children a working knowledge of Hebrew, and developing a lifelong interest in Israel. They are just as passionately determined that Israel will receive them and recognize their ways of living as are any other Jews in the Diaspora. When the State of Israel needs to engage with the American Jewish community, it will find itself addressing the philo-Israel synagogue movements, rather than the old line Zionist organizations.

And there is some change in Israel too. The hunger for non-dogmatic religious education among the people of Israel has been demonstrated, for example, by their enthusiasm for the Reform nursery schools and kindergartens and for the TALI elementary through high schools in Jerusalem and beyond. As this work and the Reform movement's many faceted educational endeavors expand, they reinforce the values of a democratic and open Judaism, which can flourish in Israel as it has in America. In addition to the TALI schools, we have perspectives that can help in those areas where Israelis are most troubled: conversion, marriage, divorce, membership on religious councils, and related subjects. In these areas, the Israel Religious Action

Center, the Israel Movement for Progressive Judaism, and the Association of Reform Zionists of America have provided significant leadership. There will also be a place for academic work in these areas.

The collaboration of Ben-Gurion University of the Negev with the Hebrew Union College in developing educational and experiential programs should be most fruitful. The University's new course in "Pluralism in Judaism" is a milestone, and its timing could not be better. The College–Institute in Jerusalem, in partnership with the other branches of the movement, supports a wide range of formal and informal Jewish learning opportunities on campus and beyond for professional educators and lay persons alike. We should act with the confidence that we are needed.

This publication is a very important step. We will make a difference.

Contributors

Steven Bayme
Director of Jewish Communal Affairs, American Jewish Committee

Avraham Burg
Chair, the World Zionist Organization and the Jewish Agency for Israel, 1995–1999; since 1999, Speaker of the Knesset

Shoshana S. Cardin
President, JTA, the Global News Service of the Jewish People

Barry Chazan
Professor, Melton Center for Jewish Education in the Diaspora, Hebrew University of Jerusalem; Jewish Education Consultant, CRB Foundation

Steven M. Cohen
Professor, Melton Center for Jewish Education in the Diaspora, Hebrew University of Jerusalem

William Cutter
Professor of Education and Modern Hebrew Literature, Hebrew Union College–Jewish Institute of Religion, Los Angeles

Gidon Elad
Member, the Center for North American Jewry, Ben-Gurion University of the Negev; Israel Experience Consultant, CRB Foundation

Daniel J. Elazar
Until his death in 1999, Professor Emeritus, Bar-Ilan University; President, Jerusalem Center for Public Affairs

Leonard Fein
Director, Commission on Social Action, Reform Judaism, Union of American Hebrew Congregations

Shaul R. Feinberg
Rabbi, Associate Dean, Hebrew Union College-Jewish Institute of Religion, Jerusalem

Allon Gal
Director, Center for North American Jewry; Professor, Ben-Gurion Research Center and History Department, Ben-Gurion University of the Negev

Yosef Gorny
Professor and Head, Weizmann Institute for Research in the History of Zionism, Tel Aviv University

Alfred Gottschalk
Distinguished Professor of Bible and Jewish Thought and John and Marianne Slade Professor of Jewish Intellectual History at Hebrew Union College–Jewish Institute of Religion

Richard Hirsch
Rabbi and Honorary Life President, World Union for Progressive Judaism

Paula E. Hyman
Professor and Director, Center for Jewish Studies, Yale University

Charles S. Liebman
Yehuda Avner Professor of Religion and Politics, Bar-Ilan University

Michael A. Meyer
Adolph S. Ochs Professor of Jewish History, Hebrew Union College–Jewish Institute of Religion, Cincinnati

Samuel Norich
General Manager, The Forward Association, Inc.

Malka Or-Chen
Argov Center for the Study of the Jewish People and Israel, Bar-Ilan University

Aviezer Ravitzky
Sol Rosenblum Professor and Chair, Department of Jewish Thought, Hebrew University of Jerusalem

Jonathan D. Sarna
Joseph H. and Belle R. Braun Professor of American Jewish History; Chair, Near Eastern and Judaic Studies Department, Brandeis University

Richard J. Scheuer
Governor, Chair of Jerusalem School Committee, Hebrew Union College–Jewish Institute of Religion

Harvey Shapiro
Assistant Professor and Dean, Shoolman Graduate School of Jewish Education, Hebrew College, Brookline, Massachusetts

S. Ilan Troen
Lopin Professor of Modern History, Ben-Gurion University of the Negev; editor, Israel Studies

David Twersky
Editor, New Jersey Jewish News, *Whippany, New Jersey*

Howard M. Weisband
Vice President for International Development, Bar-Ilan University

Deborah Weissman
Director, Kerem Institute for Humanistic Jewish Education, Jerusalem

Eric H. Yoffie
President, Union of American Hebrew Congregations

Olga Zambrowsky
Argov Center for the Study of the Jewish People and Israel, Bar-Ilan University

Sheldon Zimmerman
President, Hebrew Union College–Jewish Institute of Religion